"I don't think those of us who took part in the filming of *The Shawshank Redemption* back in 1993 had any idea that the movie we were making would go on to become one of the most beloved films of our generation. This book, *The Shawshank Redemption Revealed*, with all its rich detail and fantastic collection of firsthand accounts, gives a rare, never-before-seen look at the birth of this classic film. If you're a fan of the movie, this is a fascinating read. Enjoy."

—William Sadler, actor from *The Shawshank Redemption*

"Terrific, exhaustive work. Definitive soup-to-nuts examination of *The Shawshank Redemption*: how it got made, the story of its filming, what it means to the creators, participants, the community, and society. From extras to studio executives, craft services to critics, day players to superstars. And a point-by-point guidebook on how to support a major film on location as well as how a film company should behave on location. Great fun to read, informative, heartfelt, moving while never pulling any punches. Eat your heart out, *Forrest Gump* and *The Lion King*."

—Clancy Brown, actor from *The Shawshank Redemption*

"Mark Dawidziak's deep dive into one of the world's favorite films is amazingly detailed and complete . . . and surprisingly entertaining. Inside stories and technical details abound, but mostly it is a look at the vastness of the creative process in creating a unique and remarkable film."

—Mick Garris, director of the miniseries versions of Stephen King's *The Stand, The Shining*, and *Bag of Bones*, as well as the films *Stephen King's Sleepwalkers* and *Desperation*

"My late brother, Monty Westmore, was the makeup artist on *Shawshank Redemption*. He recalled that it was one of the most enjoyable films he had the privilege to be part of, including the cast and crew."

—Michael Westmore, Academy Award–winning makeup artist

Also by Mark Dawidziak

NONFICTION
The Barter Theatre Story: Love Made Visible
The Columbo Phile: A Casebook
Night Stalking: A 20th Anniversary Kolchak Companion
The Night Stalker Companion: A 25th Anniversary Tribute
Horton Foote's The Shape of the River: The Lost Teleplay About Mark Twain
The Bedside, Bathtub & Armchair Companion to Dracula
Jim Tully: American Writer, Irish Rover, Hollywood Reporter (with Paul J. Bauer)
Mark Twain in Ohio
Everything I Need to Know I Learned in The Twilight Zone

NOVEL
Grave Secrets

EDITOR
Mark My Words: Mark Twain on Writing
Richard Matheson's Kolchak Scripts
Bloodlines: Richard Matheson's Dracula, I Am Legend, and Other Vampire Stories
Beggars of Life by Jim Tully (with Paul J. Bauer)
Circus Parade by Jim Tully (with Paul J. Bauer)
Shanty Irish by Jim Tully (with Paul J. Bauer)
The Bruiser by Jim Tully (with Paul J. Bauer)
Richard Matheson's Censored and Unproduced I Am Legend Screenplay
Mark Twain's Guide to Diet, Exercise, Beauty, Fashion, Investment, Romance, Health and Happiness
Mark Twain for Cat Lovers: True and Imaginary Adventures with Feline Friends
Theodore Roosevelt for Nature Lovers: Adventures with America's Great Outdoorsman

THE SHAWSHANK REDEMPTION REVEALED

HOW ONE STORY KEEPS HOPE ALIVE

MARK DAWIDZIAK

LYONS
PRESS

Guilford, Connecticut

An imprint of The Rowman & Littlefield Publishing Group, Inc.
4501 Forbes Blvd., Ste. 200
Lanham, MD 20706
www.rowman.com

Distributed by NATIONAL BOOK NETWORK

British Library Cataloguing in Publication Information available

Library of Congress Cataloging-in-Publication Data

Names: Dawidziak, Mark, 1956- author.
Title: The Shawshank redemption revealed : how one story keeps hope alive / Mark Dawidziak.
Description: Guilford, Connecticut : Lyons Press, 2019. | Includes bibliographical references and index.
Identifiers: LCCN 2019008232 (print) | LCCN 2019012388 (ebook) | ISBN 9781493040995 (e-book) | ISBN 9781493040988 (hardback : alk. paper)
Subjects: LCSH: Shawshank redemption (Motion picture)
Classification: LCC PN1997.S433 (ebook) | LCC PN1997.S433 D39 2019 (print) | DDC 791.43/72—dc23
LC record available at https://lccn.loc.gov/2019008232

Groucho Marx dedicated his autobiography to
"six masters without whose wise and witty words
my life would have been even duller."
The six writers, not surprisingly, were humorists,
all of whom he claimed as friends.
So, borrowing a page from Groucho's book,
but working a slightly spookier side of the street,
this book is dedicated to the memory of three masters
I had the honor of claiming as friends
(because the universe was kind that way):

Richard Matheson
Harlan Ellison
Ray Bradbury

The iconic image used on the 1994 posters for director Frank Darabont's *The Shawshank Redemption*

CONTENTS

Dear Warden, You were right. Salvation lay within. Andy Dufresne
—ANDY'S NOTE TO WARDEN NORTON ON THE INSIDE COVER
OF *THE HOLY BIBLE: CONTAINING THE OLD AND NEW TESTAMENT*
(AND ALSO CONTAINING THE HIDING PLACE
FOR A ROCK HAMMER)

PHOTO BY BECKY DAWIDZIAK

CELLBLOCK ALERT! SPOILERS AHEAD!

THE WARDEN HAS REQUESTED THAT A GENERAL WARNING BE ISSUED TO all currently on these premises. This is in the nature of one giant spoiler alert. Revealing the secrets of what happens in *The Shawshank Redemption* is a crime worthy of, well, nothing less than a long turn in Shawshank State Prison. That is, of course, if you're revealing them to someone who hasn't seen *The Shawshank Redemption*. Nobody wants to be that kind of stool pigeon. So the assumption is that anyone joining this tour is famil-iar with the film and knows those secrets. But it's remotely possible that someone has reached these gates without having made the acquaintance of Andy Dufresne, Ellis Boyd "Red" Redding, and the other inhabitants of Shawshank. This notice is for that uninitiated person. Yes, secrets will be revealed. Key plot turns will be discussed. Indeed, you're probably here because you know what happens and love how it happens. If not, you might want to consider turning back now. Even better, you might want to consider postponing the tour, making up your loss, seeing *The Shawshank Redemption*, then returning to these gates.

OUR *SHAWSHANK REDEMPTION*

WHEN TWO CONVICTS FIRST MEET IN AN OLD HOLLYWOOD FILM, ONE IS bound to trot out that wonderful prison-yard getting-to-know-you line, "What ya' in for?" It's another of way of asking, how did you get here? So, how did you get to Shawshank?

And, come on, we both know there is every good chance that you've done a stretch in Shawshank. There's also an excellent chance that you enjoyed the experience of watching *The Shawshank Redemption* so much, you went back for another stay . . . and another . . . and another. You're not alone—not by a long shot. Again and again, fans of the 1994 movie have told me, with not much variance in wording: "I've seen it so many times, but if I happen to come across it on television, no matter where in the story it is or how late at night it is, I have to watch it all the way to the end." One of the people I've often heard say something like that is, well, me. There's even a word for this ongoing *Shawshank* experience. Paul Kennedy, who shows up well along in the film as the 1967 Food-Way manager, introduced me to the term: "I was on the phone with a friend the other day, and he said to me, 'I just got *Shawshanked*,' meaning that he had stumbled on the movie on TV and was caught. He had to keep watching . . . just got sucked in completely, even though he'd seen it countless times before. So it's now a verb: to be 'Shawshanked.'"

You might call it *The Shawshank Addiction*. This all speaks to the great attraction the film has for so many people. Fans continue to examine, explore, and celebrate this film, and it continues to grow in popularity, resonance, and, yes, affection, year after year. As of this writing, *The Shawshank Redemption* remains the highest-rated movie at IMDb with an average star count of 9.3 out of a possible 10, followed by *The Godfather*.

The film that beat *The Shawshank Redemption* at the Academy Awards for best picture of 1994, *Forrest Gump*, checks in at the number eleven spot, with an 8.8 star count. "You can't walk down the street without somebody telling you it's their favorite movie," Morgan Freeman told Seth Meyers during a 2016 appearance on the comedian's NBC talk show.

"You know, most days when I'm out and about, somebody comes up to say something about *Shawshank*," Tim Robbins said during an interview for this book. "They not only tell you it's their favorite movie, they tell you why it's so special to them. They tell you specifically how it touched them. People have told me that it stopped them from committing suicide, that it inspired them to lose weight, that it prompted them to get out of an abusive relationship. And I've heard other people connected with the film say the same kind of things. When someone approaches you in an airport or a restaurant, it's almost always to talk about *The Shawshank Redemption*. Even Nelson Mandela told me how much he loved *The Shawshank Redemption*. There's something special about this one that's really special to so many people. It's just special, to them and to us. That's a nice thing to be involved with. It rarely happens."

Other stars of the film, including Clancy Brown and Jeffrey DeMunn, told me the same thing during research for this book. "When people want to tell you about how much *The Shawshank Redemption* means to them, it's because it's so much more than a movie to them," DeMunn said.

Small wonder that, in 2015, the United States Library of Congress chose *The Shawshank Redemption* for preservation in the National Film Registry, calling it "culturally, historically, or aesthetically significant."

Given the immensity of its following nationally and internationally, it's not surprising that many roads lead to *Shawshank*, just as there are many paths that lead to redemption. It's a shared passion and yet a deeply personal, individual journey for each fan. For many, and I'm included in this number, the road to *Shawshank* began with the 1982 publication of Stephen King's collection of four novellas, *Different Seasons*. I eagerly was devouring every delectable King treat as it appeared in print, yet I was delayed a bit getting to this particular volume. It was a heady period, to be sure. I got married six weeks after the book's August 27th publication

The Shawshank Redemption is so popular, one major chain store uses the images of Andy and Red to represent the drama aisle of the home video section.

PHOTO BY BECKY DAWIDZIAK

date. My fiancée, actress Sara Showman, and I spent much of that August rehearsing and appearing in a production of *Inherit the Wind*, the play about the 1925 Scopes Monkey Trial and the state of Tennessee's attempt to ban the teaching of Darwin's theory of evolution in public schools. It was staged in a courthouse in the oldest town in Tennessee, Joneborough, during a blisteringly hot stretch of days, which went a long way in providing the proper setting, mood, atmosphere, and temperature for the show. We went directly from that production to finalizing plans for a bigger show (at least as far as we were concerned): our wedding. Once settled in our apartment, it wasn't long before we both caught up with *Different Seasons*. Sara shared my King mania, so it was difficult to occasionally pry the book from her hands. Fortunately, she's a fast reader.

The first entry in this 527-page hardcover book, featured under the heading "Hope Springs Eternal," was "Rita Hayworth and Shawshank Redemption," a gripping tale narrated by a murderer named Red. Sounds like a fairly direct route to Shawshank, to be sure, and it was a path taken by millions of readers. But as compelling as this experience was, the journey didn't end with *Different Seasons*. Turns out that the road continued taking many surprising and rewarding turns. The next major turn for me occurred in 1993, when I was the film critic at the *Akron Beacon Journal*. I received a fax from Eve Lapolla, the head of the Ohio Film Commission, informing me that a movie titled *Rita Hayworth and Shawshank Redemption* would be filming in the central Ohio town of Mansfield and other locations in the area. For three months during that blazingly hot summer (everyone who worked on the film remembers the relentless heat), Eve arranged set visits and interviews for stories in the *Beacon Journal*, including a sit-down interview with Freeman on location after a long day of shooting.

The notion of writing a book about *The Shawshank Redemption* took shape as the film gradually rose on annual polls of favorite movies. In 2015, it was voted Great Britain's favorite film by YouGov, the global public opinion and data company. Particularly intriguing was that the YouGov research proved something I long suspected: that the appeal of *The Shawshank Redemption* cut across all demographics (age, gender, race, income). It was as popular with men as women, teenagers and their grandparents. The statistics showed that the same phenomenon existed on the other side of the Atlantic.

The road back to Shawshank required another turn, however, and that leg of the journey ran through Kent State University, where I've taught the Reviewing Film and Television course since 2009. Each semester for about ten years, I've shown a variety of films and TV episodes, challenging the students with different genres and styles from different eras. A pattern soon emerged. *The Shawshank Redemption* was the only film I showed that got close to a 100 percent favorable response from those students. My students evaluated the film with an enthusiasm that mirrored its IMDb ranking (except, perhaps, their rating actually might have been a little higher) and the YouGov findings. Twice a year, year after year, the response to the movie has been the same.

Now, mind you, for the last five years or so, I've been showing *The Shawshank Redemption* to students who weren't even born when it was released in the United States on September 23, 1994. It is reassuring to see that the magic still works, especially since that movie magic was first conjured in a world far removed from their Millennial lives—a world that didn't yet know the wonders of iPhones, Twitter, Blu-ray discs, DVRs, and *SpongeBob SquarePants*. In the week before I introduce them to *Shawshank*, I show them *The Grapes of Wrath*, director John Ford's 1940 film version of John Steinbeck's Pulitzer Prize–winning novel. That adaptation of a distinctly American story always splits the room right down the middle. Half of the students find it a deeply moving, poignant, and even transformative experience. When I snap the room lights on during the final credits, it is not uncommon to see tears among this half of the class. The other half, however, look monumentally bored, completely bewildered by those blown away by the performances delivered by Henry Fonda and Jane Darwell, Gregg Toland's cinematography, Ford's Academy Award–winning direction, and Steinbeck's story of the displaced Joads set adrift during the Great Depression. They find it slow, dated, and excruciatingly dull. Some even advocate tracking down all known copies and having them destroyed, if only to spare future students the suffering they've just endured. It always makes for a lively discussion the following week, and it makes for general jubilation when, after that discussion, they learn that we're heading to Shawshank State Prison.

"Why?" I ask them one week later. "Why do you love *Shawshank* but aren't that crazy about *The Grapes of Wrath*?" Although *The Grapes of Wrath* begins with Tom Joad getting out of prison and *The Shawshank Redemption* begins with Andy Dufresne being sent to prison, these two adaptations share an awful lot of DNA. These movies, after all, are pretty much about the same thing: people crawling through shit, keeping hope alive under the most daunting, horrific, and harrowing of circumstances. Only the Joads do this metaphorically while Andy does it both metaphorically and literally. Both are laced with religious symbolism. Both are period dramas. Both are talky. Both are deliberately paced. Both edge past two hours in running time. Both feature the stunning visual work of a legendary cinematographer: Toland in *The Grapes of Wrath* and Roger Deakins, director of photography on *The Shawshank Redemption*.

They concede the points, but then make it clear that *Shawshank* speaks to all of them in a way that's more profoundly touching and, despite being set over a twenty-year span starting in 1947, more resonant.

The ending has a lot to do with that. It's an ending that dispels the darkness, and we've certainly gone through our share of that with Andy, Red, Brooks, and the other convicts in their inner circle. It is a destination devoutly to be wished. So they are one with Red who hopes to be reunited with his friend, shake his hand, and who hopes the Pacific is as blue as it has been in his dreams.

When *The Shawshank Redemption* was released, and the parents of my students had warmed to its message of hope and its celebration of friendship, times were more hopeful. The economy was good. Employment was solid. All that technology waiting around the corner was going to solve our problems, not create them. In short, overall, things looked good. Twenty-five years later, the world they are inheriting is a different world. Society seems more divided, unsettled, and uncertain. Things don't look so good, or as good. In fact, they often look downright scary. In the midst of all this, there's Andy, telling them not to give up on hope. Don't give up on the world, on the future, on the country, on yourself, no matter how distressing or bleak things may look. And the film, with its deft blend of grittiness and sentimentality, has grown more timely, more resonant, and more relevant to more people, until it has become this generation's *The Grapes of Wrath* (remember, sentimentality was a charge also levied at Steinbeck).

Hope and belief would be enough to sustain us on the journey to create this book, but this also is a film that speaks of freedom. Here, too, the message is a universal one. I mean, if one needed to have some experience of prison in order to relate to Andy and Red, the film would have quite a limited following. But we relate to the characters for the inescapable reason that we all deal with issues of somehow being trapped and seeking freedom. "I think the film powerfully speaks to what freedom is and what enslavement is—or incarceration," Robbins said. "And I don't think you have to be in jail to be in prison."

At each turn, we are strengthened by those things that sustain us as we try to make our way toward freedom and, yes, redemption. What Rod Serling might have called the signpost up ahead points us in the right directions: faith, hope, belief, friendship, education, perseverance. There are no shortcuts. You need to go through Shawshank in order to emerge at the ultimate destination, which brings us to the redemption part of the title. There is your Shawshank, whatever it might be, and, beyond it, is . . . redemption? Yes, but whose?

G. K. Chesterton famously declared that *A Christmas Carol* is a story about redemption, and, of course, it is. But Chesterton warns that it's all too easy to miss where Charles Dickens is aiming with his slim 1843 book, which also mixes grittiness and sentimentality. Those unfamiliar with the actual book may not realize how many dark, disturbing, and harrowing corners it contains. Miserly Ebenezer Scrooge certainly is redeemed through his encounter with the ghostly visitors. And yet, Chesterton tells us, the point of *A Christmas Carol* is not whether or not Scrooge is redeemed. That's almost beside the point. The real point, the real question, the real challenge behind that book is whether or not we are redeemed. Much the same might be said about *The Shawshank Redemption*. This isn't really about the redemption of any one character. It is about our redemption. It is truly *our Shawshank Redemption*.

The spiritual aspects of the story are not lost on Bob Gunton, who so chillingly portrayed the figure of evil in the film, Warden Samuel Norton. "Most people I run into recognize me from the movie," Gunton, who once thought about becoming a priest, said during a 2013 Ohio visit for a twentieth-anniversary *Shawshank* reunion. "We all share such devotion to *The Shawshank Redemption* and what it means to each of us personally— the message of hope and perseverance and friendship. I always feel like I'm a little of a priest of this particular secular cult of *Shawshank Redemption*."

The film was a box office disappointment when it initially released in September 1994. Despite that, *The Shawshank Redemption*, through word of mouth, became one of the top-rented movies of 1995 and one of the most-watched films on cable, getting a huge boost when cable czar Ted Turner secured the cable-broadcast rights and made *The Shawshank Redemption* a keystone of his "New Classics" programming. So, what Gunton calls the "secular cult of *Shawshank Redemption*" kept growing. "Mr. Turner, bless his heart, chose to show the movie every five minutes," director and screenwriter Frank Darabont quipped. Not really, but it sure seemed that way at times. The research firm of HIS found that the film occupied 151 hours of basic cable time in 2013. It has played on more than fifteen different basic cable channels since 1997, including TNT, TBS, AMC, Lifetime, Spike, USA, and A&E. That doesn't count the showings on premium channels, like HBO, or streaming services, like Hulu.

Mark Twain once observed that praise is well, compliment is well, admiration is well, but affection "is the last and final and most precious reward" that can be won by character or achievement. *The Shawshank Redemption* has been lavishly praised, complimented, and admired, but has also had that most precious of rewards: our affection.

And because of this great affection, *The Shawshank Redemption* has legions of devoted fans who regularly head for Ohio, on pilgrimage, if you will, to visit sites featured in the film. For *The Shawshank Redemption*, Destination Mansfield, the tourism-minded economic development corporation, has put together The Shawshank Trail, which boasts fifteen area stops, including the Ohio State Reformatory in Mansfield, the bank in Ashland where Andy withdrew the warden's money, the cabin at Malabar Farm where Andy's cheating wife and her lover were murdered, and the courthouse in Upper Sandusky, where Andy was tried for those murders. Those who love this film can put themselves in the exact place where the characters stood, deepening that special bond with the story. These sites also understandably justify Ohioans' view of *The Shawshank Redemption* (and also *A Christmas Story*, partly filmed in Cleveland) as "our movies." In a very real sense, they are. Yet, in sharing these locations with the visitors who flock to them with wide eyes and loving grins, we also realize these are everybody's movies, everybody's stories—and the "our" becomes universal. In every sense, it is *our Shawshank Redemption*.

"Ultimately it's what does the movie mean, not to me or to us, but to you and to the people who have seen it," Darabont said, sitting between

Robbins and Freeman during a tenth-anniversary interview on PBS in 2004. "And that's really fascinating, because we've gotten some amazing reactions through the years. The film seems to be something of a Rorschach for people. They project their own lives, their own difficulties, their own obstacles, and their own triumphs into it. They view the bars of Shawshank as a metaphor for their own difficulties and then, consequently, their own hopes and triumphs."

It's his film. It's Stephen King's story. It's Ohio's movie. But it's our *Shawshank Redemption*.

So in the spring of 2018, I took the road back to Mansfield, where, twenty-five years before, I had observed bits and pieces of what would become one of the most esteemed American films of the late twentieth century and one of the finest movies made from a Stephen King story. This time, however, I was in the company of a gifted writer and photographer named Becky Dawidziak. She wasn't around when the film was being made on Ohio soil in 1993. She showed up about three years later. We made many trips to Mansfield, Upper Sandusky, and other shooting sites, and at each stop were made to feel as if we were part of a big

Shawshank State Prison—the Ohio State Reformatory—viewed through the bars
PHOTO BY BECKY DAWIDZIAK

extended family, and I suppose we were (and still are). More than seventy interviews were conducted for this book during those months, many in person, many by phone. So this also is a book of memories, insights, and more than a little of that shared enthusiasm.

Warden Norton famously closes his welcoming speech to the new convicts by saying, "Put your trust in the Lord. Your ass belongs to me. Welcome to Shawshank."

We make no claim on posteriors or any other anatomical feature, but put your faith in this glorious reality: The story belongs to all of us. Welcome to Shawshank.

I.

STEPHEN KING, *DIFFERENT SEASONS*, "RITA HAYWORTH AND SHAWSHANK REDEMPTION"

Writing isn't about making money, getting famous, getting dates, getting laid, or making friends. In the end, it's about enriching the lives of those who will read your work, and enriching your own life as well.
—STEPHEN KING
ON WRITING: A MEMOIR OF CRAFT (2000)

STEPHEN KING, FRANK DARABONT, AND "RITA HAYWORTH"

Elderly woman to Stephen King: "I know who you are. You're the one who writes those scary stories."

Stephen King: "Yes, ma'am."

Elderly woman: "I don't like that stuff. I like uplifting stuff, like The Shawshank Redemption."

Stephen King: "Well, ma'am, I wrote that."

Elderly woman: "No, you didn't."

STEPHEN KING'S SIXTEENTH BOOK IN A LITTLE MORE THAN EIGHT years, *Different Seasons* was widely viewed as a departure for the prolific writer when it was published by Viking Press on August 27, 1982. At that point, he had published eleven novels (three under the Richard Bachman pseudonym), a western fantasy, a collection of short stories, a graphic novel based on his *Creepshow* screenplay, and a nonfiction book. This book was new territory for King, not just in form but in content. The overwhelming majority of his writing had fallen into the horror genre. *Different Seasons* was not viewed as horror, although certainly each of the four stories has its horrific aspects. Some critics suggested it was an attempt at more "literary" writing, an observation that says a great deal

Stephen King's *Different Seasons*, published in 1982, was a collection of four novellas, including "Rita Hayworth and Shawshank Redemption." Pictured here is Kinuko Y. Craft's stirring cover for the first edition.

more about those critics than it does about King. The four novellas, each assigned a season and a heading, are: "Rita Hayworth and Shawshank Redemption" (Hope Springs Eternal); "Apt Pupil" (Summer of Corruption); "The Body" (Fall From Innocence); and "The Breathing Method" (A Winter's Tale).

Of the four, the one closest in spooky spirit to a traditional King horror story is the fourth one, "The Breathing Method." A story within a story, it's an elderly doctor's tale of a patient from the 1930s. The woman was determined to give birth to her illegitimate child, and that determination is demonstrated under gruesome circumstances on a wintery night. The other stories all resonate on different levels with the horror genre.

That's certainly true of "Rita Hayworth and Shawshank Redemption," the story of Andy Dufresne, a Maine banker tried and convicted for murdering his wife and her lover. Inspirations for the novella ranged from classic Warner Bros. prison pictures of the 1930s to the 1872 Leo Tolstoy short story "God Sees the Truth, But Waits" (also known as "The Confessed Crime" and "Exiled to Siberia"). Tolstoy's main character, Ivan Dmitrich Aksionov, is a merchant wrongly convicted of murder and sent to Siberia, where his skills as a mediator win him the respect of the guards and prisoners. He spends twenty-six years in prison, dedicating his life to God and improving the lot of others when he can. While there are echoes of all of that in "Rita Hayworth and Shawshank Redemption," it is very much its own story, and that story is about the two principal characters, Andy and the teller of the tale, Red.

The mainstream reviews for *Different Seasons* were not always kind. *Kirkus* decreed, "It will take all of King's monumental byline-insurance to drum up an audience for this bottom-of-the-trunk collection: four overpadded novellas, in non-horror genres." The reviewer did concede that "Rita Hayworth and Shawshank Redemption" was the "best of the lot." The *New York Times* declared the book uneven, "flawed and out of balance," but allowed that each of "the first three novellas has its hypnotic moments, and the last one is a horrifying gem." While the *Times* reviewer's greatest praise was for "The Breathing Method," he did observe that "Rita Hayworth and Shawshank Redemption" proved that "the creator of such studies of the criminal mind as *The Shining* and *The Dead Zone* can effectively treat innocence as well as guilt."

Still, *Different Seasons* certainly won its share of rave reviews, as well, with the *Los Angeles Times* saying the book demonstrated that, "To find the secret of his success, you have to compare King to Twain and Poe, with a generous dash of Philip Roth and Will Rogers thrown in for popular measure." The *Washington Post* review heralded the book as "cause of rejoicing." And *People* said the four novellas were "fast-paced page turners" and the book was "an unqualified success." Readers agreed with the *Washington Post*, giving *Different Seasons* a nice ride on the bestseller list. It racked up sales figures strong enough to make it the eighth best-selling hardcover work of fiction for 1982. The books in front of it were novels by what the *Times* dubbed "commercial" writers, led by thrillers and historical fiction: *The Parsifal Mosaic* by Robert Ludlum, *North and South* by John Jakes, and *The Prodigal Daughter* by Jeffrey Archer.

With the luxury of taking a longer view, the leading King scholars have been better equipped and more adept at putting *Different Seasons* into some perspective, particularly in terms of the writer's long career. George Beahm, writing in *The Stephen King Companion*, points to a storytelling magic King found in the novella: "Lacking the depth and breadth of the novels, they nevertheless allow King more scope than the short stories. As a result, he is able to concentrate his attention on remarkable characters in equally remarkable settings." The author of several books on King, Beahm has this to say about Andy's story: "In spite of its horrific setting,—Shawshank Prison, with its concrete walls and cruel, sometimes stupid wardens and guards . . . 'Rita Hayworth and Shawshank Redemption' paradoxically comes across not as an exercise in gritty realism but as almost as an attempt at idealism . . . a tribute to the indomitable human spirit." Among the people who zeroed in on that element of the novella was a young screenwriter named Frank Darabont.

Sitting on the ever-expanding shelf of King publications as we approached a new century, *Different Seasons* increasingly took on a special glow, recognized as the source for the stories that became director Rob Reiner's *Stand by Me* (based on "The Body") and Darabont's *The Shawshank Redemption*. One book was responsible for two of the finest, most-praised, most-beloved adaptations of the many film and TV adaptations of King's works. Tossing in Reiner's great success with the 1990 film version of *Misery*, which boasted the Academy Award–winning portrayal of Annie Wilkes by Kathy Bates, some critics stated there was some irony in the notion that three of the greatest King adaptations were not horror stories.

To which many a Stephen King devotee would respond, "Really?" They're not supernatural in any way, but the same can be said of *Psycho, Night of the Hunter, The Wicker Man, The Silence of the Lambs,* the original *Carnival of Souls, Whatever Happened to Baby Jane?,* and another film starring Tim Robbins, *Jacob's Ladder* (directed by Adrian Lyne, the director first chosen to be at the helm of *Stand by Me*). *The Shawshank Redemption* is not a horror film? Says who? It's a horror story, all right, even if we're not using the term in the traditional pop-culture sense. Andy is living a nightmare—a brutal nightmare that goes on and on. Can you imagine a greater horror than what the innocent Andy faces at Shawshank State Prison? Probe the dimensions of that nightmare, and you sense there's much going on here that's closely related to King's supernatural tales. At least one film critic in 1994 reminded us of that, too. While many reviewers took pains to emphasize that *The Shawshank Redemption* was not a horror film, *Rolling Stone* film critic Peter Travers remarked that "the torture, rape and killing in *Shawshank* qualify as horror in my book."

"Their different tones and textures reflect the 'different seasons' of the title, yet beneath each lurks a decidedly macabre quality," King scholar Douglas E. Winter writes in *Stephen King: The Art of Darkness*. Precisely so. *The Shawshank Redemption* is much more than a horror tale, to be sure. It embraces much more in theme and genre, but you can't discount that aspect of the story. It is crucial. It is an essential part of the strong foundation on which *Shawshank* is built.

And King's story *is* the foundation on which the film and the ardency of its following are built. Darabont acknowledges the primacy of "Rita Hayworth and the Shawshank Redemption": "That's where it all started, and that's where it still lives."

Clancy Brown, who played vicious captain of the guard Byron Hadley in the film, agrees wholeheartedly. "It all starts with the script, and

Frank did such a great job of adapting that story," Brown said. "But Stephen King wrote a really great story to start with. In many ways, the story is better than the movie. The story is better only because it can be. It can go into more detail throughout the decades. It can give you more nuance. But you have to realize that I always feel the book is better. That's me. . . . The script, though, is just a brilliant job by Frank. Frank pulled off a perfect cinema adaptation. He combined characters and moved through that long, long period of Andy's incarceration, pacing it really well, but keeping the same ensemble of characters around him. That doesn't happen in Stephen King's story so much. The talent that Stephen has, which is prodigious, is perfectly suited to the talent that Frank has in adapting his stories. A few years later, he did the same thing with Stephen King's *The Green Mile*, although I don't like it as much, but then, I'm biased. Frank really is a writer's writer. He's so good at that."

Still, before we get to Darabont's screenplay, we must spend some time in Reiner's company. How did Reiner end up as the director with the keys to the King-dom?

Reiner had no film credits as a director when *Different Seasons* was published. When filming began on *Stand by Me* in 1985, he had directed just two movies: the mockumentary *This Is Spinal Tap* and the romantic comedy *The Sure Thing*. You can see in "The Body" exactly what he saw: the possibility of a lyrical and heartfelt summer story about four friends on a journey that begins in the waning days of childhood and takes them to the early, uneasy steps of adulthood. And with Wil Wheaton, River Phoenix, Corey Feldman, and Jerry O'Connell cast as the four friends, that's precisely what Reiner and his team delivered in 1986 under the title *Stand by Me*, with Ben E. King's 1961 hit song of the same name used in the film.

The perception in the mid-1980s was that Hollywood had a miserable track record when it came to adaptations of Stephen King's works. This perception led writer and King admirer Harlan Ellison to ask, in an essay penned for Jessie Horsting's *Stephen King at the Movies* (1986), "So why is it that films made from Stephen King's stories turn out, for the most part, to be movies that look as if they'd been chiseled out of Silly Putty by escapees from the Home for the Terminally Inept?"

Harlan was describing a state of affairs as frightening as anything King had conjured for his best-selling novels, but the track record was nowhere near that disastrous. *Carrie* had delivered its share of iconic moments. *Creepshow* was a solid piece of entertainment. *The Dead Zone* keeps looking better and better. Still, another perception emerged in 1986. The consensus was that Rob Reiner had delivered the first truly great adaptation of a King story (the adaptation of the novella "The Body" as the film *Stand by Me*), meaning it was both a great movie and it was faithful to the source material (something that could not be claimed by ardent admirers of director Stanley Kubrick's 1980 version of *The Shining*). Among those who stated that belief was Stephen King, who said that *Stand by Me* was the first wholly successful feature-length film based on one of his works. Reiner later told Chicago film critic Gene Siskel that, after a pre-release screening of *Stand by Me*, King was so profoundly moved, he had to excuse himself for fifteen minutes. When he composed himself and returned, he told Reiner, "That's the best film ever made out of anything I've written, which isn't saying much. But you've really captured my story. It is autobiographical."

That's not to say that young Stevie King went off with three boyhood friends to search for a body. Yet there are many autobiographical aspects to *Stand by Me*, most noticeable in young Gordie (Wheaton), who dares to dream of becoming a writer. The novella, however, is a heartfelt, richly nuanced reflection of his childhood hopes and dreams, with all its amazing potential and all the potential dangers, challenges, and snares.

The success of *Stand by Me* led Reiner and four partners to form Castle Rock Entertainment in 1987. Their film and television production company was named for the fictional town that serves as the setting for so many of King's stories. This is a moment that should be celebrated by every fan of *The Shawshank Redemption*. Without *Stand by Me*, there's no Castle Rock Entertainment, and without Castle Rock, a screenwriter and aspiring director named Frank Darabont had nowhere to take his screenplay adaptation of "Rita Hayworth and Shawshank Redemption."

Darabont first felt the pull of the movies at the age of five when his older brother took him to see *Robinson Crusoe on Mars*. The movies

9

weren't just calling; they were suggesting to him, even at that tender age, his calling.

"Even on some level," he would tell the *Los Angeles Times* in 1994, "I knew I wanted to be the storyteller. There was always something grand about it to me. My focus is to be behind the camera and pushing the buttons the way that certain people pushed my buttons as I was growing up."

A 1977 graduate of Hollywood High School, Darabont landed his first job in the movies at the concession stand of the landmark Hollywood Egyptian Theater on Hollywood Boulevard. In his spare time, he was at the typewriter. In 1980, the twenty-year-old Darabont had sent King a letter, asking permission to adapt the short story "The Woman in the Room," which had appeared in the 1978 collection *Night Shift*. A deeply personal story for King, it told of an anguished man's decision to euthanize his terminally ill and suffering mother with an overdose of painkillers. King, in his introduction to the published screenplay of *The Shawshank Redemption*, describes "The Woman in the Room" as "a kind of cry from the heart after my mother's long, losing battle with cervical cancer had finally ended."

Something in the young Darabont responded to that grief-etched cry, and something about the way Darabont expressed himself in his letter convinced King to grant his permission . . . for the grand sum total of one dollar. Yes, this was one of King's Dollar Deals.

"You can't even begin to believe how much my accountants hate this whole idea," King said.

The idea is to give young filmmakers a chance to prove themselves. For a dollar, he grants permission to film one of the short stories he has set aside for this policy. The power to assign film rights remain with King, and the aspiring directors must agree not to commercially exhibit their adaptations without his permission. King puts the resulting films on a shelf reserved for the Dollar Babies.

Darabont sent his dollar, and after having worked as a production assistant on such films as *Hell Night* (1981) and *The Seduction* (1982), he was in the director's chair for the first time. Darabont then sent the finished thirty-minute film to King, who was both greatly moved and impressed.

"You know, if I was making a list of the best films made from my stories, *The Woman in the Room* still would be on it," King said. "It was that good. It is that good."

The short film starred Michael Cornelison as the lawyer going through the anguish of watching his mother die. Brian Libby played the death-row inmate who counsels him. And Dee Croxton had the title role. Darabont used Libby in *The Shawshank Redemption* (in which he plays Floyd, one of the convicts in Red's inner circle), as well as two other King adaptations, *The Green Mile* (1999) and *The Mist* (2007). Darabont has said that Libby has a Lee Marvin–ish quality he loves (while King says it's a Neville Brand quality), and that he views him as his "good luck charm."

"Darabont obtained some exceptional performances from his actors and made a polished, well-written short film that was on the Oscar ballots," Jessie Horsting wrote of *The Woman in the Room* in *Stephen King at the Movies*, many years before Darabont had made his name as a director.

After making *The Woman in the Room*, Darabont started piling up writing credits, which included the 1988 remake of *The Blob* and the 1989 sequel *The Fly II*. He made his directorial debut with the TV movie *Buried Alive*, which aired on the USA Network and King called "a kick-ass cable movie." Darabont also penned two episodes of HBO's *Tales from the Crypt*. There had been talk following the acclaim for *The Woman in the Room* of Darabont making another King short story, "The Monkey," into a short film. Instead, he eventually got in touch with King to ask about adapting "Rita Hayworth and Shawshank Redemption."

That was in 1987. King agreed, granted Darabont an option, and waited. When months turned into years, he assumed that Darabont had given up. He hadn't. Five years later, he sat down at his computer and wrote one of the best scripts in film history over an eight-week stretch. Then he printed it out and shipped the whole thing in a huge package to King. Hard to say what surprised King more: the sheer size of the package from Darabont, or that there was a package at all. Although floored by what was inside the package, King was convinced that no mainstream Hollywood studio would touch this screenplay. But one studio would, and that's all that was needed. And, of course, it had to be the one studio that had grown out of the success of a movie based on a King story. It had to be Castle Rock. Producer Liz Glotzer, who admitted to an obsession with prison stories, was so knocked out by the screenplay, she announced her intention to quit the company if they did not produce what was then called *Rita Hayworth and Shawshank Redemption.*

"We're a script-driven company," Castle Rock president Martin Shafer told the *Los Angeles Times* when the film was released in 1994. "We just loved the script. We thought it was very moving, very intelligent, great characterizations, not like anything you've seen recently."

If you want to know Darabont's major influences as a writer, consult his introduction to the screenplay for *The Shawshank Redemption*: "In my lexicon of master yarn-spinners are names like Ray Bradbury, Mark Twain, Richard Matheson, Harlan Ellison, Charles Dickens, Shirley Jackson, Edgar Allan Poe, Saki, Raymond Chandler . . . oh, and a guy named Steve King."

It should also come as no surprise that two of the films Darabont cites as inspirations are director Frank Capra's *It's a Wonderful Life* and director Martin Scorsese's *Goodfellas*. You can sense those influences in how he transformed King's story into a screenplay. *It's a Wonderful Life* is an ultimately reassuring story with some incredibly grim aspects to it. *Goodfellas* is an edgy, violent story with some richly humorous aspects to it.

Now for the moment of truth. Castle Rock did see what King saw in the script, so much so that Reiner offered Darabont a cool $2.5 million to step aside and let him direct. That's the low figure in Hollywood lore. Some say it was $3 million. Reiner planned on casting Tom Cruise as Andy and Harrison Ford as Red, which would have pumped tremendous star power into Darabont's script. Put yourself in Darabont's place, if you can imagine it. Since making *Stand by Me*, a film King lavished with praise, Reiner had gone on a filmmaking tear, directing such films as *The Princess Bride* (1987), *When Harry Met Sally . . .* (1989), *Misery* (1990), and *A Few Good Men* (1992). This director, with perhaps the two best Stephen King adaptations to date on his resume, thinks your screenplay is magnificent and he wants to slip you a few million to direct it. Oh, and he's also going to bring two of the biggest stars in the business to the party. You're going to say no?

Unquestionably, Darabont's knees shook a trifle at this juncture. He had grown up poor. He had struggled for years to make his name in the industry. Suddenly, this was the big time. He'd be the screenwriter on a major production being directed by a red-hot director. And he'd be handed more money than he'd known in his life to deliver the screenplay into Reiner's eager hands. To sweeten the deal, Castle Rock offered to finance and green light any film Darabont wanted to direct. This is a true Hollywood story, and Darabont's reaction played out like the Hollywood script you would hope for: He turned down all of Castle Rock's offers to maintain control of his screenplay and to pursue his dream of directing. Thank goodness. Nothing against Tom Cruise and Harrison Ford, but can you imagine anyone but Tim Robbins and Morgan Freeman playing Andy and Red? Can you hear anyone but Freeman narrating the film?

Darabont held his ground. This was his moment and that meant claiming the director's chair on *Rita Hayworth and Shawshank Redemption*. How did Reiner respond? He did everything in his power to serve as a mentor to Darabont, who received $750,000 (plus a percentage of net profits) for writing and directing. The film was budgeted at $25 million (*Forrest Gump*, also made that year, had a budget of $55 million). Pre-production was slated to begin January 1993. All they needed was a cast and a place to shoot the thing.

(For more information on Stephen King's career and his thoughts about adaptations of his works, see Appendix I.)

FIFTEEN DIFFERENCES BETWEEN KING'S NOVELLA AND DARABONT'S FILM

A GREAT FILM ADAPTATION OF A BOOK ISN'T ALWAYS A MODEL OF STRICT fidelity to the source material. The jump from the printed page to the screen typically requires some reshaping and refocusing of characters and plot. The yardstick is whether or not those changes seem true to the intentions, themes, and mood of the book. The 1951 version of *A Christmas Carol* is a marvelous example of this. Starring Alastair Sim as Ebenezer Scrooge, this British production often is praised for its fidelity to Dickens. In truth, screenwriter Noel Langley changed some things and added others, particularly in the segment devoted to the Ghost of Christmas Past. (Langley and director Brian Desmond Hurst give Scrooge a motivation for resenting his nephew, Fred. In the movie, Scrooge's sister Fan dies giving birth to Fred, something Scrooge could never forgive, just as his own father had never forgiven him for being born. It's powerful stuff, and it's not in the book. Yet if not faithful in some details to the book, it is faithful to the spirit of *A Christmas Carol* [all of the spirits, in fact]).

You get the feeling that Dickens would have approved of the alterations, just as King approved of the changes in Darabont's screenplay. What was the nature of these changes? Here are fifteen examples:

1. **Andy Dufresne.** The character of Andy Dufresne in the novella doesn't quite measure up to the six-foot-five Tim Robbins. Tall and slim in the movie, Andy is described by King as "a short, neat little man with sandy hair and small, clever hands." He wears gold-

rimmed spectacles. Hearing that and picturing Robbins is a bit of a stretch, but no one's complaining, since the actor stands tall in this role in more ways than one.

2. **Red.** And Red, for that matter, is white and Irish. Morgan Freeman, not so much.

3. **Andy's Drink of Choice.** When Andy arranges for the convicts tarring the roof to enjoy bottles of cold beer, he declines to take one, telling Heywood (Bill Sadler) he gave up drinking. In the novella, Red tells us that Andy took four drinks a year, and the drink of choice was Jack Daniel's. He'd get a bottle through Red around his birthday and the holidays. He limited himself to one

One of the Stroh's Bohemian Style Beer bottles used in the movie now on display with other items at the Bissman Building in Mansfield

PHOTO BY BECKY DAWIDZIAK

drink on the morning and evening of his birthday, September 20, then gave the rest of the bottle to Red, telling him to "share it around." He'd get the second bottle for one drink Christmas night and another on New Year's Eve. The rest of that bottle also went to Red for sharing. The beer that Byron Hadley (Clancy Brown) gives the convict in the movie is an ice-cold Stroh's Bohemian Style brew. It's "piss-warm" Black Label in the novella, but, like in the movie, Andy doesn't partake, choosing to sit in the shade, watching the other convicts enjoy the beer, a little smile on his face.

4. **Brooks Hatlen, Jake, and Sherwood Bolton.** Shawshank prison librarian Brooks Hatlen is a character of far less importance in the book. He's a tough old con sent to Shawshank for murdering his wife and daughter. Not quite James Whitmore's genial Brooksie, who takes tender care of Jake the Crow. When paroled, Whitmore's Brooks tries working at a nearby grocery store. He has a room at a rundown hotel, where, tired of being afraid all of the time, he commits suicide. In the novella, Brooks, paroled in 1952, dies in 1953 at a home for indigent seniors. Jake, by the way, is also in the novella. He is a pigeon cared for by a convict named Sherwood Bolton, who is paroled a year after Brooks. After living in Bolton's cell for eight years, Jake is set free and flies away. About a week later, he's found dead, presumably starved, in a corner of the exercise yard. Darabont did include the discovery of Jake's body in his screenplay but added a touching funeral service conducted by Andy, Red, and their friends. It wasn't used in the final film.

5. **The Wardens and Prison Guards.** The movie has one warden, Samuel Norton (Bob Gunton), and one captain of the guard, Hadley. Three wardens are mentioned in the novella. Norton is the last of the three, so Darabont rolled the wardens into one character overseeing Shawshank during Andy's stay. The first warden in the novella is George Dunahy, "a prissy-looking downeast Yankee" who is fired for running a discount car-repair operation in the prison garage. He is replaced by Greg Stammas, a "cruel, wretched,

cold-hearted man" who turns Shawshank into "a kind of living hell." Hadley leaves Shawshank in 1957, taking early retirement after suffering a heart attack. In the film, Hadley remains at Shawshank until Andy escapes, and his fate is much harsher and more deserving. Stammas, about to be brought to account for his corrupt schemes, goes on the run in 1959. He is replaced by Norton, who has a Bible quote for every occasion, a sampler made by his wife, that reads, "His Judgment Cometh And That Right Early." Red calls him "the foulest hypocrite" he ever saw. "I think having continuity with the warden and the captain of the guard, as well as the prisoners around Andy, greatly focused the film and made it easy to follow," said Clancy Brown, who played Hadley. "It allowed for great continuity. That's part of the genius of Frank's script. He made all of the characters—prisoners, administration, guards—prisoners of Shawshank Prison."

6. **Warden Norton's Ending.** Like Brooks, Norton does not commit suicide in the novella. Like Brooks, he leaves Shawshank a free but broken man. He shuffles out of the prison, looking like an old con, three months after Andy's escape.

7. **Smuggled Cash.** In the movie, all of Andy's preferred treatment as a prisoner is a result of providing financial advice to the warden and the guards. That's true in the novella, as well, but Andy also has money to buy favors in Shawshank, having smuggled in $500. The realization that Andy has money was mentioned in Darabont's screenplay in part of Red's narration, but it was cut in postproduction.

8. **Bogs Diamond.** After leading an attack on Andy and beating him within an inch of his life, Bogs Diamond is given a horrific working-over in his cell. His injuries are not as debilitating in King's story as they are in the film, where he is left crippled. He suffers three broken ribs, a hemorrhaged eye, a sprained back, and a dislocated hip. Red hints that Andy bribed the guards to send a message. Red's guess is that the beating cost as much as fifteen bucks.

9. **Tommy Williams.** Like his movie counterpart, the Tommy Williams of the novella is a young convict Andy helps study for a high school equivalency test. As in the movie, Tommy once shared a cell with a high-strung convict named Blatch, who boasted to him that he was the one who killed Andy's wife and golf pro Glenn Quentin. In the film, Tommy is gunned down by Hadley when he states his resolve to help Andy. In the novella, Tommy takes a deal, presumably threatened by Norton. If he keeps quiet, he'll be sent to a minimum-security prison with a furlough program, allowing him to see his wife and child. In the movie, Tommy arrives at Shawshank in 1965. In the novella, he arrives in 1962. In the movie, Blatch's first name is Elmo. In the novella, his first name is Elwood.

10. **Prison Time.** In the movie, Andy is in Shawshank for nineteen years, arriving in 1947 and escaping in 1966. In the novella, the murders of his wife and Glenn Quentin occur in 1947, with Andy being sent to Shawshank in 1948. He escapes in 1975, having spent twenty-seven years behind bars.

11. **The Posters.** In the movie, the passage of time is represented by the three posters Andy uses to cover the tunnel in his cell wall: Rita Hayworth in *Gilda* (1946), from 1947 to 1957; Marilyn Monroe in *The Seven Year Itch* (1955), from 1957 to 1966; and Raquel Welch in *One Million Years B.C.* (1966), in 1966, the year he escapes from Shawshank. In the novella, Andy has twice as many posters: Rita Hayworth (not from *Gilda*, but a swimsuit pose), from 1949 until 1955; then Marilyn Monroe in *The Seven Year Itch*, from 1955 until 1960; then Jayne Mansfield for about a year; then English horror star Hazel Court, until 1966; then Raquel Welch (not from *One Million Years B.C.*, but, significantly, on a beach, maybe in Mexico), from 1966 until 1972; and, finally, singer Linda Ronstadt.

12. **Rita Hayworth.** In Darabont's film, the movie *Gilda*, starring Hayworth, is playing when Andy asks Red if he can get him a poster of Hayworth. In King's story, director Billy Wilder's *The Lost Weekend* (1945), starring Ray Milland as an alcoholic writer, is

playing. Darabont's screenplay followed King's lead, using *The Lost Weekend*, but Paramount Pictures asked a steep price for using a clip. So producer Niki Marvin suggested they look at the films in the Columbia Pictures library. Since Columbia would be releasing the film domestically, perhaps the studio would give them a better price to license a clip. Marvin noticed several Hayworth films on the list and honed in on *Gilda*. Darabont freely admits that, up to this point, it never occurred to him to have footage of Rita Hayworth in the movie.

13. **Mozart.** The scene where Andy locks himself in Warden Norton's office and plays a duet from Mozart's *The Marriage of Figaro* on the prison's public address system does not appear in the novella. This was Darabont's invention.

14. **Red's Friends.** Another addition by Darabont was an inner circle around Red, including Heywood (William Sadler), Floyd (Brian Libby), Skeet (Larry Brandenburg), Jigger (Neil Giuntoli), Snooze (David Proval), and Ernie (Joseph Ragno).

15. **Mexico.** When Andy finally gets out of Shawshank in the movie, Andy heads to Mexico with more than $370,000 of money he has stashed away for Warden Norton under an assumed name, Randall Stevens. He assumes the Stevens identification, cleaning out one bank account after another in the Portland area. In the novella, however, Andy tells Red that a trusted friend set up investments for him after he went to prison. The investments were made in the name of Peter Stevens, who has a birth certificate, a Social Security card, and a Maine driver's license. The friend died, but, by 1967, the Stevens portfolio is worth more than $370,000. He also tells Red that, along the base of a rock wall in Buxton, underneath a piece of black volcanic glass, there's the key to a safe deposit box. Peter Stevens is inside that box, waiting to get out . . . waiting to get out and head for a little town in Mexico . . . a place on the Pacific Ocean . . . a place called Zihuatanejo.

STEPHEN KING TALKING *SHAWSHANK*

WHILE ON ASSIGNMENT, I HAD THE CHANCE TO INTERVIEW KING almost ten years after the initial release of *The Shawshank Redemption*. Most of the conversation focused on the film and television adaptations of his works, and, since this was almost a decade after the initial release of *The Shawshank Redemption*, talk naturally got around to Frank Darabont's film. I asked King recently if he wished to revisit the subject, but, facing an incredibly busy stretch, he opted to let this stand, saying that his feelings toward the movie and Darabont's screenplay have not changed since then. For his part, Darabont expressed his hopes for the film during a September 1993 press conference in Ohio, where it was shot: "I'm drawn to him as a fan of his writing. I'm hoping that this film will broaden the perception of King's writing."

> **MD:** There was a time when a common gripe was the disappointing track record when it came to film versions of your works. If that complaint ever was true, it sort of has been wiped out by now, hasn't it? If that complaint has not been put to rest by now, it should be, right?
>
> **STEPHEN KING:** I think so. There certainly have been some good ones, and even a few great ones. [Director] Rob Reiner did a wonderful job with *Stand by Me* and *Misery*. And *The Shawshank Redemption* is right there at the top of the list. Frank Darabont not only made one of the best movies from one of my works, he made what may stand as one of the best movies, period. It seems to be well on its way to classic status, and it certainly deserves it.

MD: You've always said that the books are books, the movies are the movies, and you don't get upset when the movies turn out badly. Do you still feel that way?

KING: Absolutely. I don't get too upset when the movies don't work. What really sets my teeth on edge is when people come up to me and say, "Stephen King, I love your movies." I want to say, "Well, I do have this other little career where I write books." The book always is first with me. That's what I do. But I've never been resistant to the idea of people trying to turn one of my stories into a well-made movie. I love movies, so I'm eager with everybody else to see if someone can make a really good movie out of my work.

MD: I remember during the ABC press conference for *The Stand*, you were asked about many misses when it came to adaptations of your work, and you shared a story about James M. Cain. Do you remember that?

KING: Yeah, I've always liked that story. Some young guy went to visit Cain at his house and said something like, "Gee, Mr. Cain, isn't it a shame the way Hollywood has butchered your books?" And Cain said, "Let me show you something." And he took this guy to a bookcase and pointed to a shelf with all of his books. And he said, "See? They haven't butchered a single one of them. Look, they're all right there." That's pretty much how I feel about the movies made from my work. They can't touch the book. They can make ten bad movies based on one of them, and they still can't touch the book.

MD: Still, it must be gratifying when one of those films turns out to be *The Shawshank Redemption*.

KING: Sure. No doubt about it. I love movies. I've always loved movies. So there is a thrill when someone makes a really special movie from one of my stories. And Frank Darabont knows how to capture the essence of a book but then take the heart of that into another medium. That happens sometimes when a gifted director or screenwriter transfers a book to the screen. But I still wouldn't have bet he or anyone else could have taken that novella and turned it into a script a studio would make. No way.

MD: Why?

KING: I guess it was mostly because that story didn't have the visual elements that were in, say, *The Stand*, for instance. There's not a lot of what Hollywood would call action in the story. It's all narration. There are visual elements in the novella, but not the type or scale that makes a studio executive start rubbing his hands. It just doesn't jump out as a likely contender for a movie that would excite a big studio.

MD: So you had to have had plenty of doubts going in.

KING: Oh, sure. That had nothing to do with Frank, by the way. I already knew Frank was a terrific writer and filmmaker from what he'd done with "The Woman in the Room." It had everything to do with the nature of the work and how Hollywood does business.

MD: So when Frank asked for the rights to "Rita Hayworth and Shawshank Redemption," why did you give it to him? Was it because he'd done such a wonderful job with "The Woman in the Room"?

KING: In a way, yeah. That was a big part of it. Actually, I think one of the main reasons I said yes was because I just wanted to see what he would do with it. I was awestruck by what he did with "The Woman in the Room." That's still one of my favorite films made from one of my stories. So I knew if he could lick the novella, the screenplay would be something incredible. It would just have to be great, and it was. And I wanted to read it.

MD: But, even after you read it, you still had your doubts about this film being made.

KING: The screenplay was great, really incredible. But that didn't mean any studio would recognize why it was great. It didn't mean any studio would want to make a period drama set mostly in a prison. So now my doubts were because the screenplay was too damned good to get made. It was too smart, too talky, too nuanced, too literate to become a movie.

MD: In fact, you once called the screenplay version of your novella too novelistic.

KING: That, too. But, against all odds, Castle Rock not only let him make it, but let him make the great movie he envisioned. I sure was never happier to be proved wrong.

MD: The movie is about not letting go of hope—about Andy holding on to hope against all odds. In a way, from what you're saying, Frank's determination to make this film is mirrored in Andy's journey during the film.

KING: You're comparing a long stretch in Shawshank State Prison with making a movie? Now, that's scary. I wouldn't want to push the comparison too far. But, in some ways, I guess there are parallels there, and it's probably true for a lot of filmmakers fighting to get things made the right way. And this one sure got made the right way, thanks to Frank's vision and determination.

MD: I've heard the story about how much Frank Darabont ended up paying for the rights to "Rita Hayworth and Shawshank Redemption." I love the story and I'm hoping it's not just a story. I think it starts with Frank asking you how much you wanted for the rights.

KING: Well, I guess you could start it there. I really didn't know what to tell him, and I sure didn't know if a picture would ever get made. So I told him to send me a check for $5,000 to secure the rights. I think it was $5,000. I could be wrong about the exact amount. But I didn't cash the check. I told him that if he couldn't get the film made, I'd send him back the check. So the film gets made and we all know how it turned out. I took that check, had it framed, and I sent it back to him.

MD: And you included a note that said, "In case you ever need bail money." Is that true? Tell me that's true.

KING: Yeah, that's the way I heard the story.

II.

THE *SHAWSHANK* PRODUCTION: MAKING OF THE MOVIE

It was just a pleasure going to work every day. It was such a fun shoot. When you do this job and read the script and wonder how it will all turn out, that's when it gets exciting. If you're working with good people, which I was on this film, and the material is wonderful, which this was, it becomes so much more than a paycheck. You start to think you're part of something really special, and with The Shawshank Redemption, did that ever prove to be true.

—KOKAYI AMPAH
LOCATION MANAGER AND PRODUCTION SUPERVISOR
THE SHAWSHANK REDEMPTION

THE CAST

Planning on *Rita Hayworth and Shawshank Redemption* kicked into high gear with the dawn of a new year, 1993. At the head of the creative team were director Frank Darabont, producer Niki Marvin, and two executive producers, Liz Glotzer, the earliest Castle Rock champion of the screenplay, and David Lester. Darabont would remember this intense period started with constant talk about casting, locations, and "endless rounds of meetings with key technical people." Top priority went to casting the two lead roles, Andy Dufresne and Ellis Boyd "Red" Redding. Reiner recommended the actor he had just directed in *A Few Good Men*, Tom Cruise, for Andy. Castle Rock still was heartened by the notion of Cruise as Andy, and Cruise, like everyone, was greatly impressed by the screenplay. Intrigued as he was, however, Cruise balked at putting himself in the hands of a director making his first feature-length film. Cruise told Reiner he'd sign on if Reiner would oversee the production. Reiner told him it was Darabont's show, and Cruise passed. Among those considered to play Red were Clint Eastwood and Paul Newman. Others mentioned for the role of Andy were Tom Hanks, Kevin Costner, Johnny Depp, Nicolas Cage, and Charlie Sheen. (Hanks was unavailable because he was starring in the movie that would win the Academy Award for best picture of 1994, *Forrest Gump*. Hanks ended up making a pretty good prison picture directed by Darabont, based on a Stephen King story, featuring music by Thomas Newman, and also made by Castle Rock: *The Green Mile*.)

Darabont's top choices for Red were Gene Hackman and Robert Duvall, two of his favorite actors. Neither was available. Rob Reiner had suggested Harrison Ford for Red. It was Liz Glotzer to the rescue. She suggested Morgan Freeman, arguing that there was no reason the character had to be a white Irishman. After reading the script, a delighted Freeman eagerly accepted. And Freeman takes credit for suggesting that Tim Robbins be cast as Andy. Robbins first gained national attention in 1982, playing domestic terrorist Andrew Reinhardt in a three-episode arc of the acclaimed NBC drama *St. Elsewhere*.

"You remember that?" Robbins asked with some amazement during the interview for this book. "You're right. That is where it all began for me. It wasn't long after graduating college, and I was handed this incredible role on this show with this incredible cast and this amazing group of writers."

It took a few years, but his film career took off with writer-director Ron Shelton's *Bull Durham* (1988), director Adrian Lyne's *Jacob's Ladder* (1990), *Bob Roberts* (also his 1992 directorial debut), and director Robert Altman's *The Player* (1992). Darabont has said it was *Jacob's Ladder* that convinced him to consider Robbins. But he's willing to defer to Freeman's memory on who first suggested him.

"Morgan and I clicked immediately," Robbins said. "First of all, I was inclined to like him because I so admired his work so much, particularly in *Street Smart*, but, then again, I go back to *The Electric Company*, so. . . ." Born on October 16, 1958, in West Covina, California, Robbins had just turned thirteen when *The Electric Company* premiered on PBS with a thirty-four-year-old Freeman as a regular.

"I was just very excited about working with him," Robbins said. "When we sat down to discuss the script, I knew it was going to be a great collaboration. Both of us had a great passion for the story, and we both wanted to capture what it means to be incarcerated for a long period of time and what that does to a person's soul. And the compassion Morgan had for that was extraordinary, as was his passion for filmmaking. We both responded to the script, which was one of the most beautiful scripts we'd ever read. It was brilliant. But that also puts tremendous pressure on you. You don't want to fuck it up. You want to take the diamond and shine it in a beautiful way. There was an incredible shared sense of purpose with *Shawshank*, and we became really good friends doing that movie."

In addition to all of that, Robbins already was a major Stephen King fan.

"Oh, yes, I was, very much, yeah!" Robbins said. "Big, big Stephen King fan, so to be associated with what turned out to be one of the best adaptations of his work is particularly thrilling. Well, I remember reading *The Shining*, and being absolutely terrified in my little apartment in Hollywood, trying to read it, afraid to keep going and not able to put it down. It was a profoundly terrifying experience."

Robbins, though, also had reservations about Darabont's lack of credits as a director. He agreed to sign, with one stipulation.

"Well, none of us were yet sure about what Frank could do as a director," Robbins said. "You have to remember that Morgan and I had responded to the script. The guy wrote the best script I ever read. And when I read that script, I was filming *The Hudsucker Proxy* with the Coen brothers. I gave the script to the cinematographer on that film to read. That was Roger Deakins, who is amazing. Just incredibly talented. In fact, I used him as the cinematographer on the next film I directed, *Dead Man Walking*, which we made right after *Shawshank*. And when we were negotiating my contract for *Shawshank*, I asked for cinematographer approval. So Roger came onto the film with me. I felt that having a brilliant cinematographer was the most important thing for a first-time director. I knew that from my own experience when I directed my first film, *Bob Roberts*. You need someone who knows what they're doing in terms of storytelling with a camera. And Roger's contribution to that film is invaluable. First scene to last, look at how wonderful the cinematography is in *The Shawshank Redemption*."

So, Glotzer suggested Freeman, who suggested Robbins, who brought in Deakins. With this kind of rolling creative thunder bringing together the key players, *Shawshank* was off to a booming start.

Sixteen actors ended up with billing in the film's opening credits. In the three spots behind Robbins and Freeman are: Bob Gunton, who plays the evil Warden Samuel Norton, William Sadler, cast as the funniest of Red's inner circle, Heywood; and Clancy Brown, portraying the brutish captain of the guard, Byron Hadley. Brown was no newcomer to films destined to inspire passionate fans and followings. Two such pre-*Shawshank* movies for the actor were *The Adventures of Buckaroo Banzai Across the 8th Dimension* (1984) and *Highlander* (1986).

"I've played a few villainous characters in films, but the only one that had close to the impact of Hadley was maybe Kurgan in *Highlander*," Brown said. "I don't know if the villains I had played made them think about me for Hadley. Kurgan was a pretty show-boaty villain. I still get asked about him a lot, but not like *Shawshank*. I've never been in a movie that had the same kind of resonance as *Shawshank*."

The versatile Brown's hard-as-prison-bars Hadley is such a memorable presence in the film, many are stunned to discover that, for twenty years, he has been providing the voice of Mr. Krabs, the notoriously cheap owner of the Krusty Krab on Nickelodeon's *SpongeBob Square-Pants*. When a newspaper interview with Brown ran in his home state in 2018, one reader left the comment, "OK, you've officially blown my mind. Byron Hadley is the voice of Mr. Krabs."

Even more villainous is Gunton's Warden Norton. After serving for two years (1969–1971) in the Army, earning a Bronze Star for valor and the Vietnam Service Medal, Gunton turned his attention to acting. He won a 1980 Tony nomination for playing Juan Peron in the original Broadway production of the musical *Evita*. Other Broadway credits that decade included the King in the original production of *Big River*, the Tony-winning musical based on Mark Twain's *Adventures of Huckleberry Finn*, and the title role in the 1989 revival of *Sweeney Todd*. He also had appeared as General Harper in *Glory*, the 1989 film featuring Freeman, and as Captain Benjamin Maxwell in a 1991 episode of *Star Trek: The Next Generation*.

"I'm so grateful for this movie myself, to be a part of it," Gunton told a group celebrating the film's twentieth anniversary. "Earlier on, I thought my only possible bid for kind of semi-immortality would be that I once played Juan Peron on Broadway. And now I think I may have scratched into my tombstone, 'This dude was the Warden. His ass now belongs to God.'"

After *The Shawshank Redemption*, Gunton played Ethan Kanin, a character who served as secretary of defense, White House chief of staff, and secretary of state over three seasons of Fox's *24*. His first film following *The Shawshank Redemption* was another acclaimed adaptation of

Rita Hayworth keeps her secret as she looks at Warden Norton (Bob Gunton) visiting Andy's cell in *The Shawshank Redemption*.

a Stephen King story, *Dolores Claiborne*. It was well received, but his role had nowhere near the impact of Warden Norton.

Gunton took a day off from playing Chief George Earle in the Sylvester Stallone–Wesley Snipes action thriller *Demolition Man* to audition for Darabont and Marvin. His head had been shaved to play Earle, so Gunton wore a wig for a screen test made with Robbins and filmed by Deakins. Everyone was deeply impressed with his take on Norton.

"I thought this was the best character I'd ever been given to portray," Gunton said during the twentieth-anniversary stay in central Ohio. "He was very rich—not just a bad guy, but an interesting bad guy . . . his being drawn to Andy so strongly, and his own crisis of a very warped conscience when he has to blow the kid away. He's so in control for three-quarters of the movie, and then just loses it, and the deliciousness for the audience of watching this guy . . . coming up against another proof that he was the one who was obtuse and didn't know what was going on. And that was fun to play."

The "kid" Warden Norton has blown away is young convict Tommy Williams, played by sixth-billed Gil Bellows. Brad Pitt had been cast as Tommy, but he dropped out of the production (he costarred with Cruise in director Neil Jordan's film version of Anne Rice's *Interview With the Vampire*, which opened in theaters two months after *The Shawshank Redemption* in 1994). Turning twenty-six during the shoot, Bellows was making his film debut in *The Shawshank Redemption*. Next in the credits were Mark Rolston (*Aliens, Lethal Weapon 2*), cast as prison rapist Bogs Diamond, and Jeffrey DeMunn (Harry Houdini in *Ragtime* and Mayor Jacobs in *Newsies*), playing the 1946 district attorney. If you're keeping track of the *Shawshank* cast that might have been, consider that future *Sopranos* star James Gandolfini turned down the role of Bogs.

William Sadler's name appears just before Gil Bellows. He had appeared in the 1990 action thrillers *Hard to Kill* and *Die Hard 2* and took on the role of Heywood, who loves Hank Williams tunes but doesn't like Andy at first. He gradually warms to Andy and grows to admire him, as do the other members of Red's gang. Sadler later recalled that Darabont approached him in 1989 about being in the cast for a Stephen King story he was planning to make into a film. Given that King often cites the *Tales from the Crypt* comic books of his youth as a major formative influence, it's appropriate that this conversation took place on the set of HBO's series version of *Tales from the Crypt*. Darabont wrote two episodes of that fun fright show, "The Ventriloquist's Dummy" (1990) and "Showdown" (1992).

The next five spots in the opening credits belong to the other actors playing members of Red's group of friends: Larry Brandenburg (Skeet), Brian Libby (Floyd), Neil Giuntoli (Jigger), David Proval (Snooze), and Joseph Ragno (Ernie). Libby's association with Darabont went back to the short film *The Woman in the Room*. Giuntoli had appeared in his *Tales from the Crypt* episode "Showdown." The next two spots were for actors playing Shawshank guards: Paul McCrane (Trout) and Jude Ciccolella (Mert).

The sixteenth spot was reserved as special billing for the actor adding a bit of Hollywood and Broadway royalty to the production, James Whitmore, "as Brooks." That would be Brooks Hatlen, the aging con lifted from a brief passage in King's novella and shaped into a likable and sympathetic character by Darabont. Whitmore, a World War II veteran, reported for duty on *Shawshank* at the age of seventy-one. He had won a Tony award. He had won a Grammy. He had portrayed Will Rogers, Harry S. Truman, and Theodore Roosevelt in one-man shows. He had appeared in such films as *Battleground* (1949), *Kiss Me Kate* (1953), *Them!* (1954), *Battle Cry* (1955), and *Planet of the Apes* (1968). He had starred in an acclaimed episode of *The Twilight Zone* penned by Rod Serling. He already had a star on the Hollywood Walk of Fame. And, for more reasons to count, he had special billing in *The Shawshank Redemption*.

Many a late night was spent debating the casting choices. Darabont recalled that "the only thing that made all those way-past-midnights really worth it was that our casting director, Deborah Aquila, could make us laugh our asses off and vice versa."

Dozens of smaller but nonetheless important roles needed to be filled, so casting notices were published and auditions held in Los Angeles and Ohio. One of the key roles that proved difficult to cast was that of a character known only as Fat Ass. This is the pathetic new convict who falls apart his first night in prison and is savagely beaten by Hadley. They found just the right actor for this crucial part during the California auditions. Thirty-three-year-old Frank Medrano auditioned at the Castle Rock office on Maple Drive in Beverly Hills.

"I was relatively new to professional acting, so I had just signed with an agent," Medrano said. "And I didn't have a car at the time, which is a sin in Los Angeles. So I recruited a friend to drive me. The scene called for crying, and I had learned some techniques in my acting training to get there. I have a couple of memories that seem to open the floodgates. So as I was waiting, I was doing my acting thing, and I started crying. And that was when the producer, Niki Marvin, went walking by and she saw me. So she tried to quickly get everybody together, because I was at that moment of great emotion. They couldn't get everybody, so they sent out a casting assistant to ask me if I could come back in about an hour, because so many people were at lunch. I agreed, but my friend who had driven me had left by then."

His agent's office was about a half a mile away, so he walked over there. When he got there, everyone was in a panic. Castle Rock had been calling. Where had he gone? Why did he leave? How soon could he get back? They were ready for his audition, for crying out loud. Medrano high-tailed it back to Castle Rock, only to discover that the "they" ready for his audition was one person.

"It was the casting assistant's assistant," Medrano said. "So I walked back and did the big crying scene for the casting assistant's assistant. And that went well, so then they had me read for the casting assistant. And that went well, so then they asked me to read for the casting director, Deborah Aquila. And I bawled again. That did it. I got the part. They later told me they saw hundreds of people for that role. I think they were most impressed that I could cry that many times in one day."

Filming wasn't scheduled to start for several months, so they sent Medrano on his way with a full version of the script and instructions to work on his part.

"It was the longest script I'd ever read," Medrano said. "It was like 120 pages. But it was incredibly compelling. You had to keep reading it. You couldn't stop. But there wasn't much to go on about the character in the script, not even a real name. Just Fat Ass. I begged Frank Darabont to change the character's name. Who wants to be referred to as Fat Ass?

But while working on the character, I never gave him a name in my mind, because there was something about his being nameless that actually helped me. So I never named him, but I did give him a job. I had taken an accounting 101 class and they told us about this problem when people routinely switch two numbers. So I thought this guy went to jail for a simple accounting error that led to big trouble. I used that because the punishment for a mistake was so enormous."

The preparation and planning phase for the film covered five months: three primarily in California and two primarily in Ohio (although, as early as March, there was steady activity in Ohio to prepare for the mid-June start date). When the Ohio State Reformatory in Mansfield was selected to be Shawshank State Prison in the movie, the Ohio auditions drew busy stage actors from the Cincinnati and Cleveland areas. They claimed many key roles. Located in the center of the state, Mansfield is about eighty miles away from Cleveland, to the northeast, and about 172 miles from Cincinnati, to the southwest.

Most of the Cleveland area actors traveled to downtown Mansfield to audition on May 5. The casting notice sent out in late April said that only those interested in speaking parts should audition (casting calls for extras were held later in May under the direction of extras casting director Ivy Weiss, including ones in downtown Mansfield and at the high school in Upper Sandusky). More than three hundred actors and wannabe actors showed up for the casting call overseen by the casting director for Ohio and day players, D. Lynn Meyer. Among the announced roles to be cast, for men age twenty-five and older, were prison guards, inmates, parole board members, a judge, and a supermarket manager. The announced roles for women, thirty-five or older, were a landlady and a supermarket shopper. Those cast in the film that day included Scott Mann (as golf pro Glenn Quentin), Morgan Lund (the driver of the laundry truck that delivers Andy's rock hammer to Shawshank), James Kisicki (the bank manager at the end of the film), Dorothy Silver (the 1954 landlady who lets Brooks into his hotel room), and Rohn Thomas (the editor of the *Portland Daily Bugle*, although this was not the role he was originally assigned).

"I was sitting in a breakfast nook with a friend in Cleveland Heights when I saw the notice about auditions in Mansfield," Lund said. "So I said to my friend, 'Hey, you look like a convict. Why don't we go down to Mansfield and end up prisoners in this thing?' So we went down to audition, and my friend didn't get in, but I did. At first, the casting person said, 'The director wants you, but he doesn't know where yet.' And I thought, 'Yeah, that makes a lot of sense.' I left thinking they'd never cast me. But, lo and behold, they call me and I end up being the laundry truck driver."

Silver and her husband, Reuben, were both pillars of the Cleveland theater community. Both auditioned for *The Shawshank Redemption*. Both were offered parts.

"It was my first film audition," Dorothy Silver said. "I read well for Darabont. I had every reason to believe I'd be cast as the landlady who admits James Whitmore into that dreadful room. And I was. Reuben was cast as the newspaper editor. He would have been in it, but he had a time conflict and couldn't do it. He was so disappointed, because he wasn't a film actor, and it would have been a wonderful experience for him. I know he would have enjoyed it."

Thomas, a stage actor whose film credits included the horror-comedy romp *Innocent Blood* (1992) and director George A. Romero's *The Dark Half* (another Stephen King story), also made the trip from Cleveland to audition in Mansfield.

"I was given a sheet with a few lines to read, like 'fish, fish, fish' or 'you want to double bag that,' so they obviously were thinking of me for several different characters," he said. "I eventually was cast as the center parole board man when Red finally gets paroled at the end of the film. Now, at the same time, I was cast in *Roommates*, which was shooting in Pittsburgh at the same time. But this was going to be a day-shoot on *Shawshank* late in the film so, no problem."

But Thomas didn't end up on the parole board, so there had to be a problem. There was. *Roommates* was a comedy-drama mix starring Peter Falk, D. B. Sweeney, Julianne Moore, and Ellen Burstyn. Thomas was making the two-hour drive from Cleveland to Pittsburgh to work on that film.

"Then the *Shawshank* people called me and said that Tim Robbins had had an allergic reaction to makeup, and they wanted to shoot the parole board scene the next day," Thomas said. "I told them, 'Look, I'm working in Pittsburgh and I have to stop at home first. I have two children. I have things at home to take care of.' Two or three hours later, I was home and packing a bag and I got a call. They said they didn't need me anymore. But when you're called to the set like that, it's a verbal agreement. According to SAG [Screen Actors Guild] rules, they owed me that day. So I called my agent and said, 'Look, I had a verbal agreement with these people. I had to take care of my kids. I packed a bag and was on my way when they called and canceled.' So when this was brought to their attention, someone on the film actually said, 'You'll never work in Ohio again.' I said, 'Oh, okay, that's interesting. We'll see how that plays out.'"

This is how it played out. Reuben Silver had a conflict and couldn't play the editor. Thomas, replaced on the parole board, was called in at the last minute to play the newspaper editor. It was one of the very last scenes shot in Mansfield. He not only worked in Ohio again (many, many times), he worked on *The Shawshank Redemption*.

Among those cast at the Cincinnati auditions were Claire Slemmer, who played the bank teller in 1966, and Paul Kennedy, who was cast as the 1967 Food-Way manager. Both had worked at the Ensemble Theatre Cincinnati.

"I was doing *A Streetcar Named Desire* at the time," Kennedy said. "I read for both the 1954 and 1967 Food-Way manager, not realizing they were two different characters. I thought they were the same part. So I got to play the 1967 Food-Way manager, who had a name, by the way. It's on the name tag they gave me to wear, so I always knew his name. It's Tom Briggs, although he's only billed as the 1967 Food-Way manager. So when people ask me what part I played in *The Shawshank Redemption*, sometimes I just say, Tom Briggs. Tom Briggs. Don't you remember Tom Briggs?"

Slemmer decided to audition when Ohio casting director Meyer got in touch with her agent about auditions.

"I was doing a lot of voiceover work, corporate films, theater for Ensemble Theatre of Cincinnati," Slemmer said. "So I went down to the theater where they were holding auditions, and there was this big long line. It was a cattle call. Well, I had an appointment, so I walked out, thinking, 'Look, with all of these people, they're never going to cast me anyway.' A week later, I get a call from Lynn, who said, 'They still haven't cast that part and they'd like to see you on film.'"

The part was the bank teller who Andy asks to put a package of incriminating evidence against Warden Norton and his whole corrupt system in the outgoing mail.

"I ended up auditioning in the bathroom of a house across the river in Kentucky, being filmed with a hand-held camera," Slemmer recalled. "Lynn just kept telling me, 'Be as natural as possible.' Again, I thought, under these circumstances, I'm never going to get this."

Like Lund, she was pleasantly surprised when the call came a few days later. Along with the good news came a copy of the screenplay, not just her scenes in the bank.

"They sent me the entire script, and I laughed and cried all the way through it," Slemmer said. "But I'd never heard of Frank Darabont. So I had no clue that it was going to turn out how it did: spectacular."

Charlie Kearns, who had done a number of commercials in Los Angeles, was a graduate student at Ohio State University at the time. He was cast as the 1966 district attorney at auditions held in Columbus, but he went into the audition thinking the movie was a horror flick.

"I wasn't sure I wanted to be in it," Kearns said with a laugh. "I end up being in one of the most loved movies of all time."

Piece by piece, top to bottom, the *Shawshank* cast fell into place. Yet one major role couldn't be decided by readings and script interpretations and filmed auditions in bathrooms. And this was as crucial as casting Andy and Red. What structure had the mood and presence to play Shawshank State Prison?

THE PRISON THAT WOULD BE

KING'S SHAWSHANK

It quickly was decided that *Rita Hayworth and Shawshank Redemption* would be filmed at an actual prison, not at a Hollywood studio, so the search was on for a suitable candidate. Producer Niki Marvin took the lead in scouring possible prisons in North America. A wide field of contenders was narrowed down to three—one in Montana, one in Tennessee, and one in Ohio.

The Montana prison was rejected because it seemed too western for a story set in Maine. And then there were two. The finalists were the Ohio State Reformatory (OSR) in Mansfield and the Tennessee State Prison in Nashville. Each had recently been closed: the OSR in 1990, the Tennessee prison in 1992. Knowing that there was great interest in OSR, Eve Lapolla, manager of what was then called the Ohio Film Bureau (later the Ohio Film Commission), worked on a strategy to make Mansfield the frontrunner. She put together a box of pictures and related material for Darabont and Marvin to peruse. She lugged the box out to Los Angeles for a massive expo attended by producers and representatives of the country's many state and local film commissions, arranging for Darabont and Marvin to meet her at the crowded event. It was the right move at the right time. But when the right time came, with Darabont and Marvin standing before her, the box went missing. Lapolla promised to send the pictures to them. They thanked her and moved on. Not five minutes after they had left, she found the box and went tearing down the packed aisles after them. Luck was with her. They were still in the building and very interested in seeing the pictorial evidence of OSR's star quality.

Looking through the box, Darabont kept saying, "Perfect, I love it, perfect, I love it." The next step was getting him to Ohio to tour the prison grounds.

This was not the first time that the massive OSR had attracted Hollywood's attention. And with good reason. Designed by prominent Cleveland architect and Civil War veteran Levi Tucker Scofield, the impressive structure used three styles of architecture: Victorian Gothic, Richardsonian Romanesque, and Queen Anne. The sprawling front part of the reformatory housed the administrative offices, a formal dining room, and living quarters for the warden, the chaplain, and their families. Using sandstone, limestone, and brick, Scofield incorporated design features from medieval castles, fortresses, and chateaux that fascinated him while studying in Europe. Built on a site that had once been a Civil War camp and training ground, OSR welcomed its first prisoners in 1896 (although construction, which started in 1886, was not complete until 1900).

In her book about the Ohio State Reformatory, Nancy K. Darbey titles a chapter about Scofield, "A Building Fit for a King." A king? Or maybe a count.

"Scofield's design of the Ohio State Reformatory was intended to create a sense of spirituality within the inmates so as to allow them to leave the institution better than when they arrived," Darbey writes. "Unfortunately, the prisoners saw the building as less spiritual, naming it 'Dracula's Castle.'"

The nickname stuck, and Dracula's Castle it became to not only the prisoners but many of the locals. Still, during its early years, OSR was a model prison guided by a genuine philosophy of reformation. By the late 1980s, however, the OSR had gone from reformatory to maximum-security prison. It also was suffering from age and overcrowding. A new prison, the Mansfield Correctional Institution (MANCI), was built on grounds adjacent to OSR, opening in 1990.

"The whole idea of the architecture was to point skyward, to promote looking skyward and to pray for redemption," said Dennis Baker, who worked as a corrections officer at OSR and later was the warden of the Mansfield Correctional Institution. "Everybody was given a Bible and forgiveness and a job to do, so there was a lot of spirituality mixed

The impressive front of the Ohio State Reformatory, nicknamed Dracula's Castle and used as Shawshank State Prison in *The Shawshank Redemption*

PHOTO BY BECKY DAWIDZIAK

up with the reformatory philosophy back in those days. That's not how it ended up, but it's fitting that those original ideas of spirituality and redemption also are reflected in the film most associated with it, *The Shawshank Redemption*."

Harold Cope spent five years as an officer at OSR, making sergeant after just twenty months on the job. He saw the old building at its worst before working at the new prison from 1990 to 2006.

"And I much preferred the old prison," Cope said. "The new prison was a very different atmosphere. I was not as pleased with the new prison. People were tighter and closer at OSR, prisoners and guards. I'm not saying there weren't brutal aspects to the place. Look, I was stabbed with a pencil and hit on the back of the head with a pipe during my days at OSR. But OSR had a tradition and feel. The old place had a lot of nostalgia for me, and a lot of the guards who worked at both prisons will tell you the same thing. It was special. It was a unique experience. It cost $87 million to build the new prison. For me, that money would have been much better spent renovating the old prison."

Cope and other guards were enormously helpful to the actors eager to have a better fix on the physical, emotional, and psychological aspects of prison life.

"They had opened the other prison not far from there, so some of the extras had been guards at the old prison," Robbins said. "They were able to give us great insight into what the whole system was and what it was like to be in that system."

Even during its final days, OSR, according to Cope, never completely lost the sense of one community it had during those days as a model prison.

"With some of the stupid stuff I pulled as a kid, I could have ended up in there as a prisoner instead of a guard," said Cope, who ended up with a speaking part in the film, as a guard, with one line. "One wrong turn can make all the difference. So I never wanted to know what someone was in for. I wasn't in their shoes. I didn't know what road they took. From the day I started to the day I retired, I took that into consideration, even if you were an inmate. We were all people at OSR."

Long before it closed its doors, however, OSR and its remarkable architecture had caught the eye of a Hollywood location scout. In August 1975, eighteen years before Darabont and his crew set up shop there, the prison was used for scenes featured in *Harry and Walter Go to New York*, a comedy starring James Caan, Elliott Gould, Michael Caine, and Diane Keaton, and directed by Mark Rydell. The film was set in the 1890s, and OSR fit the bill and the timeframe. Unfortunately, the film was poorly received. The dud landed with a resounding thud, and Caan took to calling this flop, "Harry and Walter Go to the Toilet." Not the most auspicious start for OSR's Hollywood career. Still, the two weeks Rydell's cast and crew spent filming in Mansfield poured an estimated $500,000 into the area economy. And the stars all made favorable impressions on their hosts, who enjoyed the fun and diversion of having a movie filming in their own town. It was an experience worth repeating.

And they did. Fourteen years later, Mansfield again hosted a film crew for two weeks, and the Ohio State Reformatory again was used for scenes in a major Hollywood movie. It was called *Set Up*. Never heard of it? Well, *Set Up* was what it was being called when filming at OSR began in mid-July 1989. By the time it hit movie screens at the end of that year, it was called *Tango & Cash*, starring Sylvester Stallone and Kurt Russell. When Warner Brothers first expressed interest in filming *Tango & Cash* at OSR, then in its final year as an active prison, Lapolla arranged a meeting with the warden, Eric Dahlberg.

"The new prison was close to being completed, but they weren't able to move into that yet," Eve Lapolla said. "When Warner Brothers came in to scout the location, Eric told them, 'There are three things you can't do here. You can't shoot an escape scene. You can't use my prisoners as extras. And you can't shoot in this one particular part of the yard.' And, of course, they wanted to do all three things. The fellow from Warner Brothers said they would pay a location fee."

"You don't understand," Dahlberg told him. "A location fee doesn't mean anything to me. It would go into a general state fund and then get split up by every penitentiary and reformatory in the state, so I wouldn't get much out of that."

The Warner Bros. representative then asked the key question. He asked Dahlberg what he wanted to close the deal.

"And Eric said he didn't have anything in his budget for a computer system for the new prison," Lapolla recalled. "The production company set up an account with a local store in Mansfield and deposited $100,000 in the account. That was his to spend as he wanted. So the new prison got its computer system. And Warner Brothers shot all three things."

Yet *Tango & Cash* fared no better than *Harry and Walter* with critics. The high-octane, high-action film was widely roasted in reviews from coast to coast. The box office also was disappointing. It was, however, another happy shoot for a Hollywood film crew in Mansfield. Lapolla said at the time that the prison officials' cooperation had boosted the chances for more films being made at OSR.

"The people in Mansfield, specifically from the superintendent on down at the reformatory, went the extra mile in cooperation," Lapolla said at the time. "There were several things they initially said couldn't be done that got done, thanks to the warden. Warner Brothers certainly left here happy. We would like to try to sell OSR as a location. It's a great piece of architecture. A period film could be done there with no problem."

Four years after the filming of *Tango & Cash*, Lapolla was contacted by Castle Rock about OSR possibly being used as Shawshank State Prison.

"I didn't recognize the title 'Rita Hayworth and Shawshank Redemption,'" she said. "So I called my son, who was in college at the time and a big Stephen King fan. He knew it right away. And when I read the script, I thought, 'This is wonderful.' It was a fantastic script. You don't know who is going to be cast, and that's everything, but the first order of business for me was to get the filmmakers to Mansfield."

Lapolla put together her box of photographs and had her meeting with Darabont and Marvin in the chaos of that noisy expo. She soon learned that OSR was one of the two finalists. Darabont and Marvin wanted to make a decision in March so they could begin filming in June. Her key ally in making the case for OSR was Lee Tasseff, executive director of the Mansfield-Richland County Convention & Visitors Bureau (the economic development corporation now known as Destination Mansfield). She placed her first call to Tasseff in early February.

Tasseff had been on the job since the fall of 1990. He started in the bureau post the same year OSR ended its days as a prison. He had met Lapolla through acquaintances at the state tourism office. He immediately recognized what a long film shoot would mean to Mansfield. This wouldn't be any two-week stay, like *Harry and Walter Go to New York* and *Tango & Cash*. This would generate more money for the area than both of those films.

Dennis Baker, the warden at the Mansfield Correctional Institution and a former corrections officer at the Ohio State Reformatory, had worked with Lapolla on other projects, including *Tango & Cash*. He also was brought into the loop.

Tasseff also put Lapolla in touch with Lydia Reid, Mansfield's first woman mayor.

"Part of the job is finding the location the production company wants and securing it," Lapolla said. "Lee was great in this regard. And Lydia Reid also understood immediately what was needed to be done. She couldn't have been more cooperative."

On a chilly Friday in March, Lapolla called Tasseff to say, "I've got four people coming into town from Hollywood to tour the old prison. I've got the director, Frank Darabont, and three others. We'll be there Monday. Meet us up there."

The three others were producer Niki Marvin, executive producer David Lester, and production designer Terence Marsh (a two-time Oscar winner for art direction in the 1960s, first for *Doctor Zhivago*, then for *Oliver!*). The prison had been empty for three years, and it wasn't in the best of shape when it closed. And the Hollywood visitors would be seeing it during one of those Ohio March stretches when winter refuses to loosen its icy grip. Baker was summoned, and he and Tasseff led Darabont and his three colleagues through every frozen corner of OSR on that frigid Monday, March 8.

At one point, Marsh, a soft-spoken London native, looked up at the wintry sky and said, "This place would look smashing with an opening

Director-screenwriter Frank Darabont, Mansfield mayor Lydia Reid, and producer Niki Marvin pose in front of the Ohio State Reformatory before a screening of the film in September 1994.

PHOTO COURTESY OF EVE LAPOLLA

43

helicopter shot" (thereby planting the seed for one of the movie's most famous scenes).

The OSR took their breath away, all right, but so did the blast of winter. Or, as Darabont would put it, the California visitors were "abjectly freezing our butts off and picking sleet out of our teeth."

"There was snow on the ground," Tasseff said. "There was snow inside the prison. It was cold, nasty, drippy, rainy. It looked every bit the abandoned hellhole as you might imagine. We spent eight hours in that place. Frank was everywhere, exploring and looking at everything. He was relentless. Every now and then, David Lester would say, 'Hey, I need to make a phone call.' And Frank kept scouring the place. I knew he was thrilled with what he was seeing, but I couldn't tell if they'd found what they wanted."

Baker got a stronger vibe. He was fairly certain OSR was knocking the proverbial socks off their Hollywood visitors.

"They fell in love with it," Baker said. "They really fell in love with it. It was cold, all right. It was a hellhole at the end of its time as a prison. In the wintertime, you had ice on the walls. There were rats and roaches and cats running around. It was overcrowded. East cellblock was the world's tallest free-standing cellblock. And it was like a human factory. The stench and the screams and the isolation. You get a bit of a feel of that in Shawshank. They loved the prison because it had the feel."

They did. Darabont, though, had yet to see the Tennessee State Prison. They told Lapolla, Tasseff, and Baker that they would be touring that site the next day. They'd make a decision right away and let them know no later than Tuesday night.

As good as his word, Lester called Tasseff on Tuesday. "If you can find me a warehouse, we'll bring you the movie," he said.

A warehouse? Darabont had determined that, as vast as the cellblocks in OSR were, controlling lighting and sound would be a nightmare. The small, dark, cramped cells couldn't be properly lit or shot. Also, Darabont wanted rows of cells facing each other, something that's not part of the OSR cellblock design. The plan was to construct an entire four-story cellblock with two hundred cells in a local warehouse, duplicating the general look inside OSR. Tasseff knew an ideal location. The downtown

Mansfield Warehousing & Distribution, a Westinghouse building, had plenty of space and a forty-foot ceiling.

"It was mainly used for storage, hauling things in and out, for companies that didn't have their own warehouses," Tasseff said. "It wasn't vacant, so they had to move some of their customers out to make room for the set. But it sure had the height they were looking for. So only David Lester came back on Wednesday, and he talked to the fellow who controlled the warehouse.

"Lester told the warehouse owner, 'Look, we know we're inconveniencing you, and we need to accommodate you and pay for that. But don't start gouging me. Tell me what you need. Tell me what's realistic. And we'll accommodate you.' And that's it. It was done. Eve called me on a Friday to show up on Monday, and on Wednesday I'm watching this all unfold with a guy I only met two days ago. You read about this kind of thing. You hear about it. But how on Earth do you end up in the middle of something like this? I walked out, and we know they need houses where the stars can stay, hotel and motel rooms for cast and crew. My head was just buzzing. I was thinking, 'Wow, this is good.' But I was scared."

There was one other minor stumbling block not yet mentioned. Going into 1993, OSR was scheduled for demolition.

"It literally was down to minutes before the wrecking ball was coming in," Lapolla said.

Actually, the wrecking ball already was there. Baker called Lapolla and said, "Eve, you're going to have to call the governor, because I have a wrecking ball sitting here."

Sounds like something out of a Hollywood movie, yet the idea was to move fast so they wouldn't lose a, well, Hollywood movie.

"Wires got crossed and the right people weren't informed," Baker said. "The day they wanted to start shooting was the day it was scheduled for the wrecking ball. So, wow, we had to jump through a lot of hoops. We went to the governor and got it stopped, or we'd never have had a *Shawshank*, at least not one filmed here."

The calls to Columbus saved the start date for the film company, and, in return, the film saved the Ohio State Reformatory from demolition.

"No question, the film saved the prison," Baker said. "The only thing that ended up being torn down were the outbuildings, where you had factories, textile shops, shoe repair, slaughter houses, canning, chicken coops. Because back in the old days, the prison was self-sustaining. It was a state-of-the-art prison at first. All of that was still standing for the film, as was the wall going around all of the prison and the outbuildings. But if it hadn't been for the movie, the main building and cellblocks wouldn't still be standing."

The Shawshank Redemption not only rescued OSR from its date with the wrecking ball, it ended up generating about three times the original estimated revenue for Ohio. The early calculation was about ten times what *Harry and Walter Go to New York* had kicked into Ohio coffers. *Harry and Walter* had only been in Ohio two weeks. *Shawshank* was a three-month shoot, with more than two months of pre-production in Mansfield and other area locations. Local media gleefully projected in March that the film would spend about $5 million in the area.

"When it was all over, we estimated that they spent between sixteen and eighteen million dollars in Ohio," Lapolla said. "Remember, it was primarily shot here, so they left most of the production money here."

Oscar-winning production designer Marsh hired Sebastian Milito to be the film's construction coordinator. They had worked together on *The Hunt for Red October* (1980), and it would be Milito's job to build what Marsh envisioned. Milito headed for Mansfield in February with location manager and production supervisor Kokayi Ampah. Beginning a seven-month stay at the Holiday Inn, they were tasked with overseeing preliminary location preparation.

"The prison was a mess and the warehouse presented all sorts of challenges," Milito said. "The unit manager, David Lester, asked me by phone, 'You ready to quit? You ready to come back?' But I was energized by the challenge. They gave me a blank slate. And the first thing I did was tear everything out, demo the old floor, and poured a new concrete floor. It was a six-inch floor. I hired a local contractor—an old Italian guy in his seventies. And the studio didn't give me any flak about anything. They let me do what I thought best. I'm a hands-on Brooklyn guy, so this whole experience was freaking exciting."

By the end of March, the Marsh-led team was building the cellblock set in the warehouse.

The walls, floors, and bars were painted a dark and dismal gray and treated to give them an aged look. Wood was used for some cell bars, fiberglass for the brick walls, and plastic for steel pipes. But Marsh's crew worked their magic to engineering specifications that accounted for the weight of dozens of men. And the cellblock was brought to life in great detail, right down to names on the wall, peeling paint, and imitation rust. Propshop foreman Isadoro Raponi came up with an air-pressure system that opened and closed the cell doors. Several real prison guards working on the film remarked on how realistic the warehouse set looked.

"If I had my eyes closed and was just dropped in here, I'd think it was a prison," Mansfield Correctional Institution officer Lieutenant Rick

The magnificent cellblock set designed by Terence Marsh takes shape in Mansfield's old Westinghouse warehouse.

PHOTOGRAPHS COURTESY OF SEBASTIAN MILITO

Brawley told the Mansfield newspaper. Brawley had worked at OSR from 1979 until 1990. Darabont later said that Marsh probably was passed over for an Academy Award nomination because almost no one realized what a marvel this set was in look, design, and ingenuity. It was so good, most people just assumed they shot the film in an actual prison.

"That cellblock set in the old Westinghouse warehouse was an art direction masterpiece," Ampah said.

Indeed, it was. It's what made the location shoot in Mansfield possible.

"It was an immense job," Milito said. "Tim's cell and Morgan's cell had actual metal bars. I had welders working day and night on that. Then a little back was steel frame. Then way back, we used wood and made it look like metal. But working on this movie was the best experience of my career."

Meanwhile, back at the actual prison, OSR, forty-three honor inmates from the Mansfield Correctional Institution were rewarded for their good records by being put to work. They were taken out of MANCI and over to the old prison, where they joined the battle against the damage and ravages of neglect in the areas Marsh and the Castle Rock team indicated they'd be filming. The company then hired contractors to paint and spruce up those areas, making them camera-ready. That included the reclamation of the prison yard, where so many scenes would be shot.

"The prison had been abandoned, so the yard was overgrown with grass and weeds, and this was supposed to be yard that had 2,000 men walking over it every day," Milito said. "So we weed sprayed everything, and then I had twenty or thirty truckloads of gravel dumped in. We made it look like a prison yard is supposed to look."

(It should be noted that Darabont also was impressed with what he saw in Nashville, and although the Tennessee State Prison lost out to OSR in the *Shawshank* sweepstakes, it would one day be ready for its close-up, thanks to Darabont. The writer-director filed it away, pulling it out of the file when looking for a prison to use in *The Green Mile*. But June of 1993 was the beginning of the Ohio State Reformatory's star turn.)

"It was in pretty bad shape, so I got there long before the shoot started to oversee the cleanup," Ampah said. "There were a lot of factors that went into the decision to shoot in Mansfield. One was the cooperation we got from the Film Commission and Mansfield. But, primarily, you look at that old castle appearance and those outbuildings, and it just has an incredibly distinctive look. Your jaw just drops when you're standing in front of that place. You look at that fantastic aerial shot early in the film, where you approach the prison, then go over it, and that says it all."

As the actors showed up in Mansfield, they were taken on tours of OSR. All felt the weight of the memories and ghosts clinging to the structure.

"I remember walking into the cell block with my son, Jack, who was four at the time," Robbins said. "And I remember him saying, 'Daddy, it's really sad in here.' And you could feel it. He was feeling what I had felt when I had walked in there."

And what had he felt? It's not an easy thing to put into words.

"You know how when you're looking for a house or an apartment, and you get that feeling?" Robbins asked. "You get that feeling of, 'Nah,

One tier of one cellblock at the Ohio State Reformatory
PHOTO BY BECKY DAWIDZIAK

I don't want to live here.' Then you find out somebody was murdered in there or something horrible happened there. It's a palpable thing. And walking into that cellblock, you could feel the pain and the suffering and the misery that had been between those walls. Now, we didn't shoot in that cellblock. It was easier for the production to build the cellblock as a set. There were safety issues, too. But the exteriors certainly made you feel like a prison and made you feel the history that was there."

Actor Jeffrey DeMunn put it another way: "We toured both the old prison and the new prison, and that gave me religion. I resolved at that moment not to even roll through a stop sign. But you couldn't help feeling the immensity and the history of the old prison."

In Hollywood terms, OSR had tremendous screen presence. If those gray walls could talk, they might have said, "I'm ready for my close-up, Mr. Darabont."

"It has an incredible presence in the film," Baker said. "It not only has a lot of character, it is a character unto itself, no question about it. The movie wouldn't be the same without it."

Lapolla puts it even more strongly: "This reformatory, this amazing building, to me, is the main character in the film. After all, it has the title role. This is Shawshank."

THE FILMING SITES

PRODUCTION OFFICES FOR *RITA HAYWORTH AND SHAWSHANK REDEMPTION* were set up in a downtown Mansfield building, 166 Park Avenue West, near the historic Renaissance Theatre (where the film would have a premiere showing in September 1994). With the casting directors looking for day players and extras, the locations team had to find various places for scenes set in everything from a bank and a pawn shop to a courtroom and a newspaper office. What they found contributed mightily to the success of the film.

Ashland University assistant professor Maura Grady, the coauthor of *The Shawshank Experience: Tracking the History of the World's Favorite Movie*, believes that the importance of the Ohio locations can't be underestimated. "The Ohio locations played a huge role in the success of the film, because each of those locations have a real history, and that affects the actors' performances and imbues the film with a realistic sense that people feel," she said. "It's not something built on a green screen. It feels real. It feels authentic, and that makes you believe you're experiencing something that's authentic. It's a tremendously important contribution to the film."

Grouped by areas, this is what they found and used in the film:

MANSFIELD

1. **The Ohio State Reformatory:** Even though the cellblock set built in the old Westinghouse warehouse was used for all of the scenes of Andy and Red in and around their cells, OSR was put to constant use in the film. It is believed that the only cell scene filmed inside OSR was the one of twitchy Elmo Blatch (Bill Bolender) confessing

that he murdered Andy's wife and golf pro Glenn Quentin. But all of the many prison-yard scenes and various Shawshank exteriors were the OSR grounds, including, of course, the memorable flyover shot showing the entire grounds early in the film. An assistant superintendent's room in the west administration wing of the main building became Warden Norton's office (a false wall was put in for the safe where Norton stores records of his financial schemes, and it remains there to the delight of visitors). The nearby staircases and hallways (with their distinctive floor designs) were used for scenes near Norton's office. The east cellblock showers, nicknamed "The Car Wash," were used for the scene where Bogs (Mark Rolston) first approaches Andy. The second-floor west-wing Protestant chapel, nicknamed "the Jesus Room," was where Red and other convicts are watching *Gilda* when Andy asks Red about getting Rita Hayworth smuggled into the prison. Other memorable scenes filmed inside the prison include Norton's welcoming speech to the new convicts, Red's three parole board hearings (1947, 1957, 1967), the projection room attack on Andy, and the prison library sequences. One still-standing set inside OSR is Brooks Hatlen's hotel room. The distinctive downtown Mansfield building used for the halfway house Brewer Hotel was not, in fact, a hotel, so Darabont's team found a space in the prison, near the immense Catholic chapel, and the veteran production designer turned it into the room where Brooks will hang himself. Nowhere on the OSR grounds seemed right for the woodshop where Red works or the prison laundry where Andy toils during his early days at Shawshank. Both were locations found outside of Mansfield.

2. **The Bissman Building:** Although only the exterior of this grand structure was used for the Brewer Hotel in *The Shawshank Redemption*, a ground-floor front room did become the *Portland Daily Bugle* office where the editor, played by Rohn Thomas, receives Andy's package of information exposing the corruption at Shawshank State Prison. Completed in 1886, the distinctive structure with its early Romantic Gothic style housed the Bissman family business for several decades. "We were kind of like the Wal-Mart of the 1800s," Ben

Bissman said while sitting in the room that became the newspaper office. "We had a little bit of everything from beverages—beer, wine, whiskey—to corn, produce, meat, clothing, hats. We were a wholesale grocer. We were a coffee roaster. We had spices. You name it." One day in 1993, he was in City News, the downtown newsstand and tobacco shop, and overheard a woman with the film company telling the owner they needed a big building to use as a boarding house. "We were already doing some signs for them," Bissman said. "So I walked

The distinctive and historic Bissman Building in downtown Mansfield doubled for the Brewer Hotel in *The Shawshank Redemption.*
PHOTO BY BECKY DAWIDZIAK

over and told her we had a great big building. I walked her down the hill a couple of blocks, and she looked at this and said, 'Perfect!'" *Shawshank* fans who visit the Bissman Building often ask if they can see the room where Brooks Hatlen, then Red, stayed after getting out of prison. They sure can, but it requires a quick drive to OSR. "I had a guy who insisted that he knew that room was in this building, and he was going to find it," said Amber Bissman, Ben's wife. "He was hell-bent. Thank goodness some people who just toured the reformatory came in and said, 'Oh, no, it's at the prison. We just saw it.' Even then, you could tell he didn't quite believe them."

3. **The Pawn Shop:** The Main Street building that is now home to Mansfield's Carousel Antiques was redressed by the *Shawshank* team to become the pawn shop where Red gazes through the window and sees the compass that later guides him to the rock wall and oak tree.

4. **Central Park:** The downtown Mansfield park was home to the bench where Brooks feeds the birds, hoping Jake will stop by and say hello.

5. **E&B Market:** Another downtown location, this actual market was used as the Food-Way, where Brooks works bagging groceries. Red later gets the same job in the same place. "We kept looking for a store to use for the Food-Way," location manager Kokayi Ampah said. "We kept looking and looking. It turned out, we found just the right one around the block from our production offices." In fact, many members of the production team had purchased groceries there. Shuttered for many years, it was renovated and reopened in 2018 as the KV Market, again a full-service supermarket.

UPPER SANDUSKY

1. **The Wyandot County Courthouse:** The historic structure became the Maine courthouse where Andy is tried for murder. Most of the film's locations were in or near Mansfield, but that city's century-old courthouse had been torn down in 1969 and replaced by a modern building. The *Shawshank* team went searching for a more suitable

candidate and found it in Upper Sandusky. They fell in love with the Wyandot County courthouse with its old judge's chair and leather jury-box seats.

2. **The Woodshop:** An actual brick woodshop, the Stephan Lumber Company, was used as the Shawshank prison woodshop. The original lumber company was built on this site around 1905. A fire in 1978 destroyed much of the building. It now houses a museum dedicated to *The Shawshank Redemption*. "We had to find a woodshop and a laundry, and both ended up being a good distance from the prison," Ampah said. "But they had the perfect look. You watch the film, and you have no doubt that these are in the prison."

ASHLAND

1. **The Farmers Bank:** An actual working bank in downtown Ashland was used for the Maine National Bank, where, at the end of the movie, Andy cleans out the account with Warden Norton's ill-gotten money. The Farmers Bank's massive vault, with its thirteen-ton door, was featured in the movie, behind the bank manager (played by Jim Kisicki). The building now is the home of Crosby Advisory Group, LLC, which is accustomed to fans stopping by for a glimpse at the vault.

2. **Downtown Store:** A building that now houses the Revivals 2 Thrift Store was transformed into the Trailways Bus Station where Red buys a ticket to Fort Hancock, Texas.

BUTLER

1. **Corner of Snyder Road and Hagerman Road:** This intersection was used for the road where Red gets out of the red pickup truck in Buxton, Maine, and begins to make his way toward the rock wall and oak tree.

2. **Route 95 near Hagerman Road:** This stretch of road was where you see the Trailways Bus carrying Red toward Fort Hancock, Texas. It's fitting that Red is on the road to finding renewal in the scenes filmed

in Butler. This was the town where Morgan Freeman stayed on a rented farm during the summer of 1993. He found a regular source of renewal here by going on horseback rides.

LUCAS

1. **Pugh Cabin at Malabar Farm:** Some Hollywood history already had been made at Malabar Farm, the home of Pulitzer Prize–winning novelist and screenwriter Louis Bromfield. This was where his friends Humphrey Bogart and Lauren Bacall were married on May 21, 1945. During filming, actors James Whitmore and Clancy Brown were given a private tour of the main house. But the quaint wooden cabin on the property, now a state park, was used for the opening scene, where a drunken Andy Dufresne sits in his car with a revolver and a bottle of whiskey. The cabin's interior was used for a passionate glimpse of cheating Linda Dufresne (Renee Blaine) and golf pro Glenn Quentin (Scott Mann).

2. **The Oak Tree:** Not far from Malabar Farm, on private property, the *Shawshank* team found the mighty white oak more than one hundred feet tall. It suggested Andy's description of looking "like something out of a Robert Frost poem." The rock wall wasn't there. It had to be built by the film crew. "It was a guy in my department, Chris Cozzi, who found the tree, and what a find," Ampah said. "And I learned a lot during that negotiation. There was a whole learning curve about putting that tree thing together. There was a field rented by a farmer who grew alfalfa, and there was the land owner. I learned that there are three cuttings of alfalfa: one in the spring, one in the beginning of summer, and one at the end of summer. And they degrade in quality, so the first spring cut is the best grade. So we let the farmer cut the first one. Then we asked him not to cut other ones, so then I had to find out from the agriculture department to estimate how much he'd get for the other cuttings. And we compensated him. Because we wanted it to be overgrown when we shot. Terry Marsh designed that wall and put a watering system in the wall, so we could grow things in the rock to give it that aged look. His team built it piece by piece.

"Like something out of a Robert Frost poem," the mighty white oak tree that
became another iconic image from *The Shawshank Redemption*

Then it was incredible to see how Frank used all of that to make the most of what we had: the field, the wall, the tree."

Building the wall fell to construction coordinator Sebastian Milito.

"The rock wall was one of my great pleasures," Milito said. "I told Terry we had to build it early because, we were going to bring in tons and tons of rocks with trucks and heavy equipment. It would trample all of that surrounding area down and will look like we just built it. So we had to do it early and let everything grow up around it and not look like a construction crew just left yesterday. Nature took over and made it look perfect."

Another non-human star of the film, the oak, estimated to be about two hundred years old, was split by heavy winds on July 29, 2011 (not struck by lightning, as is often reported). Rot was blamed for weakening the tree. "I don't know how pervasive this rotting is," Louis Andres, the regional manager for Ohio State Parks told the *Columbus Dispatch* at the time. "If it's pretty major, the next storm could knock down the rest of it, as well." His comments were prophetic. It was knocked down by wind storms on July 22, 2016. What remained was cut down on April 9, 2017. Clancy Brown, who grew up in Ohio, provided the three-word epitaph echoed by those who prize the movie: "That poor tree." But *Shawshank* fans still travel to where the tree stood, gazing at the site from a fence on Pleasant Valley Road.

ST. CROIX, US VIRGIN ISLANDS

1. **Sandy Point National Wildlife Refuge:** The only two scenes not filmed in Ohio occur near and at the end: Andy driving his car as a free man and the reunion of Andy and Red on the beach in Zihuatanejo, Mexico. The search for Zihuatanejo proved to be an adventure. The characters had to earn it in the movie, and so did the film's location manager. "I went away a couple of times to scout locations for the ending, for those two scenes," Ampah said. "I actually scouted in Mexico for beaches, and I had my car stolen. Now I'm six-three, and at that time I weighed maybe two-hundred-and-fifty. I had a Mayan guide who was maybe five-feet. We parked the rental car on the road and walked about a quarter of a mile to look at a beach." When

they returned, the car was gone. They had no choice but to walk to a small town nearby. "So imagine the two of us walking down the road, ending up at this small police station with a *Casablanca* fan and a comandante typing with two fingers on a Royal typewriter," Ampah recalled. "So we decided to go somewhere where English is spoken and they dealt directly in dollars. We got to St. Croix, but we picked a beach that had nesting leatherback sea turtles. So now we have to coordinate with the people there for when the turtles will be released from their next hatching and head for the ocean. It's just amazing what you learn when you do this job, from alfalfa crops to the nesting patterns of leatherback sea turtles."

SCENE ONE

THE FIRST WORDS YOU HEAR IN *THE SHAWSHANK REDEMPTION* ARE THE lyrics of songwriter Jack Lawrence's "If I Didn't Care," sung by high tenor Bill Kenny of the Ink Spots. The 1939 hit plays as a drunk Andy Dufresne sits in a car outside the cabin where his unfaithful wife (played by Renee Blaine) is in a passionate embrace with golf pro Glenn Quentin (Scott Mann). But the first actual lines of dialogue are spoken by Jeffrey DeMunn as the 1946 district attorney cross-examining Andy, on trial for murdering his wife and her lover. DeMunn's unnamed prosecutor then summarizes the case against Andy to the jury. It's a strongly worded final summation, and it results in Andy being given two life sentences in Shawshank State Prison.

It's the only time DeMunn is seen in the movie, yet his presence is crucial. He must make the case with absolute authority. He must make the evidence sound overwhelming, despite Andy's claims of innocence. He must get the film off to a compelling start. And does he ever, more than earning his billing in the opening credits. How did DeMunn end up with this crucial assignment? Well, trust had a great deal to do with it. Indeed, trust has meant a lot to the actor throughout his career. It led to a long, continuing association with a writer-director named Frank Darabont. That started with the 1988 remake of *The Blob*.

"That came out of left field," DeMunn said. "Frank was a writer on *The Blob*. They suddenly needed to replace someone on the film. I got the call, and I really needed a job. I had young children, and I was just trying to get through the month, month after month, every month. I asked, 'How much?' Because at that point my goal was just trying to make a living for my family. I got there, had a blast, and thought, 'Well, that's

Tim Robbins on the stand, playing Andy Dufresne in a scene filmed at the Wyandot County Courthouse in Upper Sandusky

that!' Then, a few years later, I got a call out of the blue to do *Shawshank*. That's when I was able to put two and two together. I thought at the time, 'Why would this man call me to do this role? How would he even know me?' It was because of *The Blob*."

The name may not be instantly recognizable, but you probably know Jeffrey DeMunn's work, and not just because of *The Shawshank Redemption*. Perhaps you know him as Dale Horvath in the early seasons of the hit zombie drama *The Walking Dead*, or as Russian serial killer Andrei Chikatilo (the Butcher of Rostov) in the acclaimed 1995 true-crime cable movie *Citizen X*, or as well-connected power player Chuck Rhoades Sr. on Showtime's *Billions*. DeMunn, who grew up in Buffalo, has established a solid reputation as one of Hollywood's most reliable team players.

"That's why I love acting," DeMunn said. "I had no desire to be the center of anyone's attention. When I went to college, I was picturing being part of a group of people trying to do the impossible. I really didn't find that in education, but when I discovered the theater, there it was. It was a group of people working toward a common goal, trying to do the impossible. I said, 'I'm home. This is it.' I had no desire to be a star—none. I wanted to be part of everyone pulling together to do the impossible. That's what *The Walking Dead* was in the early going. That's what *Billions* is like. And that's what being part of *The Shawshank Redemption* was like. It was being part of a great team."

Darabont directed Robbins and DeMunn in a third-floor courtroom of the magnificent Wyandot County Courthouse in downtown Upper Sandusky, located about forty-five miles west of Mansfield. A striking example of Beaux-Arts classicism, the impressive structure was constructed in 1899 and 1900. Darabont opted not to show the exterior of the courthouse, which, today, boasts a 2017 Ohio historical marker commemorating the part it played in *The Shawshank Redemption*. The courtroom he selected, however, had just the right atmosphere for the moment that blind justice blindsides Andy Dufresne.

This is also where principal photography began, with the first scenes shot for the movie on June 16. Many residents from the Upper Sandusky area packed that courtroom during the two blisteringly hot days they filmed at the courthouse. These extras were dressed in 1946 fashions to play jury members and spectators. They were more than a little starstruck when Robbins's partner of five years, Susan Sarandon, showed up for one of her Ohio visits that summer. The outgoing Sarandon chatted up several of the extras while standing with them in the food line for lunch.

"My wife and I had been in Florida, and we got home to see the newspaper story about them needing extras," said Robert Nachbar, an appliance store owner cast as a courtroom spectator. "So I told her, 'I'm going to go out and see if I can get into this picture.' I was never interested in the movies, so it was all about the new experience for me. Now I look at the film and realize I have a little part in something incredibly special. They told us not to talk to any of the actors, unless they talked to us first, and not to ask for autographs. But after Susan Sarandon and the kids stopped by, I found myself standing right next to Tim Robbins, so I said, 'Tim, were those your kids?' And he said, 'Yeah.' I guess it was

The Wyandot County Courthouse in Upper Sandusky, with its statue of Lady Justice, now boasts an Ohio historical marker that tells of its association with *The Shawshank Redemption*.

PHOTO BY BECKY DAWIDZIAK

violating the rules, but it's not like I was risking a big career in movies. But everyone was exceptionally nice during those two days."

That's the consensus, all right. The overall mood with the locals and their Hollywood visitors was extremely congenial.

"Frank Darabont later made a point of commenting on how gracious and welcoming everyone in Upper Sandusky was during their stay here," said Bob Wachtman, hired as an extra for those two days. "We certainly embraced the film, and why not? It doesn't happen very often that a rural farming community gets into the movies. So we really rolled out the red carpet and the hospitality in a big way."

Wachtman, a former weather officer with the US Air Force, was then the owner and president of Wytech, Inc., an Upper Sandusky security and fire alarm business. He had a ringside seat for a good deal of the courtroom shoot. He played the bailiff, so he spent much of those two days in uniform, sitting at the actual bailiff's station, located to the judge's left, under a large gold rendering of "The Great Seal of the State of Ohio." What's that? You don't remember a bailiff in the film? Quite right. You've stumbled on the case of the missing bailiff. Despite being tantalizingly close to camera range, Wachtman never made it on screen.

"There's a medium shot of Jeffrey DeMunn, and I'm about eight feet away," Wachtman said. "That's the closest I got to being in the movie. It would have been nice to have been immortalized in the final product, so it was disappointing not to be seen in it. But just the experience of being able to see how a professionally done movie is made, how all the arts and crafts have to come together in just the right way for things to work, that was one of the highlights of my life."

Of course, there were times when Darabont was filming tight shots of Robbins and DeMunn, and didn't need the extras to be in the courtroom. At those times, the extras gathered in an area set up in an old heating plant located across the alley.

"Since that's right across the way, it was crucial that everyone there be very quiet so no background noise would be picked up during filming," Wachtman said. "So the assistant director in the courtroom would call, 'Rolling!' And there was a man out in the hall on the third floor, and he'd yell down to the first floor, 'Rolling!' And then the man on the first floor would yell to the guy at the south door of the courthouse, 'Rolling!' And that guy would yell it out to all of us: 'Rolling!' And we were told, when that happened, not a sound. Absolute quiet. But one of our extras, Kenny Delaplane, a retired appliance store owner, was somewhat hard of hearing."

Sure enough, on one occasion, the extras listened as the "Rolling!" relay rolled its way from the third floor toward them. One "Rolling!" after another, they grew more and more quiet, until the last one finally reached them. The silence was complete, until, after a pause, it was broken by a puzzled Delaplane, who shouted out his question: "What did he say?!" You couldn't stop people from breaking up, yet the laughter didn't delay shooting in the courtroom.

Locals unaware of the film and driving by the courthouse would be puzzled by the strange appendages it seemed to have grown. On one side of the building, they would have seen two odd looking four-wheeled machines with metal arms reaching all the way to a bank of third-floor windows. These were yellow telescopic boom lifts, and they were lifting lights that could be aimed into the courtroom. On two sides of the building, they would have seen two white tubes snaked from the ground into third-floor windows, pumping in badly needed air-conditioning. It was summer. There were actors, extras, and crewmembers in the courtroom. And there were all of those lighting units, the cameras, and all of the filmmaking equipment. Those tubes were a matter of survival.

Remember the bailiff in the courtroom scenes of *The Shawshank Redemption*? No? Well, Bob Wachtman, holding a picture of himself in uniform, was on duty the whole time, but he didn't appear in the final film.

PHOTO BY BECKY DAWIDZIAK

Actor John Horton, who, two years later, would play a judge in another film based on a Stephen King book, director Tom Holland's *Thinner*, played the judge who found Andy to be "a particularly icy and remorseless man," sentencing him to serve two life sentences, "back to back, one for each of your victims." Nachbar approached Horton during a break, again bending the rules. "I had a notebook with me, so I got the judge's autograph," Nachbar said. "He wrote, 'Boy, I hope this is worth something someday.'"

The actual judge whose courtroom was used for filming, John Greer Hunter, was cast as one of the jurors. The Wyandot County Common Pleas judge played Juror No. 7. It was one way of saying thank you to the man who had given an enthusiastic "Come on!" when producers asked if they could take over his courtroom for filming. With Darabont presiding as the true judge during that shoot, DeMunn quickly felt comfortable in this setting.

"I immediately took to Frank and immediately trusted him," DeMunn said. "I liked him, but I also trusted him. And I think he trusted me. I didn't feel any pressure at all doing those scenes. I just zeroed in on playing this attorney who was absolutely intent on nailing this guy—just nailing him. It was such a clear and strong motivation, it gave you an immediate fix on how to play it."

To tighten up the whole opening sequence, Darabont cut what he described as a "swell" tracking shot in the jury room, as well as a few of DeMunn's lines while cross-examining Andy and while delivering his final summation to the jury. Darabont said DeMunn was "gracious enough" not to hold the dropped dialogue against him.

It was, in fact, the beginning of a beautiful professional relationship. Darabont also used DeMunn in his film versions of King's *The Green Mile* and *The Mist*, as well as the 2001 Jim Carrey period drama, *The Majestic*. *The Green Mile* and *The Mist* featured another *Shawshank* star from Buffalo, William Sadler. *The Mist* featured three other actors Darabont recruited for *The Walking Dead*: Melissa McBride, Laurie Holden, and Juan Gabriel Pareja.

It was in 2010 that DeMunn got a call from Darabont, who was the executive producer in charge of an AMC horror series based on the comic book *The Walking Dead.* "I was doing a play down in Texas," he said. "And Frank called and said, 'Hey, you want to come to Atlanta and kill zombies?' I didn't have to think about it. It was Frank. I knew it was going to be quality. I didn't know the comic books. I didn't know what I was getting into. And I didn't care. It was Frank. He asks and you're thinking, 'I want to come to your party. You betcha.'"

Although DeMunn's work on the movie was done, and Robbins had no more scenes in Upper Sandusky, the courtroom shoot did not end the city's association with *The Shawshank Redemption.* The crew returned in August with Morgan Freeman, Gil Bellows, and other actors and extras cast as Shawshank inmates to film scenes at the lumber company woodshop a few blocks away from the courthouse. It doubled for the prison workshop, and it's where Red and his fellow prisoners pause in their labors, transfixed by Andy playing Mozart's *The Marriage of Figaro* over Shawshank's public address system. In that scene Andy has locked

The lapel cross purchased in Upper Sandusky is worn by Warden Norton (Bob Gunton) as he welcomes new prisoners to Shawshank State Prison.
PHOTOFEST

himself in Warden Norton's office. The room used for that office was forty-five miles away, in the Ohio State Reformatory. Today, that former woodshop houses a museum packed with *Shawshank* memorabilia.

Upper Sandusky contributed something else to *The Shawshank Redemption*.

"We have an antique store here in town, Woods' Antiques 'N More, and one of the props people went in there when they were in town and bought a little gold lapel cross," said Wachtman, a familiar face at the Shawshank Woodshop. "And you'll see that cross on Warden Norton's lapel when he welcomes the new prisoners to Shawshank. The way they lit that scene, when he emerges from the darkness, that cross almost seems to be glowing. It just jumps out at you."

CABIN FEVER: LINDA DUFRESNE AND GLENN QUENTIN'S LOVE AFFAIR

VERY FEW FILMS ARE SHOT IN SEQUENCE, MEANING IN THE PRECISE chronological order mapped out by the screenplay. Strictly speaking, *The Shawshank Redemption* was not one of those rare films to claim that cinematic distinction. But director Frank Darabont did try, as much as possible, to film scenes in the order of the overall time periods, 1940s to 1960s, that the story encompasses. So, one of the earliest shoots in mid-June 1993 was at Pugh Cabin, the log cabin on the Malabar Farm grounds that became golf pro Glenn Quentin's place. It is where we glimpse the passionate encounter between Linda Dufresne (Renee Blaine) and Quentin (Scott Mann), and where they are found in bed the next day, riddled with .38-caliber bullets. The passionate lovemaking was shot, not the shootings. And the scene that starts Darabont's screenplay is slightly delayed, shown when the district attorney (Jeffrey DeMunn) is grilling Andy on the witness stand.

But when the roles were being cast during the Mansfield auditions on May 5, there was no way of saying how far the scene would go. The script called for some lovemaking exclamations by Linda. It called for a barrage of grunts, groans, gasps, and laughter. It called for Quentin to carry Linda, legs wrapped around him, across the room, falling into bed. The actors trying out for the roles were told there might be some nudity. And there might be a scene showing the naked bodies discovered in the blood-soaked bed. Both Blaine and Mann were represented at the time by the Cleveland acting and modeling agency David and Lee.

Both were contacted by the agency about auditioning. A David and Lee representative asked Mann if he was uninhibited enough to do a nude sex scene in a movie. His immediate question was, "Well, what kind of movie is it?" He was told that they thought it was some kind of B horror flick being shot in Mansfield.

"I think they thought that because it was a Stephen King story," Mann said. "So I wasn't too thrilled about it, and I wasn't going to go. But I was single at the time, and I thought, 'Now, wait a minute. Maybe there would be girls auditioning for this, too. Maybe I should go down and audition, just for the hell of it.' So I went down to Mansfield and immediately got paired up with Renee."

Blaine had recently moved from Colorado to Ohio with her eleven-and-a-half-month-old baby. Having worked in Japan and Italy, she was confident of finding modeling work. "We were rounding up local photographers and getting my book out there for local work, and this audition came up for *Rita Hayworth and Shawshank Redemption*," she said. Blaine, though, was told that this was a Castle Rock production starring Tim Robbins and Morgan Freeman.

"I knew Morgan Freeman from *Driving Miss Daisy* and had seen the film *Jacob's Ladder* with Tim Robbins," Blaine said. "I knew Castle Rock Entertainment was Rob Reiner, who was from *All in the Family*—an old family favorite—but even bigger the director of *The Princess Bride, Misery, Stand by Me* and other great films."

So she was excited about the prospect of being in the movie. Believing many others would be, too, and that this would be a "cattle call" audition, Blaine arrived so early in Mansfield that day, she was the first one in line. Mann showed up a short time later.

They spent a little time talking and sharing portfolios when a casting manager approached them with a white piece of paper outlining the cabin scene. There wasn't much more than the basics.

"They just gave us a one-page scene that just said, 'Couple comes in drunk,'" Mann said. "No title of the movie. Just the one page. There seemed to be a lot of couples there, and I saw a couple of different couples rehearsing, and they were just kind of going off script and being giggly."

After looking over the description of the scene, Blaine told Mann, "Let's really do this. Let's really kiss and see where this goes." Mann didn't need any encouraging. Her take on the audition lined up perfectly with his instincts.

"Okay!" he replied without hesitation. "Look, it says we come in drunk and go at it. I think we should just do it that way. Since you don't know me and I don't you, let's just go at it."

Then the call came to audition for casting director Deborah Aquila.

"Scott and I hadn't known each other for more than twenty minutes and just went at it," Blaine said. "We pretended that we were coming in the cottage and couldn't wait to get one another naked and in bed—groping at each other's bodies and clothing, and kissing hot and heavy, and then. . . ."

Then Mann lifted Blaine up against the wall and her back hit the light switch, and, yup, out went the lights.

"We were all stunned for a moment, and then laughed and laughed," Blaine recalled.

Mann turned to Aquila and said, "I think that's a cut." Aquila told them, "I'm kind of glad you guys stopped when you did, because I didn't know how far you were going to go."

Everyone felt good about the audition, and Mann was told by someone with David and Lee that he definitely was in the running to get the part. Mann gave an unenthusiastic, noncommittal response. "Aren't you excited?" the agency employee asked.

"Why?" Mann asked. "So what? No big deal. It's just a B horror flick in Mansfield."

That's right. He still didn't know. They told him just what kind of film was being shot in Mansfield.

"Then I got excited," he said.

But the wait on a final decision was excruciating, at least for Blaine. When finally contacted, she learned that Mann, too, had been cast. They had auditioned so well together, Aquila wanted them "for the real deal." Copies of the screenplay arrived in the mail, and the Castle Rock logo on the front suddenly made everything seem real. Although billed in the credits as "Andy Dufresne's wife," the character's name in the novella was Linda, and Blaine was told that was her name in the film, as well.

"She was to have a line, something like, 'Oh, baby, you're so good,' that I never got out during filming," Blaine said. "The rest of the script was amazing, and I fell in love with Red, Heywood, Brooks and Jake the crow."

Both Mann and Blaine credit costume designer Elizabeth McBride with getting them through the ninety-minute evening shoot. McBride had been the costume designer on *Driving Miss Daisy, Thelma & Louise,* and *Fried Green Tomatoes.*

"When it was time to find the period clothing, she was the best," said Blaine, who was twenty-four at the time. "Elizabeth was so kind and hip and friendly and funny. I am sad that cancer took her away [at age forty-two in 1997] as she would still be a shining star in this business."

Blaine was told to be at Malabar Farm at 4:00 p.m. on the day of filming and report to makeup. The goal was to be filming before sunset. Key makeup artist Kevin Haney was talking to Blaine about her eyebrows when in walked Tim Robbins and Susan Sarandon. Robbins walked right up to Blaine, leaned over, and jokingly said, "How could you do this to me?" He was smiling, of course. The only thing she could think to say was, "I don't know." They both laughed.

"I had my boyfriend and daughter in the trailer with me," Blaine said. "Of course, the attention went to Susan Sarandon, her nanny and their little boy Miles, who was my daughter's age. She asked, 'What is her name?' Riley Rae we said, and she said, 'Oh, this is Miles, but we sometimes call him Miley.' It got hot in there for me. I was at a loss for words for a few minutes and then we all got on with it."

Understandably, it seemed unreal and a bit surreal to Blaine that she was casually chatting with a star she'd seen in such films as *The Rocky Horror Picture Show, The Hunger,* and *Thelma & Louise.*

Hair and makeup done, there was some time to kill in the hurry-up-and-wait manner typical with filmmaking. Robbins and Mann came out, and they all chatted about movies, including *Bob Roberts.* Blaine was tickled to have her own trailer, even if her name was spelled *Blain* on it. Mann took a picture of her sitting on the steps to the trailer, misspelled name and all. Then it was time to get into costume and head over to Pugh Cabin. All the way over, Mann kept saying, "I am nervous. Are you nervous?"

Right before her big scene, Renee Blaine, who played Linda Dufresne, poses on her trailer steps (name misspelled on trailer) for a picture taken by Scott Mann, who played golf pro Glenn Quentin.

"Elizabeth McBride, the costume designer, was like my rock," Mann recalled twenty-five years later. "Because I was freaking out. Renee kept saying she wasn't nervous."

And she wasn't, at that point.

"I am thinking, 'I've been around a lot of lights and production folks in my career,'" Blaine said of that moment. "So, I wasn't nervous. We're waiting on the front porch for our call and Scott again tells me he's nervous. I keep saying, 'I am not nervous. What's there to be nervous about?' But he insisted that he was nervous."

At that moment, Darabont poked his head out the door and good-naturedly asked, "You kids ready?" Mann told him the truth: "Frank, I'm shittin' in my pants right now." Darabont replied, "Yeah, me, too. This is my first film, too." The director disappeared behind the door, and they waited to hear the yell for "Action!" That was the moment Blaine got nervous, as well.

"Oh, okay, Miss-I'm-Not-Nervous," Mann kidded her. "Let's just do it the way we did it in the audition."

And that's precisely what they did.

"The only effect that nervousness had on me was I acquired the driest mouth in the universe," Blaine said. "Knowing that we would be kissing and my mouth just dried up like a cotton ball."

Like everyone who worked on the film, Mann and Blaine remember the heat.

"That cabin was not air-conditioned back then," Mann said. "It had to be in the nineties that day. It was humid, near dusk, and we were dressed in 1940s-style clothes. And with all the people in there, with the cameras and the lights, it was just scorching hot in there. They had to wipe us down after every take."

Fortunately, there weren't many takes.

"We did the scene as you see it in the movie, but it goes on a little longer, where I carry her to the bed and get on top of her," Mann said. "So they shot that sequence from different angles. And it isn't easy to do a sex scene where you're constantly thinking, 'All right, whose jacket comes off first and when.' You're trying to remember the order while doing this passionate scene. There was one point where Frank said, 'That's a take.' And a woman came over and said, 'Nope, his jacket came off before hers, so we can't use that.' But after the first couple of takes, I started settling into it."

Then, all of a sudden, Mann saw Robbins in the corner, watching them. It shook him for a moment, but Robbins later told them: "Sorry to barge in on you while you're doing the scene. I know how difficult it is to do a scene like that. But I just wanted to see what my character was in all this turmoil over."

They understood. "He's a very method actor," Mann said of Robbins. "But he scared the crap out of me, watching us."

They did the entire scene, wide angle, start to finish, a couple of times.

"And we had gold," Blaine said.

Then they did an assortment of takes of various little movements from different angles.

"There was some talk of moving us to the bed and creating some bloody scene where we would be lying there naked and dead," Blaine said. "But that scene was never shot."

It was a wrap. Blaine and Mann were done on the film. It had been an exhilarating experience, but, a little more than a year later, the whole experience had faded for Mann. Then in July 1994, he took a date to see the Arnold Schwarzenegger action thriller *True Lies*. Before the movie started, there was a trailer for a familiar film.

"And there Renee and I were on the big screen," said Mann, who still lives in Cleveland but now pursues a career as a visual artist and photographer. "I called my mother and all of my friends, and everybody had to go see *True Lies* to see the trailer for *The Shawshank Redemption*."

ON THE SET WITH MORGAN FREEMAN

Twenty-five years ago, I was working as a film critic in Ohio. Eve Lapolla and her team at the Ohio Film Commission helped coordinate trips to Mansfield for stories about this "prison flick" being filmed in the Buckeye State. The title still was Rita Hayworth *and* Shawshank Redemption. *One August day, she asked me if I'd be interested in interviewing Morgan Freeman. So, on a scorcher of an August day, I jumped in my car and pointed it in the direction of Mansfield, about a sixty-nine-mile trip from my home in Cuyahoga Falls to the front gates of the Ohio State Reformatory. Listening to the tape recording of the interview, poring over my notes from the day, and looking through the related material in the boxes of* Shawshank *items from then and now, I realized this was a snapshot of Freeman in the heat (literally and figuratively) of putting together his most beloved performance. Here were his thoughts on playing Red while he was playing Red (much of it never published before). Filming had gone much longer than expected that day, so Freeman didn't break free until well past the scheduled time for the interview:*

MORGAN FREEMAN IS TIRED. THE LOOMING WALLS OF THE OHIO STATE Reformatory behind him, he walks across the prison yard still dressed in the convict uniform of his character. The day's filming has gone much longer than expected, and he's many hours late for this interview. As he nears a scattered collection of chairs in a relatively quiet area of the grounds, the sun is flirting with the horizon, mercifully taking with it a few of the degrees that pushed the day's temperature into the mid-eighties.

"Sorry you had to wait so long," the six-foot-two actor says in a voice dripping with fatigue. "What a day."

A rough shoot?

Morgan Freeman on location at the Ohio State Reformatory in 1993: "I've got to tell you, this was one of the best scripts I've ever read, period."
PHOTOFEST

"No, no, not at all," says the star of *Rita Hayworth and Shawshank Redemption.* "I'm tired because of the long day, not because of the working conditions. It was just a long day and a lot of takes. In fact, this has not been a particularly rough shoot at all, not in a physical sense. You know what makes for a rough shoot? Action sequences. They can really pound away at you. Action sequences are what really take it out of you. Action is just the toughest on you physically, and there's not a lot of that in this film. This film is about emotionally challenging territory, not physically challenging. And there's a lot of that kind of ground to cover, so you can be tired at the end of a long day, but it's a good kind of tired."

So this isn't what he'd describe as "doing hard time"?

The weariness had been fading from his face as he warmed to his subject, and this prison reference made in the shadow of a prison inspires a tremendous smile, followed by an explosive laugh that turns the heads of nearby crewmembers stowing film equipment.

"Not at all," says Freeman, who turned fifty-six on June 1. "Not even close. You know what was the only thing that proved a bit tough physically? Now, this doesn't sound like much. You're going to laugh, considering what other people have to do in this film. But there's a scene early in the script. It's just a conversation that takes place when a few of the prisoners are throwing a baseball around in the prison yard. Nothing to it, right? Well, we did a lot of takes, covering things from all different angles. You do that. So you're throwing and catching a baseball, hour after hour. Easy."

Freeman kept tossing, not realizing the toll it was taking. The next day, he showed up with his aching arm in a sling.*

"We're not working in a manned prison, so it hasn't been psychologically tough, either," says Freeman, whose blue denim shirt bears the prisoner number 30265. "All the ghosts are there, that's for sure, but it's not like working a live prison. That would be tough."

Unlike most of King's tales, the novella "Rita Hayworth and Shawshank Redemption" is not a supernatural spooker.

"Although I wasn't familiar with this particular story, I wasn't surprised that Stephen King had written a wonderful character piece about hope and friendship and the human spirit," says Freeman, who is riding high on the rave reviews for his portrayal of Ned Logan in director Clint Eastwood's Oscar-winning *Unforgiven*. "I'm a reader, so I already knew that King could write stuff that wasn't horror. But his horror stories work for the same reason. He gives you great characters you care about and wonder about. He gives these characters great challenges, exploring and illuminating the themes behind these stories. And he makes you feel as if you're really in the places you get described. That's what all great writing has in common: great characters, great themes, and great sense of place. This story certainly has all of that, and more."

In the novella, the character of Red is, well, a red-headed Irishman. That didn't stop Darabont, producer Niki Marvin, and their team from casting Freeman as Red opposite Robbins as banker Andy Dufresne.

---

* Many years after this interview, I saw estimates that put the all-day baseball shoot at nine hours. Darabont said it was an "entire day" of shooting, and it didn't occur to him how sore Freeman's arm must have been getting, but "not once did he complain."

"I've got to tell you, this was one of the best scripts I've ever read, period," Freeman says, leaning forward in his chair. "My representatives sent it to me, and I was just floored. I wanted to be part of it, so when they asked me what I thought about the script, I said, 'It's fantastic. No question, I want to be part of this. By the way, what part do they want me to play?' And that's when I was told they wanted me for Red. That floored me. I said, 'Red? Really.' I was beyond delighted. He tells the story. He's the narrator. The character doesn't need to be Irish. He became black. He became me."

That must be somewhat refreshing.

"Somewhat?!" Freeman says with another laugh that turns heads. "It's entirely refreshing. As the world progresses, so does Hollywood. Clint Eastwood did the same thing in *Unforgiven*. That character wasn't black, either. If you look at the movies being made today with Forest Whitaker, Wesley Snipes, Denzel Washington, Laurence Fishburne, Danny Glover, and others, you see change, but, then again, you also see that Hollywood always has been the same. If you make money for them, you work. If you're good box office, you work. I don't want that to sound overly optimistic on one hand or overly cynical on the other. It's just recognizing the reality of how things are. The positive aspect of the change is that more kinds of people are being allowed to make money for them."

Born in Memphis, Tennessee, in 1937, Freeman made his Broadway debut in the all-black 1968 production of the musical *Hello Dolly!* It starred Pearl Bailey and Cab Calloway. Three years later, PBS viewers got to know him as a regular on the children's series *The Electric Company*. He played such popular characters as book-loving hipster Easy Reader, disc jockey Mel Mounds, and Dracula-like Vincent the Vegetable Vampire.

Freeman started getting regular film work in the early 1980s. His career was kicked into high gear with an Oscar nomination for the thriller *Street Smart* (1987). In 1989, he had starring roles in three acclaimed films: Sergeant Major John Rawlins in *Glory*, Paterson, New Jersey, high school principal Joe Clark in *Lean On Me*, and Hoke in *Driving Miss Daisy*. Since then, he has had made memorable contributions to such films as *Robin Hood: Prince of Thieves* and, of course, *Unforgiven*.

No stranger to Ohio, Freeman has been in three previous films shot in the Buckeye State. And the first two also were prison pictures: the 1980 TV movie *Attica* and the 1980 theatrical film *Brubaker*, which starred Robert Redford as the new warden of an Arkansas prison. He also was in the cast of *Teachers* (1984), filmed in the Columbus area.

Before arriving in Mansfield, Freeman finished work on his directorial debut, the Paramount Pictures production, *Bopha!*

"The transition from actor to director was not at all difficult," Freeman says. "In fact, it was like putting on a well-tailored suit. Many actors have great directorial instincts, and somewhere along the way, I began to think about directing. And you learn a lot from working with great directors. From Clint Eastwood, for instance, I learned to let people do what they know how to do. Don't get in their way."

Freeman is not only riding the acclaim of those rave reviews these days, he's also making time for riding horses, one of his favorite pastimes. For the three-month shoot in Ohio, he's living in a rented house on a farm in Butler, about fifteen miles south of Mansfield. Most important is the farm has a stable for a couple of his riding horses.

"Got to have my horses with me," Freeman says. "I have a farm in Mississippi, and I wanted to make sure there was a place for my horses here. That's been another nice thing that has helped make this shoot anything but tough. I couldn't live in a hotel for three months. That would drive me crazy. You get to go stay in a real home at the end of a long day. And I get to ride when the schedule allows. It keeps you centered. It renews you. There's nothing like being on a horse to relax and renew you. There's nothing better for the weary spirit."

JAMES WHITMORE: THE OLD PRO AS THE OLD CON

No one connected with *The Shawshank Redemption* had more show business experience than James Whitmore. The legendary actor was treated with great deference and respect by everyone in the cast and crew, but he asked for and expected neither. At seventy-one, he clearly was having trouble staying on his feet for long stretches, especially in the brutal summer heat, but, if he ever uttered a complaint, no one remembers it.

And it's not as if his contribution to the film amounts to little more than a glorified cameo. In the early sequences, the aging Brooks Hatlen is in the meal scenes with Red and his gang. He's in the prison library scenes. He delivers a book to Andy's cell, completing the smuggling chain for the rock hammer. He has the emotional attack on Heywood (William Sadler) upon hearing that his parole has come through. He has an entire sequence to himself after getting out of prison: dodging traffic, working at the Food-Way, sitting in the park, and wrestling with the terrors of being institutionalized while in his hotel room. Whitmore's Brooks is by turns charming, sympathetic, humorous, and heartbreaking. Other actors might have been able to play Brooks, but it's difficult to imagine one hitting so many levels and making so much of his screen time. He's everything Darabont could have wanted for Brooks, "a used-up old con with arthritis in both hands"—a man who got used to leaning his old bones on prison walls, and then the walls were taken away from him. It's an amazing performance that stands as towering evidence of why the short, craggy-faced star was known as "the supporting actors' Spencer Tracy." He resembled Tracy both physically and in dedication to craft.

Some of the busiest people during the *Shawshank* shoot were the local barbers and hairstylists. The first order of business for actors and extras was to get period haircuts. Extras were handed no-nonsense memos bannered with a message in capital letters: "AFTER WARDROBE FITTING, YOU MUST GO AND GET YOUR HAIRCUT!!!" This would be followed by directions to Wilma's Cosmetique or some other downtown establishment, or perhaps a trailer on location. The memo concluded with capital letters: "NO HAIRCUT . . . NO WORK!!!!!!!!" That's right, eight exclamation points to drive home the point. The no-haircut-no-work rule was evoked often and emphatically. The one exception was Whitmore. But that wasn't without a fight.

"The first time James Whitmore came on set, he was wearing bright yellow pants," recalled Brian Connell, a member of the "Core Con" extras (meaning he was on hand to play a convict for most of the shoot). "One of the hair and makeup ladies told him to go with her to get his hair cut. He politely refused."

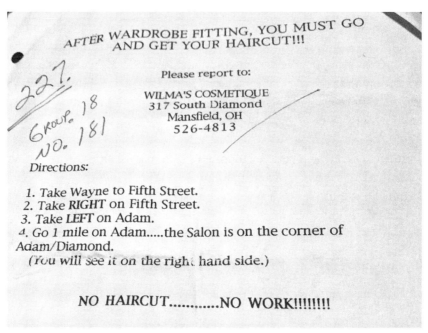

PHOTO COURTESY OF BRIAN CONNELL

The hair and makeup person told him that he needed to have a hairstyle appropriate to the late 1940s and early 1950s. Whitmore laughed aside the request, explaining he was "alive and well" in the late 1940s and his current hairstyle was the same as it had been back then. It was expert testimony, all right, but it didn't seem to carry much weight with the insistent representative of the hair and makeup department. She protested and repeated her demand, until Darabont walked in and said Whitmore's hair was just fine.

"The hair on my arms stood up when he first came in," Connell said. "And I thought, 'This is a real movie star.'"

Most of Whitmore's days on the film were spent at the reformatory, where areas were used for the hotel room and the prison library, and in downtown Mansfield, where the street, park, and Food-Way scenes were filmed. Among those who got to observe Whitmore at these two locations were Cleveland actress Dorothy Silver, cast as the 1954 Brewer Hotel landlady, and Ben Bissman, whose downtown family building doubled for the Brewer.

Silver was a day player who reported for filming at OSR and the set for the hotel room. All you see of Silver on screen is the very moment when the dour landlady opens the door and lets Brooks into his room. In Darabont's screenplay, however, the scene starts with them walking up the hotel stairs to the room, the landlady outlining the rules as they go. And all of this was shot that day.

"It was essentially setting forth a list of restrictions on Whitmore's rental of the room," Silver said. "It was supposed to be shot as a reflection of his life in the prison, done as we climbed up the stairs. I could see he was having a lot of difficulty going up and down these steps. I know how older bodies move, because I have one. I'm fairly certain he was suffering from arthritis. We did about seven or eight takes, going up and down these steps. And, after each take, Frank Darabont would ask with great solicitude for Whitmore, 'Mr. Whitmore, do you think you could do another take?' Whitmore always said yes. That was my first introduction to a real trouper, that he was able to do this without complaining. I was tired at the end of the day, and that was twenty-five years ago."

Brooks (James Whitmore) awaits visitors in the hotel room set built inside the Ohio State Reformatory.

PHOTO BY BECKY DAWIDZIAK

Whitmore often told interviewers that he preferred the theater to film work. His first love was the stage, without question, but he also found the long waits between takes to be incredibly boring. His favorite remedy for this boredom was to talk with fellow actors and crewmembers. He'd tell them stories, yet it never turned into a monologue. He'd ask them questions, and never in a perfunctory way. "Where did you grow up?" "How did you end up here?" "Do you have kids?" "Do you like doing this?" "Where did you go to school?"

In the long stretches between takes, Silver and Whitmore got to know each other a bit. Silver was married to actor-director Reuben Silver, and they often appeared together in plays. Whitmore had been married from 1972 to 1979 to Audra Lindley, best known for playing a landlady on the hit ABC sitcom *Three's Company* (but also a distinguished stage veteran whose credits included productions of *Long Day's Journey Into Night* and *On Golden Pond*).

"It turned out they'd done many of the same plays I'd done with Reuben," Silver said. "So we bonded over that. He was such a sweet guy. We went to lunch together that day, and we sat near about eight fellows dressed as prison guards. And Whitmore went over to them and started chatting with them. He said, 'Boy, what great casting. You guys actually look like prison guards.' They said, 'We are prison guards.' They were guards from the new prison. And that's the way he was. He'd go up and talk to anybody. It was a wonderful experience. Since then, I've done a lot of day-work roles on films, but, in many ways, the first one was the most memorable."

Flash forward to October 1994 and the nationwide release of *The Shawshank Redemption*. Silver sat in a Cleveland theater, waiting for her scene with Whitmore.

"I realized all of my lines had been cut," she said. "I was just there looking like the landlady from hell. My first reaction was, 'Oh, all of my lines are gone.' My second reaction was, 'Great cut.' They didn't need all that stuff. All they need was what you saw, which was a dismal room and bitchy landlady." As fleeting as her appearance in *The Shawshank Redemption* is, Silver still gets recognized for it.

Ben Bissman spent even more time in Whitmore's company. Noticing the toll long shoots had on the actor, Bissman put together a comfortable resting corner in a room on the ground floor of the Bissman Building. It was the very room that later would become the office of the *Portland Daily Bugle* editor-in-chief. Bissman brought in a big comfortable La-Z-Boy recliner and end table. And he put an air-conditioning unit in the room.

"We made him his own little spot," Bissman said. "It was a place for him to escape the heat and relax and hold court while smoking a pipe or a cigar. He liked to hang out in this building. He just sat and talked to all the people on the crew, sound and lighting guys, everybody. He told stories about Jayne Mansfield and Cary Grant. He'd answer questions about all of the films and television shows he'd done. He was wonderful. He wasn't getting around very well at that point. He was moving mighty slow. I think it was arthritis. So this was a little corner of peace and solitude and comfort."

The irony is that Brooks was desperately unhappy at the Brewer Hotel while Whitmore found a happy place in the building cast as the Brewer. There's also some symbolism in the realization that the set for Brooksie's room was back at OSR, as if to underscore that the poor fellow never really got out of prison.

Brooks (James Whitmore) forever haunts the Bissman Building (the Brewer Hotel in the film), standing in the doorway and catching the eye of fans visiting the filming sites.

PHOTO BY BECKY DAWIDZIAK

Darabont also took Whitmore's advice, dropping some casual swearing in the mess hall scene where Brooks is telling Red and the other cons how a guard asked Andy for financial advice in the library. Whitmore argued that Brooks was of an older generation that wouldn't have been given to casual cuss words. He also thought that this would make a later scene, when an upset Brooks is holding a knife to Heywood's throat, more effective because his swearing here would have greater shock value. Darabont immediately saw the wisdom in this.

Always looking to again use favorite actors, Darabont cast Whitmore, along with *Shawshank* players Jeffrey DeMunn and Brian Libby, in *The Majestic* (2001). When he died in February 2009, his *Oklahoma!* costar Shirley Jones told the Associated Press how he emphasized to her the importance of learning and working at your craft. It was similar advice from Whitmore that James Dean credited with his desire to take acting seriously. "And he never stopped learning," Jones said of Whitmore. The obituary published by *Playbill*, the magazine of his beloved theater, mentioned only one role in its lead paragraph: "a memorable late-career role as a grizzled prison librarian in the movie *The Shawshank Redemption*."

THE SHOOT

One key decision made before the cameras started rolling was to record all of Morgan Freeman's voiceover narration during the pre-production phase. Frank Darabont reasoned that many scenes would depend on timing with the narration, so it would be best to have it readily available while filming. With most films, such a narration would be recorded in postproduction, but, in this instance, pre-recording ensured that action would match narration. The schedule also allowed for two weeks of acting rehearsals on location before filming. Darabont is a strong proponent for rehearsals on film shoots, knowing how useful it is in fine tuning dialogue, delivery, timing, and characterization.

"It was during this time that Tim decided he wanted to spend a night in solitary," said first assistant director John R. Woodward. "He wanted to know what it was like to go through that for a night. And the solitary cell was in a horrible place in the old prison, terribly dark and terribly dank. I don't know how long he was in there, but he had to be taken out. He could not take it for a night."

One of the first scenes filmed at the Ohio State Reformatory was the unloading dock of the laundry truck that is smuggling in Andy's rock hammer. Cleveland actor Morgan Lund had been hired to play the laundry truck driver, but since his character had no specified lines in the screenplay, he wasn't sent a script or even an explanation of the scene. He arrived on set and was sent to costume. They gave him a gray fedora hat, a bow tie, suspenders, and gray pants. From costume, he was sent to makeup. After makeup, he was told to get his haircut ("NO HAIRCUT

. . . NO WORK!!!!!!!!" the posters off scene declared). He got his haircut, so it was time to work. Ready?

"Uh, I don't have a script," Lund told them. He was immediately enveloped by a chorus of voices.

"No script?!" "What?" "This guy doesn't have a script." "How did that happen?" "This guy needs a script!" "Get this guy a script."

"I'm ready to go on set, and I don't have any lines, but I'd like to know what the scene is all about," Lund recalled. "The director walked up at that moment, and I remembered him from the audition."

Although there were no lines in the screenplay for the truck driver, Darabont wanted Lund's character to be pushing along the convicts who were unloading the sacks of laundry.

"We're just going to do this," Darabont said of the scene. "Can you improv it?"

Lund was happy to oblige. They did the scene, then Darabont asked for another take, encouraging Lund to "do what you want and say what you want."

"So all of the lines and all of the blocking are mine," Lund said. "They changed the camera angles a couple of times, and we were done. That was it. It was really quick and easy. The director was just a sweetheart, and, as an actor, you love that level of trust and cooperation. But I still didn't have a script, so I still didn't know how this laundry truck driver fit into the story. I didn't even know what the story was. So I went home and read Stephen King's novella. I thought, 'Whoa, this could be pretty good.'"

This didn't end Lund's work on the film. After Darabont and his team returned to California, he got a phone call from the production company.

"We have to change the dialogue in your scene," Lund was told.

When he asked why, Lund was told that the lines he improvised were too contemporary for the time period. Instead of hiring an actor to dub over new lines, they flew Lund from Cleveland to Los Angeles.

"I made up some new lines and matched them to what had been filmed," he said. "They were happy with it, but they wanted me to wait for the director to approve it. I said, 'Look, I don't really want to sit here all day.' And they said, 'Well, you got it on the first take. Go ahead and leave.' So I left."

Lund, therefore, was one of the first and last actors to work on *The Shawshank Redemption*. In between his contributions, Darabont was working fifteen-to-eighteen-hour days, six days a week. And on his "day off," he was thinking and planning what scenes to shoot in the coming week—and how. "'Exhausting' is too wimpy a word to describe it—they have to invent a new word that applies," Darabont wrote in "Memos from the Trenches," a guest essay for David J. Schow's "Raving & Drooling" column in *Fangoria* magazine (the piece was reprinted with Darabont's published screenplay). "Sleep becomes a dim memory. The mental and physical stamina required is awesome. The stress is beyond belief."

And, remember, this was his first feature-length film. "Trial by fire" also seems too wimpy a phrase to describe it. This wasn't lost on Clancy Brown, playing feared captain of the guard Byron Hadley.

"I don't think it was that difficult, at least not for me," Brown said. "It had its difficult days, like any shoot. There were some long days. But it was very civilized. And we all got along very well. It was a bunch of guys in the middle of Ohio. We palled around a lot. I think it was mostly tough on Frank. He never stopped. Frank got more than a little tired. The challenge at that level was a little new to him, and, even if it wasn't new to him, this was an incredibly big job. So I think he got a little bit exhausted."

Brown was more than a little impressed with how Darabont rose to the challenge.

"It definitely was a new challenge for him at the time," Brown said. "He had to come in and lead Tim Robbins and Morgan Freeman and Roger Deakins. All these masters of the craft suddenly are looking to him to say the words that will answer their questions. That's intense. But he definitely was up to the challenge. He was exhausted, but he was up to it."

The principal actors remember the long days and the often-brutal heat (of course), but, for the most part, they recall a pleasant and positive stay in Ohio.

"It was arduous," Robbins said. "It was hard work. They were extremely long shooting days, and there was an awful lot of moving parts to this. But the story and the script were so good, and all of the actors really loved the script so much, we all wanted to serve the script and make it as truthful as we could."

First assistant director John R. Woodward remembered it as "a challenging shoot."

"But in truth, every film is a challenge," he said. "It wasn't a tough shoot, but, whenever you're paying attention to detail over twenty years of time, it's going to be challenging. And scheduling was one of the most challenging aspects on this film. You know, you get tornado warnings in the summer in Ohio. So, on days when it looked bad, we put a production assistant up in one of the prison towers with binoculars. He was on tornado watch. We also had to be careful about lightning storms, which you also get in Ohio that time of year. Generators attract lightning, and we were using a lot of generators. Scheduling and safety issues are a big part of what an assistant director does, so you had to stay on top of those."

That's not to say the heat wasn't an issue. The temperatures soared so brutally high in the OSR room used for the warden's office, it became a necessity to keep the windows open as much as possible. That, however, attracted another problem for cast and crew: flies . . . swarms of flies. It got so bad, everyone on duty was issued a fly swatter.

"I can't tell you how many times we had to break a take because a fly had landed on an actor's face or one flew through frame," Woodward said. "It was like the old West. We took to notching our fly swatters for body counts."

Because of the relentless heat, Niki Marvin would have craft services fill ice chests with ice cream treats. She'd bring them over to the prison every day around two o'clock. It got so everyone depended on the tasty afternoon morale booster, but, one day, the ice cream failed to show up and the crew jokingly rebelled. "No ice cream, no work," they told the producer, arguing that such an outrage must lead to a work stoppage.

And the craft services folks were among the unsung heroes of *Shawshank*. After the heat, the first thing many people connected to *The Shawshank Redemption* remember was how well everybody ate.

"I got a big kick out of the meals," said Dennis Baker, the warden of the Mansfield Correctional Institution and an adviser on the film. "The spreads were incredible with all kinds of food, and it was all great."

So, among the unsung heroes of this campaign were the craft services team of Mark Moelter, Don Speakman, and Brian Boggs, as well as caterers Joe Schultz, Carlos Garcia, and Jose Lopez—all of whom end up with on-screen credit.

"The food was the high point," said David Lessig, an extra hired to play a convict cutting with a saw in a prison woodshop scene. "We had to be here at six-thirty in the morning for an entire day of shooting at the woodshop, and that entire day lasted eleven hours. We ate like kings the whole day."

Another extra hired to play a prisoner, Max Gerber, said the food was so good during those three months, "I must have put on twenty pounds."

MAKING MANSFIELD HOME

Despite the heat, cast and crew were treated well in Mansfield, and Mansfield was happy to have so many visitors for three months.

"They quietly and seamlessly fit in," said Lee Tasseff, executive director of the Mansfield-Richland County Convention & Visitors Bureau. "If you weren't at the warehouse or hanging out at the prison, which most people didn't, you might not have even known they were in town. They shut down the square for a day to film the scenes with Brooks in the park and walking around town, then for Morgan walking around downtown. That was when people most noticed them being here. But mostly you'd hear they were out at the prison that day, or Malabar Farm, or in Upper Sandusky, or out in the country. There would be sightings of the stars now and then, but nothing really interfered with daily life in the town."

Cast and crew were able to go about their business without fear of interruption by gawkers and stalkers.

"There was no social media back then, either," said Jodie Snavely, who also was with the bureau in 1993 (and still is, as the group tour and media director for what is now called Destination Mansfield). "And that really helped them to be under the radar while they were here."

Modern stoplights and signage had to be removed from downtown for the scenes of Brooks and Red struggling with life outside of prison. A fleet of vintage cars were deployed for these scenes. Then everything was put back as it was.

"Everyone here was friendly and accommodating, and it was the same with the film people," Tasseff said. "It was an extremely agreeable situation, really. Other than the heat and the humidity of that summer, it was a fairly smooth operation."

Every spare hotel and motel room in the area was occupied during these three months, with many members of the cast and crew staying at the Holiday Inn, the Best Western, and the Park Place Hotel. People in town grew accustomed to seeing crewmembers walking around town, maybe strolling near the production office, around the park, or down to the Bissman Building.

"The community was great," said location manager and production supervisor Kokayi Ampah. "I stayed at the Holiday Inn, but how often was I there? I really enjoyed myself on that film. I had a tremendous amount of work to do, and Mansfield was nice. I grew up in Minnesota. It's not Los Angeles or New York. So I was accustomed to the pace of life and such. A lot of happy memories of Mansfield and working on *The Shawshank Redemption*."

The major stars who were in Mansfield for most of the three months stayed in rented homes. Freeman had his ranch and horses in Butler. And Robbins?

"I rented a house from a Seventh Day Adventist dentist," Robbins said. "I remember there was a tornado that went through at the time. That was a little scary. But it was a comfortable stay. We were working so hard and I was a young father with two small boys, so I really didn't get out much to see the town. There wasn't much time for fun. I did go to the State Fair, which I really liked. I saw a tractor pull for the first time, which was quite an experience for a city boy."

Clancy Brown was no stranger to Ohio summers. He grew up in Urbana, a drive of about one hundred miles to Mansfield.

"Mansfield is far enough away from Urbana that I didn't have to go to my parents' house every weekend," Brown said. "I remember the heat, but I also remember it being a typical Ohio summer. I never felt uncomfortable. One thing that freaked out the New York and L.A. dudes was that there was a big rabid raccoon infestation at some point. It brought me back. The New York and L.A. dudes didn't quite understand land with endless rows of corn."

Brown and Larry Brandenburg, who played Skeet, rented a farmhouse near Loudenville, about twenty miles southeast of Mansfield.

"It was really nice," Brown recalled. "It was a long shoot, and to go back to a hotel every single night would have been intensely depressing. So Larry Brandenburg and I found this great farmhouse. Larry is from rural Minnesota, so he knew what country was, too. We went out there, watching ballgames and shooting stars, playing basketball, drinking too much. That was fun."

Every Sunday, Robbins invited cast and crewmembers over for half-court basketball games and pool parties.

The "bunch of guys" camaraderie also is recalled by Max Gerber, who worked as a stand-in and extra on the film: "We played basketball with Tim Robbins and softball with Clancy Brown. My wife was getting a little put out, because we had a young daughter, and I was leaving early and getting home late. We played two-on-two basketball: me and Tim against Clancy and Morgan's stand-in. One time, the cast and crew played the actual prison guards in softball. There was a lot of chances to hang around and have fun."

Woodward, like Ampah and Molito, stayed at the Holiday Inn.

"Everyone kind of ended up in the bar at the end of the week," Woodward said. "People came and went. You know, Mansfield was very good to us. It really was a terrific place to film, and I've worked on a lot of films in a lot of places."

Echoing something Gunton has said, Brown believes that the lack of diversions found in a major city created a strong sense of camaraderie among the cast and crew. "We made our own fun," he said. "We hung out together. And we got close. We laughed and we played and we talked."

Gunton said that they inevitably talked about work and their characters. It was kind of an informal actors workshop that strengthened and deepened all of their performances.

"And Frank would have people over to his house on Saturday morning, and do you know what he would do?" construction coordinator Sebastian Milito said. "He was so dedicated to making *Shawshank*, he'd screen movies. He was such a creative and artistic guy, that he'd look at these movies and say, 'How did he do that?' He was endlessly analyzing other people's movies, looking for insight. He was incredibly passionate about it."

SHOOTING IN THE PRISON YARD

The most challenging and complex shot for everybody was the one that inevitably gets singled out when fans talk about the film. This was the amazing shot first imagined by production designer Terence Marsh during that frigid first tour of OSR in March. The sequence would include a helicopter flyover showing the entire prison grounds, the arrival of the prison bus taking Andy to Shawshank, the emergence of five hundred extras playing convicts rushing to greet the "new fish," and the taunting of the just-arrived convicts as they are removed from the bus and marched toward their introduction to Warden Norton. For the all-important flyover, three major elements had to be perfectly timed (helicopter, bus, and extras), but the sky needed to be consistently over-cast for the entire sequence.

Getting the flyover to work took a month of planning with pilot Robert "Bobby Z" Zajonc, aerial camera operator and gyrosphere oper-ator Mike Kelem, and assistant directors Woodward and Tom Schellen-berg. (Darabont later said it was like "diagramming the world's largest football play"). All of the planning paid off. It took about eight takes, but the play eventually was executed perfectly.

"Weather is weather, and the day we picked was rainy," Woodward said. "It wasn't what Frank wanted, but we went ahead and shot it any-way, timing through the cloudburst. Coordinating that was a bit of an effort. We had the helicopter sat down where I was. We had cars and about four hundred extras in movement. Getting the cues out and get-ting them right took an effort. I was in contact with Frank, who would tell me where the helicopter was, so I could cue the release of different extras at different times. It's never quite perfect, and Frank always wanted to try it again. But you run out of day and you've got what you've got. And, really, it's only the filmmakers who see the tiny little imperfections. Roger Deakins was pleased with it. And it was Niki Marvin who finally persuaded Frank, 'Hey, we've got it.'"

But the rest of the sequence tested the crew's patience, taking more than a week to complete. The problem, often enough, was, again, the weather, which was either too nice or too rainy. And the rest of the sequence had to match the overcast skies of the flyover. Most days started out overcast, and that's when Darabont rushed to grab shots before things suddenly switched to bright sunshine. When that happened, he'd try his best to use the precious time by working on other prison-yard scenes, especially ones requiring lots of extras, since they already were gathered for work. The first conversation between Andy and Red, with the baseball being tossed around, was grabbed in this manner (note how sunny the skies are in that scene). So was the scene where the prisoners in the yard are listening to Andy play Mozart's *The Marriage of Figaro* on the prison's public address system. Again, brilliantly sunny skies.

The marching of the chained prisoners through the yard took two days to shoot.

"That was tricky," said Jodiviah "Joe" Stepp, an extra hired to play the new convict walking ahead of Andy. "We really were dodging the rain one day. I think we got about ten takes in over those two days. In the first take, I'm wearing a fedora hat, and you can see that in a couple of the publicity pictures they took for the movie. But then someone noticed that, even though I'm shorter than Tim Robbins, from certain angles, the hat was blocking his face. So we lost the hat."

Stepp also was in the delousing scene, which turned out to be a good thing for Robbins.

"There's an extremely quick glimpse of me—naked guy in the back, standing near Clancy Brown and the guards—when they're turning the fire hose on Tim and delousing him," Stepp said. "You can just spot my right arm and leg, and it looks like they've already put the delousing powder on me. Well, they had. They tried the fire hose on me first. When the powder they used for the delousing mixed with the water, it made the floor extremely slippery, and, sure enough, down I went, hard. I was all right, but it made everybody aware of the danger when Tim stepped into the cage. In some ways, I think it was a fortunate slip . . . fortunate for Tim, anyway."

Tim Robbins and Jodiviah "Joe" Stepp (minus his fedora) get ready for another take as "new fish" marched through the prison yard.

PHOTO COURTESY OF JODIVIAH STEPP

Also in the "fresh fish" scene is Morgan Freeman's son, Alfonso. He's the grinning con who further unnerves Fat Ass by chanting, "Fresh fish! Fresh fish today! We're reeling 'em in!" He's billed twice in the film credits, first in the cast as "Fresh Fish Con" and later as "assistant to Morgan Freeman." He makes another notable appearance in *The Shawshank Redemption*—they took a picture of Alfonso Freeman to use for the prison mug shot of young Red.

FIRST NIGHT IN SHAWSHANK

The "first night" in the cellblock scene includes a close-up of a guard giving the shouted "lights out!" command. That's John E. Summers, who had been a guard at OSR and then was a guard at the new prison. Key to the success of this scene was the powerful performance by Frank Medrano, cast as the new convict known only as Fat Ass.

"When the day came to fly to Ohio, they sent a limousine to take me to the airport," said Medrano, who also stayed at the Holiday Inn in Mansfield. "Now I had only done one film before this, and that was an independent. I was really feeling it. I was on top of the world. I was only thirty-three years old and I was in a major film. They treated me like gold. I was pampered."

One of the first things Medrano did in Mansfield was take the tour of OSR.

"It was overwhelming," he said of the old prison. "I remember thinking, 'I hope I never have to stay in a place like this.' And even though we didn't film the cellblock scenes there, going through it really helped feed my performance. It wasn't difficult to imagine how horrible it would feel to be marched into a prison for the first time."

Medrano was in Mansfield for a month in the early part of the shoot. But only six of those days were spent filming his scenes.

"The scenes in the cellblock where I start crying and Clancy beats the daylights out of me, that took three days," Medrano said. "But the actual crying part took a day. They wanted multiple takes. We did it about five times. They'd go to absolute quiet and then give me all the time I needed to get the crying going. And with the later takes, as you might imagine, it took a little longer."

Then came the part where Byron Hadley drags the crying Fat Ass out of his cell and savagely beats him with the baton, adding some vicious kicks to the attack.

"We were rehearsing and I was padded," Medrano said. "They gave Clancy a rubber baton, so he could just go crazy and not hurt me. So he kept hitting me harder and harder, and I didn't feel a thing. Not a thing. I thought. 'This is working great. Let's do this.' In the actual take, though, a couple of the blows actually hurt. And when I was taking the padding off in my dressing room, I noticed two marks on my chest that crisscrossed. And they turned into bruises. There was a couple of real bruises. I guess those were the ones that hurt. But I didn't mind. These were badges of honor."

Indeed, the injuries during filming tended to be minor, like Freeman's sore throwing arm and Medrano's badges of honor.

"There were tough days," Brown said. "There were a couple cases of heat stroke, because it was hot. And maybe the fellow who played Bogs and the fellow who played Fat Ass, the guys I beat senseless, they may have gotten a couple of extra bruises during the filming of those scenes. But actors love that stuff. They love showing off that stuff."

THE ANIMALS OF SHAWSHANK

Working with animals always presents its own set of challenges on a film, and there are birds, dogs, and rats, among other non-human stars, in *The Shawshank Redemption*. Local trainer Therese Amadio was asked to be an animal trainer on the film. Scott Hart, who was responsible for the main animal star, Jake the Crow, got billing as "animal trainer." Amadio, now Therese Backowski, was billed as "additional animal wrangler," and that covered a lot of animals. The *Shawshank* team didn't need to look far for a trainer. Amadio had a business right next door to the film's Park Avenue production offices in downtown Mansfield.

"I had a retail dog-training, dog-cleaning, pet-grooming pet store in Mansfield, and when Castle Rock Entertainment came to town, they paid the business next door to move out of the building so they could use it for their production offices and wardrobe," Backowski said. "So I started making friends with people involved with the production. They used to come over and give silly names to some of the equipment we used in the grooming room. For instance, we had an integrated vacuum system, so that when we groomed dogs, the hair immediately went into a receptacle, as opposed to into our lungs or all over the store. The guys called that the Auto Suck."

Chatting with the pet store owner, they soon learned that she was not only a trainer but a trainer who had worked on commercials. She had experience, and she was their next door neighbor. Marvin soon arranged a meeting. It all began with the rats.

"There are rats in the movie and I trained those rats," Backowski said. "Niki Marvin asked me to train some sewer rats for a scene with Tim Robbins. Well, I didn't think anyone in their right mind would work with wild rats, so I suggested we use domestic rats and I dye them to make them look like sewer rats. She agreed to that, and then began the great rat dyeing project, which became pretty silly after a while."

So, ever try to dye a rat? Getting domestic rats to cooperate isn't the tough part. Getting the formula right can drive you crazier than the proverbial outhouse rat (to use the polite term for the rodent denizen of an outdoor commode).

"Essentially, human hair dye doesn't behave the same way on rat hair as it does on human hair," Backowski explained. "So, as I experimented, I was getting rats coming out lilac or somewhere between blue and purple. Eventually, I got the right combination and we ended up with rats that looked like sewer rats."

When animals are used in a movie, a representative of the American Society for the Prevention of Cruelty to Animals or the American Humane Society will show up to supervise filming and guarantee the movie earns the familiar end credit: "No animals were harmed during the making of this film."

"The ASPCA was, of course, involved with the filming, and they were very pleased with how careful and responsible we were with the rats," Backowski said.

She and her assistant, Rhonda Heimberger, began working with the rats as babies, handling them and taming them and teaching them. They gave them names like Jake, Clyde, and Clarence. The rats were being trained for a few scenes, including one not used in the film. The rats were supposed to figure in the tense moment where Andy emerges from his tunnel and begins the climb down to the sewer pipe. In Darabont's screenplay, when Andy reaches for a steel conduit while crawling out of the tunnel, a rat goes for his hand. While he makes his way to the sewer pipe, rats scurry, darting this way and that. You'll notice a decided absence of rats in the way it was finally shot. Darabont shortened the process because of time. In his notes for the published screenplay, he said that, if there was one thing in the movie he could improve, he'd make more of Andy's trip from tunnel to sewer pipe.

Another cut scene the trainer had prepared for was one in Brooks Hatlen's hotel room. No, not rats this time.

"Ants," Backowski said. "There was supposed to be a scene where ants crawl up the side of a dresser in the hotel room. For that you needed a colony of ants and a sugar trail of some kind. I'd figured out how to do it, but they decided not to film that, either."

A scene that was shot and stayed in the film was the one where the guard goes down to the solitary confinement cell and tells Andy that Tommy has passed his high school equivalency test. A rat runs in front of the guard carrying the tray with bread and water.

"That was one of my rats," Backowski said. "I trained three rats for that scene. And there was a rat I knew would do the scene, because he was very gregarious and he always came when I called him. The minute I put him down in that corridor and he saw all the people and all the lights, he just stood up and preened, as if to say, 'Finally, everyone knows that I am the star.' So he wouldn't do what many movie animals do—what they're asked to do. When I tried the second rat, who I thought was too shy to do it, he turned out to be perfect, because, every time I called him, he came running to me. And I thought he would be the unlikely one to make it work."

She also trained the pigeons that Brooks feeds in the park. Why not just send James Whitmore to Mansfield's Central Park and let the pigeons gather to be fed? What city's downtown doesn't have pigeons showing up when food is around?

"The problem with that was that Mansfield had just recently instituted a pigeon eradication program," said Backowski, who ended up serving as a wrangler, trainer, animal advocate, and handy technical adviser. "They eliminated all of the pigeons in downtown Mansfield, and now I had to bring twenty-five pigeons into the square and turn them loose. I knew a person who bred pigeons, so that was no problem. Naturally, one of them became one of my favorites. We fed them only from our shoes or a paper bag, so, as soon as they saw shoes or a paper bag, they stayed right there in one place, ready to be fed, and that scene could be shot. But we had a crew ready to corral the pigeons so they wouldn't get loose. Because I had to live here, and I wasn't going to leave a stray pigeon behind in the park."

The toughest shoot was with the bloodhounds being used to search for the escaped Andy.

"The bloodhounds, the day we shot that, honestly, it felt like it was two hundred degrees out," Backowski said. "They had dammed the stream, so it would be deeper than normal, and treated it with chlorine. One of the bloodhounds was just ancient. The dogs were so exhausted running through that stream, I had to stuff liver in my bra and lay on a sewer pipe and call them. I finally told them, 'You have to get this shot this next time. These dogs are exhausted.' And do you know? They got it the next time."

Jake's scenes were not without issues. The adult bird had a tendency to give out a "caw!" without understanding the concept of stepping on another actor's line. And then there was the scene where Andy finds a maggot in his food. Brooks asks him if he's going to eat it and asks if he can have it, then slips it to the baby version of Jake, secreted in his jacket. "Jake says thanks."

Yes, but the person overseeing animal safety said, "Hold on." Something here endangering the bird?

"They had warned me that no animal could be harmed during the making of the film, and that meant not even the waxworm that was supposed to be fed to the crow," Backowski said. "That was a bit of a dilemma. Even though the crow was the only animal I didn't work with in the movie, I had arranged getting the waxworms. Almost all of the feedback from the ASPCA was favorable and positive, but this turned into a problem."

The waxworms had been purchased from the Clearfork Marina in the nearby village of Lexington. They were sold there primarily as bait for fishermen. That explanation did not cut any slack. It was decreed that no live waxworm could be fed to the bird. It would have to be a dead one, and one that had died from natural causes. The impasse was resolved when a dead waxworm was found in the batch, although an impatient Darabont suggested having the deceased waxworm autopsied to determine it had indeed died of natural causes. By the end of the day, some grips had fashioned a small director's chair out of matchsticks, for the comfort of the waxworms.

MAKING A WINTER SCENE IN SUMMERTIME

Challenges come in big and small packages on a movie set. Delays were caused by everything from waxworms to planes flying overhead at inopportune moments.

There was one challenging scene that required a lack of sunshine . . . and summer. Darabont wanted a winter shot in the film, partly because the story is set in Maine and partly to show a desolate Andy at a particularly bleak moment. No problem grabbing such a scene in Ohio, at least not in early March, when Darabont had first seen OSR. That would have been a perfect day to depict icy winter at Shawshank. But the stretch from mid-June to early September is not quite so accommodating in this regard. Still, Darabont was not to be denied his winter scene. For one day, Robbins and extras playing prisoners put on extra layers of clothing and wandered around the prison yard as a giant fan blew buckets of potato flakes around them, simulating snow.

"While being bundled up with jackets and wool hats, we were told to 'act cold,' all the while dying in the heat," Connell said.

The scene was shot away from the direct sunlight, using a shady side of the prison yard and a long lens that provided strong focus on swirling "snow."

INTERACTIONS WITH THE ACTORS

As weeks stretched into months, certain actors emerged as favorites with the extras and the people in the community. Top honors for *Shawshank* charmers went to Morgan Freeman, James Whitmore, and William Sadler, as well as the two actors playing the nastiest villains, Bob Gunton and Clancy Brown. Each is invariably described by the extras as gregarious, warm, funny, and extremely approachable.

"Bob Gunton couldn't have been nicer," said Jane Imbody, a local television reporter and anchor cast as a reporter in two scenes. "He made a point of talking to us and was so sweet. No airs at all about him. And everybody you talked to was completely charmed by Morgan Freeman. Tim Robbins kept to himself. But Morgan went to church here and constantly chatted up everyone. I'd have to say he was everyone's favorite."

The dozens of people interviewed for this book confirm that assessment. The extras were told that they were strictly forbidden from talking to the actors, unless they talked to you first. Freeman took care of that by initiating conversation after conversation . . . in the prison yard . . . in the makeup trailers . . . walking around town . . . in restaurants . . . at the lunch table.

Among the Shawshank convicts enjoying the ice-cold Bohemian Style beer are, at center back, Floyd (Brian Libby) and, center front, Heywood (William Sadler).
PHOTOFEST

Others recall Robbins joking around before and after shooting, but remaining distant and focused while on set.

"Tim was very playful and up in the makeup trailer," said Claire Slemmer, who was in the bank scene with Robbins near the end of the film. "But on the set, he was very reserved and quiet and stayed in character."

"Tim Robbins was very quiet and shy," Ohio Film Commission manager Eve Lapolla said. "He usually kept to himself. He also was playing a character who seems aloof and is thrown into a horrible situation, and, being more of a method actor, you have to call on great concentration to stay in character and feel the character. I'm sure that was not easy."

Freeman, on the other hand, quickly emerged as the film's goodwill ambassador. He left behind a lot of friends and warm memories in Ohio, hosting a barbecue at his rented digs in Butler near the end of the shoot. One person who never forgot his kindness was Mike Koser, who, in 1993, was a twenty-one-year-old college student. Between his sophomore and junior years, he was working as a waiter at the Olive Garden in Mansfield that summer. One weekend night, a large group strolled in at a point when the wait for a table was about two hours.

"I stopped dead in my tracks," Koser said. "I couldn't believe it. Standing right in the middle of the entourage was Morgan Freeman. I walked up to the person who appeared to be the leader and told him not to worry, I would find his group a table immediately. I wasn't about to disappoint Morgan Freeman."

He knew better than to bother the actor during dinner, but, the whole time, an idea was forming.

"After what seemed like forever, Freeman and his party collected their things and made their way to the exit," Koser recalled. "Here was my chance. Palms sweaty. Heart racing. Feet moving and then. . . ."

"Um, Mr. Freeman, sir. My name is Mike and I am a communications major in college. I guess you are filming a movie here in town. And it, um, well, it would mean a lot to me if maybe I could come to the set and interview you and then maybe I could play the interview back on my college radio station this fall."

Freeman turned to his assistant and told him to take Koser's number. Heading for the door he said that they would be in touch. Much to Koser's surprise, unit publicist Ernie Malik called him the next day and said: "Look, I don't know what you said or did, and, frankly, I can't believe this is happening, because Morgan Freeman has only done one other interview so far from the set, and guess what? You are going to be the second. But Morgan had one thing he wanted me to tell you . . . you better know your stuff!"

Koser spent the next two days at the library, preparing for the interview. He arrived on set confident that he'd done his homework. Freeman was about to shoot a scene with Robbins, who passed Koser, saying "Hey, kid." After the scene was completed, Freeman walked Koser to the makeup trailer and said, "So, my aunt makes the world's best peanut brittle. She just sent me this package. Here try some."

Then it was over to Freeman's trailer for the interview. Freeman plops down on the couch, kicks off his shoes, and opens an ice-cold Diet Coke. "So, tell me Mike, what do you wanna know?"

"Well, I guess when you're done shooting here you're probably gonna head south and hop aboard *The Sojourner*, and enjoy a little time off," said Koser, whose research had revealed the name of Freeman's boat.

"Wow! You know your stuff," Freeman said after a pause. "I like that."

Looking back on this interview a quarter of a century later, Koser related, "I make my living doing the thing he is so incredibly gifted at: voiceovers. So, in a way, we've come full circle. And it all began on a hot summer night in an Olive Garden in Mansfield, Ohio."

Eve Lapolla had met Freeman about ten years earlier, when director Arthur Hiller was filming the 1984 satire *Teachers*. Shot mostly at the former Central High School in Columbus, Ohio, the United Artists movie featured a cast led by Nick Nolte, JoBeth Williams, and Judd Hirsch. Also in the film were Ralph Macchio, Lee Grant, and Freeman.

"One of the producers on *Teachers* rented a house that was right next door to the governor's mansion," Lapolla said. "There ended up being a regular nightly poker game at the producer's house, and it usually fell to me to round up players for the game."

Hirsch, Freeman, and Lapolla were regulars at the poker table. One night, Lapolla ended up winning $90 from one of the actors in *Teachers*. During the *Shawshank* shoot at OSR, the manager of the Ohio Film

Commission went up to Freeman and said, "I don't know if you remember me." Without a pause, he replied, "Yeah, I remember you. You took $90 of my money. I haven't played poker since."

The Freeman stories are endless and always served up with delighted smiles. Brian Connell, an extra playing a convict, summarizes the prevailing impression when he says, "Morgan was a blast and funny."

Sadler also was a favorite in Mansfield.

"It was a long shoot," Connell said. "Bill Sadler and I got along fine, as we both are guitar collectors. Bill was looking at photos I brought in for him to see, and while he was looking at them, we heard 'Actors to the set!' And he grabbed me and dragged me into the scene where they are passing around Tommy's letter on whether he passed his equivalency test or not."

Morgan Freeman on set with Eve Lapolla
PHOTO COURTESY OF EVE LAPOLLA

One day, Freeman and Sadler summoned eighteen-year-old Chris Hershberger to have lunch with them.

"I was teaching martial arts at the time," Hershberger said. "And that's what they wanted to talk about the whole time. They wanted to ask me questions about the martial arts. You couldn't ask to meet two nicer guys."

Doug Wertz, a Mansfield actor hired to play the part of "The Tower Guard," remembers conversations with Freeman and Whitmore, sharing a table for dinner and a show with Sadler and his wife, and having drinks and lively conversation with Clancy Brown.

"The few of us that got together were making comments about his [Clancy's] Harley-Davidson shirt he was wearing, and he got a kick out of telling us it was a pajama top," Wertz said. "The cool thing about it all is that those who took the time to chat to us regular folk turned out to be some of the nicest, down-to-earth people. Regular humans themselves."

Darabont, Marsh, Ampah, and other key members of the behind-the-camera creative team also made many friends in Mansfield.

"Frank always was very friendly and down to earth," Tasseff said. "I remember driving through town, and seeing Frank, Kokayi, and others just walking around Central Park. I beeped and waved and shouted, 'What the hell you doing?' And Frank shouted back, 'Making a movie, man.' And Kokayi is like, 'Come on over.' So I parked and walked over, talked a while, then it was, 'OK, see you guys, goodbye.' That's the way it was with them. You might not see them for days, but they were always glad to see you and catch up with you. Nothing pretentious at all."

Marsh was the same way.

"Terry Marsh was fantastic, so welcoming and friendly," Amber Bissman said. "He was awesome. I mean, he was the one who figured out how to build that cellblock and make it work. I was drawn to his office because it was like a candy store to me. He had the reformatory on one wall, pieced together with pictures. He had stacks of *Look* and *Life* magazines, for research and references. He had all kinds of bits and pieces and odds and ends. He was super-cool. As you went out his office door, you'd notice this weird shape on the wall. It took me to a few years ago to realize that it was the size of the hole that Andy crawls through."

Marsh would not only graciously welcome crewmembers and locals to his office, he would welcome their input and solicit their ideas.

"That was Terry Marsh, a prince among men," Milito said. "He was the kind of guy who would take input. I walked into his office one day, and he was drafting two wonderful drawings of details on arches. And he said, 'Which one do you like?' So I picked one. And he said, 'Fine, take that one, throw the other one out, and we'll build the one you like.' That's the kind of production designer he was. That's why people loved him."

Tasseff and Jodie Snavely (then Jodie Puster) sometimes would leave their Convention & Visitors Bureau offices to catch a glimpse of filming.

"I love how things are built," Tasseff said. "I love processes. And I was fascinated about learning that with a film, but I just thought the process was so slow and methodical."

Snavely agreed: "We watched the scene up at OSR where the warden tells Tim Robbins to shine his shoes. They did that over and over and over. And I remember thinking, 'I thought it was perfect the first time.'"

Robbins sometimes had that precise thought. Both Robbins and Freeman had directed movies and understood the pressure, and both wanted to be careful about not stepping on the shoes of a first-time director. Yet they did think there were occasions when Darabont was asking for one take too many.

"I guess the standard answer is that everything went beautifully, but it was challenging," Robbins said. "I don't want to take anything away from Frank, because he did a phenomenal job with an immense production and a lot of stress. And he came up with this great vision on how to take Stephen King's story to the screen, and then he was able to make it all work and draw out these wonderful performances that run all through that film. But, sure, there were times Morgan and I thought he already had what he needed, and we may have voiced that opinion a couple of times. We may have voiced it in strong terms. But, all things considered, it was an amazing collaboration. All credit to Frank, first as a screenwriter, then for what he accomplished as a director."

If a warden's opinion holds any weight on such filmmaking matters, Baker always was impressed with how quickly and effectively Freeman could get into character and deliver the dramatic goods. "He was a real pro," Baker said. "He always nailed it on the first take."

ROLES FOR THE REAL WARDEN AND GUARDS

Dennis Baker, the former corrections officer at the OSR, got a small taste of acting. The warden agreed to be an extra, if he could play, of all things, a convict. He's sitting on the 1960s prison bus, right behind Tommy (Gil Bellows). Harold Cope, who spent five years as an officer at OSR, is in the film, too, but not as an extra. He got a line and on-screen billing. Billed as the "Hole Guard," he's the officer who gets Bogs out of solitary, saying, "Time's up, Bogs." This was a prison scene shot at OSR. A solitary cell was built near the bullpen, a pass-through area that was selected as the setting for Warden Norton's "welcome" speech to Andy and the other new convicts.

"I did the 'Time's up, Bogs' line in one take," Cope said. "Because it was a speaking part, I had to join the Screen Actors Guild. But I was getting five hundred dollars a day, and I ended up working six days on the film. I had my own trailer. And I still get royalty checks." Other guards playing guards included Donald E. Zinn as "Moresby Batter," the Moresby Prison guard who learns that his gun and holster are deductible items, and Chuck Brauchler as the guard who yells, "Man missing on tier two!"

All of which makes Baker say, "I wished I had held out for a speaking part in it. I'd still be getting checks for it."

Cope also worked on the film that shot at OSR after *The Shawshank Redemption*, *Air Force One*, the 1997 thriller starring Harrison Ford, Gary Oldman, and Glenn Close. This wasn't a long stay at OSR, which was doubling for a Russian prison, although other Ohio locations were used, including Severance Hall in Cleveland, the Rickenbacker Air National Guard Base near Columbus, and the Cuyahoga County Courthouse in Cleveland.

"I had a lot of working knowledge of that prison, and that came in useful for filmmakers," Cope said.

It also came in useful for cast and crewmembers who wanted to ask him question after question about what OSR was like as a working prison. He'd been given the "don't speak to the actors unless they speak to you" command, but one actor kept him talking for a half-hour. Not surprisingly, that was Morgan Freeman.

"I've met a lot of celebrities, working events as security or working on movies," Cope said. "And Morgan Freeman was just the most genuine, down-home, caring individual I ever met among movie folk. That's not to say I haven't met other nice people. I met a lot of them, but Morgan Freeman was in a class by himself. If anyone was at all condescending to the locals, Morgan Freeman would jump in and defend us. He wasn't going to have it."

THE DAY THE AMBULANCE NEEDED FIRST AID

Although he collected a bruise or two thanks to the baton swung by Clancy Brown's Byron Hadley, the actor who cut such a menacing figure as Bogs, Mark Rolston, ended up faring better than the ambulance used to take away his crippled character. The ambulance was crippled during the filming of that scene. Darabont recalled that the engine block cracked, leaving them with "a giant paperweight instead of an ambulance." Stepp, on hand as an extra that day, said the vintage vehicle started smoking, giving the impression that it was catching fire. Although some remember this as "the day the ambulance caught fire," it never actually reached the point of flames. Brian Connell, also on hand that day playing a convict, just remembered that, once arriving on the scene, the ambulance wouldn't start. It was going nowhere under its own power, and Darabont had a schedule to keep. He quickly enlisted the help of about six people—grips, electricians, and extras—and they pushed from behind until it had enough "extra" power to coast through the scene. Stepp and Connell were two of the extras giving emergency aid to the ambulance in the form of a mighty push.

"That was under our power," said Stepp, one of those recruited to push. "And it worked. It glides by in frame, past Red and his friends behind the fence, with just enough power to get it past them. That's all it needed."

And all Darabont and his fellow pushers needed was to stop short and stay out of frame. They managed to keep out of camera range, but it

The ambulance that broke down during filming on *The Shawshank Redemption,* now on display at the Shawshank Woodshop in Upper Sandusky

PHOTO BY BECKY DAWIDZIAK

required some wild acrobatics, waving of arms, and awkward movements. What most impressed Darabont was that Freeman continued to deliver his lines without cracking up. That ambulance now is on display at the Shawshank Woodshop in Upper Sandusky.

The ambulance wasn't the only thing that broke down during filming. A huge section of the wall around the prison collapsed in the middle of that summer.

"I was working outside and heard this rumble," Milito said. "And I thought, 'That isn't good.' And there's a big hole right where we need to shoot. The lime and cement just collapsed."

Milito quickly assembled a cleanup crew and then set about repairing the gap. To shore up the damaged area, he hired a pool company to gunite the new construction (gunite pools use a rebar framework sprayed over with a concrete and sand mixture for durability).

"When we were finished, you'd never know something that big had given way," Milito said. "That's the challenge of working on a location like that, but it's also the fun. How do you solve the problem?"

BREAKING OUT OF PRISON

Prison break scenes were filmed for both of the previous films shot at OSR, *Harry and Walter Go to New York* and *Tango & Cash*, and *Shawshank* would make it three-for-three. The sewer pipe that Andy escapes through was built to be camera and actor friendly. The fifteen-foot "pipe" remains on display at OSR, along with the cone-shaped addition used to create the illusion that the pipe was longer than it was. The addition was attached to the pipe for the moment when Andy first looks in the pipe. The gradual reduction of size toward the cone tip made it appear that the pipe stretches on many yards instead of a few feet. There have been erroneous reports that Robbins was crawling through a mixture that, while not sewage, was in some way potentially harmful. But if Robbins was going to get sick, it would have been from, ironically, how sweet it smelled in there. Doubling for sewage was a mixture primarily made from water, sawdust, oatmeal, and, the secret ingredient, chocolate syrup.

While shooting the pipe crawl, Robbins looked over at Darabont and said, "I don't know, maybe I don't want to take a shower. This stuff smells pretty good."

What was potentially harmful was the stream that Andy falls into when he emerges from the sewer pipe. It was tested by a chemist, who found toxic elements in the water samples. That was why, as Backowski recalled, it was treated with chlorine to kill contaminants and make the shoot safe for both human and canine actors.

"We had the water tested, and the chemist told us, 'The water in that stream is kind of like water but not quite,'" Milito said. "He told us it was loaded with bacteria because waste from cattle in the area had been washed into it. So, in order to shoot those scenes, I had to dam up that stream and dump chemicals like chlorine into it, just to make it safe. That was the water that Tim ran through for that iconic scene."

It's such a triumphant, exultant scene, with the water symbolizing cleansing and purification—an almost ritualistic washing away of years tainted by abuse, brutality, and corruption. And yet, Robbins had to be talked into going into that water, which itself had to be cleansed.

"I wasn't completely sure of it, but I was sure enough to give it a try," Robbins said. "Looks like I lived to tell the tale."

WARDEN NORTON'S DELETED SCENE

Bob Gunton's last filmed scene was the one where Warden Norton accepts the pie-and-cash bribe while his convict crew works in the background. Connell said there was more shot than what ended up in the movie.

"I am in several scenes but my best one was cut from the film," Brian Connell said of this sequence. "It was shot on prison land north of the prison. Several of us were down the hill on the warden's left, and a tree falls and pins a con. I was right there in the middle of it all, rushing over to help the injured man. The tree was rigged so that they could crank the thing back up, so they could shoot it several times. On about the second take, an older man tumbled down the hill after losing his footing while he was coming to aid the pinned con."

The moment was meant to underscore how the pious Norton felt nothing for the prisoners (a point already amply made). And it does appear in Darabont's screenplay. A winch snaps dramatically behind Norton, whipping through the air and almost severing a convict's leg. Norton barely takes notice as the man is pinned and the other cons run to help him. That's how the scene is described in the script.

There was a well-earned round of applause for Gunton, and the production headed for the last scenes filmed with Robbins and Freeman, both of whom left Mansfield in late August. The remaining cast and crew left in early September.

WRAPPING UP THE SHOOT

Freeman and Robbins weren't the only ones doing some artistic pulling and tugging with first-time director Darabont. There also were differences of opinion between Darabont and Deakins over the visual style of the film. Darabont, however, again and again credits choices made by Deakins resulting in memorable moments throughout the film, including the creative way the mess hall scene is shot after Andy gets out of "The

Hole" for playing Mozart on the public-address system and the quick cut to Norton slamming down the newspaper exposing his corruption schemes. Both of these instances eliminated needless camera setups, and Darabont later described such lessons as attending "the Roger Deakins School of Visual Economy."

"I'd done a movie with Frank before that, a TV movie called *Buried Alive*," Woodward said. "And Frank, like a lot of directors, asked for a lot of takes. I won't say they're over-shooting. They want coverage. They want to machine-gun out everything they do. Roger Deakins is the opposite end of that spectrum. Roger doesn't believe in a lot of setups. He believes in spending more time planning to get one good shot. That was the tension between them. Frank wanted more coverage. Niki wanted more coverage. The studio wanted more coverage. But Roger didn't. And the film certainly didn't suffer because of that. The different approaches probably helped. It was an advantage. Remember, Roger wanted a lot of time to plan, and Frank gave it to him."

Milito believes that the differing viewpoints and filmmaking philosoophies made for a better film.

"The success of that whole film owes to the gathering of talents on that film, starting with Frank, Terry Marsh, and Roger Deakins," Milito said. "Frank had a great team around him, and he relied on them. It was his first feature film, so he was learning, but he wasn't the kind of director to think no one could tell him anything. That's what allowed him to take full advantage of the experience of guys like Terry and Roger. And you see that in the film."

One of the last scenes shot was in the Ashland bank. Andy walks in and is greeted by a teller (Claire Slemmer). The scene then moves to the desk of the bank manager (James Kisicki), who tells "Randall Stevens" he's sorry to be losing his business. Andy, as Stevens, then asks the teller if she will put a package in the outgoing mail.

Slemmer came perilously close to falling out of the film. The Cincinnati actress drove to Mansfield for her one day of work on the movie. Upon arrival, she had a wardrobe fitting and a meeting with the hairstylist.

"They wanted the hairstyle to be authentic 1960s, so they gave me a jar of Dippity-Do and a package of brush rollers," Slemmer said. "They asked me if I knew how to use them. I did because it's what I did all throughout high school, from 1962 to 1966. I had that hairdo, that bubble hairdo. And he said, 'You need to sleep on them.' Well, that's what I did in high school."

Given a room at the Holiday Inn, she decided to explore the town the night before.

"I had my roller blades in the trunk of my car," Slemmer said. "So I'm tooling around the downtown and it started to get dark. And I thought, 'I'd better get home.' I was going down a slope and hit a pothole. I flew into the air and thought, 'Oh, shit. I won't be able to do this tomorrow. Protect your face.' I did end up injuring my shoulder, but my face was fine and I could walk the next day."

The next day, she reported for work in Ashland and was put at ease because "everyone was really nice, relaxed, and calm." The script called for Andy to enter the bank, and the teller, looking up and noticing him, says, "May I help you?" Andy replies, "My name is Peter Stevens. I've come to close out some accounts." By then, of course, the switch had been made from Peter to Randall.

"And when we rehearsed, Tim came up to the counter and immediately said his line," Slemmer said. "He didn't give me the chance to say my line. And I was too shy to say, 'Tim, I have a line before you. Don't take my line away from me. I have so few.' That happened a couple of times, so I called the assistant director aside and said, 'I know I'm just a local actor. This may not be important. But I'm not getting a chance to say my line.' So he talked to Tim. I said my line, and then they ended up cutting his line."

When the scene switched to the bank manager's desk, Slemmer was able to sneak in a line that wasn't in the script. As Andy asks the teller about mailing the package, it seemed natural for Slemmer to respond, "I'd be happy to." So she did.

"It felt right, so I kept saying it in rehearsals and through the takes, and nobody told me not to," Slemmer said. "So I ended up adding four words to my fourteen words. So I had eighteen words."

And she added a line of dialogue to an American screen classic.

"Oh, that's right," she said with a laugh. "I hadn't thought of it that way. Isn't that an actor for you? When I first saw the film, I was most concerned about whether my scene would still be in the movie. You always wonder if you'll end up on the cutting room floor. Once you know you haven't been cut, you can go back and realize you ended up in a great movie."

The package Andy has her mail then lands on the desk of the *Portland Daily Bugle* editor-in-chief, played by Rohn Thomas. (You can spot Thomas as the coroner in the vampire comedy-crime mix *Innocent Blood* [1992], as a doctor in another film version of a Stephen King story, *The Dark Half* [1993], and as a police sergeant in *Telling Lies in America* [1997].)

"It's a little embarrassing to say, 'I was in *Shawshank Redemption*,'" Thomas said. "It's probably the best film I'm in, and it's one of my shortest times on camera. But I'm amazed at how many people recognize me. I know people who watch it twice a year or more. Who knew it would have legs like it did?"

The screenplay called for the editor to open the package, scan the cover letter, dash to the door, and yell, "Hal! Dave! Get your butts in here!" The line wasn't used and the scene was tightened in order to jump more quickly to the warden's reaction. Amber Bissman had hoped to appear in the scene, which would have been appropriate, since the editor's office was on the ground floor of the Bissman Building.

"It was an easy scene," Thomas said. "You just have to open a package. A lot of the crew had already gone at that point. Darabont directed it. All in all, it took about three hours."

Paul Kennedy made the trip from Cincinnati late in the shoot to play the 1967 Food-Way manager. The scene was filmed in downtown Mansfield, at the E&B Market, but, upon arrival, Kennedy was offered a tour of OSR. He arrived when they were filming the scene of Red working in the prison cemetery. This poignant patch of ground had been in continuous use since 1896. The families of prisoners who died in custody could claim their bodies, but bodies not claimed were buried in OSR cemetery. The tombstones identified the prisoners only by their inmate numbers, a realization that led Sadler to observe how these inmates didn't even

Ben and Amber Bissman reminisce about *The Shawshank Redemption,* sitting in the ground-floor room of the Bissman Building used for the newspaper editor's office.

PHOTO BY BECKY DAWIDZIAK

get their identities back in death. Darabont knew from the start that he wanted to use the "pauper's graveyard" in the film.

"Frank couldn't figure out where to use it in the film, and we talked and talked and talked about it, because we were constantly walking by that little cemetery," Woodward said. "Finally, I said, 'Frank, why don't you have Red here as just one of the group of prisoners cleaning up? Because, basically, he's lost his best friend, and Red is expecting to live out his years there.' That turned out to be a really wonderful scene. I love it."

Darabont agreed. Andy has escaped, after all, and this was the ideal way to strike what the director called "a haunting chord of melancholy and loss."

"There was a cut scene in the Food-Way where a kid is shooting a toy gun at Red," Kennedy said. "And, of course, the scene that remained in the film is where Red asks me permission to take a piss and I tell him he doesn't have to ask. People say to me, 'Oh, you're so mean to him in that scene.' I always say, 'Really? Mean? I think I was trying to be the nice guy.' I think they mash up my character with the earlier Food-Way manager. But I've lost count of how many people have asked me permission to take a piss."

During a break, one of the actors kept Kennedy talking for about twenty minutes. Come on, you know it was Morgan Freeman.

"I would have never presumed to go up and talk to him," Kennedy said. "But he came up to me and said, 'So, what's your story?' And he really wanted to hear it."

Another scene cut from the movie featured first assistant director John R. Woodward as a tower guard with a bullhorn. He orders Red and his friends, worried about Andy, to move out of the prison yard and get back to their cells. Darabont looked at Woodward and said, "You need to do that because you know how to use a bullhorn. Right?" Then it was a fight between Darabont and Marvin over who would break the news to Woodward that his scene had hit the cutting room floor. But to make sure he'd still receive his Screen Actors Guild residuals, they left his name in the billing, "Bullhorn Tower Guard." If you're a credit watcher and you've wondered where this guard appears in the film, now you know he doesn't.

An improvised scene that shows up late in the film is Freeman's stroll through the overgrown alfalfa field that Ampah had found. They had filmed the moments showing Red at the wall and the tree. They had packed up the equipment and were leaving. As they made their way through the field, grasshoppers started to jump all around Darabont.

"We were wrapping, and now we could actually walk through the field and beat it down," Woodward said. "Going in, we didn't want to ruin anything with our equipment and everything, because you never know what kind of shots you're going to get. Now we didn't care."

Darabont looked at his watch. They still had twenty scheduled minutes left for filming. He quickly conferred with Deakins. They laid down a dolly track, loaded the camera, and grabbed a shot of Freeman walking across the sun-dappled field. And not one grasshopper put in an appearance. They had been scared by all of the activity. With only minutes left on the clock, Darabont sent Freeman back to his start-mark. This time, however, Darabont and members of the crew were in front of Freeman, out of frame, madly yelling and dancing and waving their hands and doing what they could to get the grasshoppers to hop. And they did. It was what Darabont described as "a veritable grasshopper kaleidoscope."

"It was kind of crazy, but it sure resulted in a great shot," Woodward said. "It's such a quiet, poetic scene, but right in front of it was what looked like absolute madness."

King's novella ends with Red making his way toward Andy and Zihuatanejo. And, originally, this is where Darabont's screenplay ended. Producer Liz Glotzer, who always seemed to be stepping in at crucial moments with just the right opinion, lobbied for a final scene depicting the reunion of Andy and Red in Zihuatanejo. She argued that the audience would want to see the friends reunited, particularly after all they'd been through. Darabont wrote it and filmed it but remained doubtful about whether to use it. A test screening erased all doubt. The audience didn't just love this moment. They were crazy in love with it. Darabont did, however, wisely cut what were to be the last lines of dialogue in the film. Seeing Red approach the boat, Andy was to say, "You look like a man who knows how to get things." Then Red would reply, "I'm known to locate certain things from time to time." Darabont ruled that this exchange not only undercut the beautiful simplicity of the final images, it also came off as rather cutesy. One battle during this shot was over that harmonica Andy gave Red as a gift earlier in the film. The studio wanted Red playing the harmonica as he approached the boat. Freeman argued vehemently against this.

"Leave the harmonica the way it is in the movie," Freeman said.

The studio argued that it would be an affectionate touch, with Red, years later, playing this gift presented to him in prison. It all struck Freeman as obvious and sophomoric.

"This was a big fight," Woodward said. "They went round and round about it. And I think Roger Deakins agreed with Morgan, because he stalled and stalled. We already had got everything else, and this scene would have to be captured late in the day. We just sat around waiting for the right light, and the clouds were rolling in, and, pretty soon, you know, the day had just gone to crap and we couldn't do it. So Morgan's choice won out. And I think he had the right instinct there, because the ending is perfect."

The final day of shooting was on the Sandy Point National Wildlife Refuge beach found by location manager and production supervisor Kokayi Ampah. Cinematographer Roger Deakins and first assistant director John R. Woodward were on hand, and helicopter pilot Robert "Bobby Z" Zajonc again was called in for duty. With the only scene not filmed in Ohio now in the can, that was a wrap.

EXTRAS, EXTRAS! READ ALL ABOUT 'EM!

THE SHAWSHANK REDEMPTION REQUIRED ENOUGH EXTRAS TO CONVINC-ingly suggest an entire prison population. That meant the production needed a lot of area residents to play convicts and guards. And many of them had to be available for the entire shoot. If you were an extra playing a prisoner in several scenes, you became part of what was known as "the Core Con." A technical adviser of sorts was never far away, since some of the extras playing guards were actual guards from the nearby Mansfield Correctional Institution (some of them having been guards at the Ohio State Reformatory), and some of the extras playing prisoners were former prisoners. Other roles required extras to be around for only a day or two: jurors, courtroom spectators, reporters, downtown shoppers, and travelers on buses.

The guards playing guards weren't the only extras typecast in *The Shawshank Redemption*. Two of the extras playing reporters were report-ers working in Mansfield: Jane Imbody and Lou Whitmire. Imbody was an anchor and reporter at WMFD, the local television station, so she was well aware of the three casting calls for extras in May.

Finally, in July, Imbody got the call from extras casting director Ivy Weiss. "Oh, what am I going to play?" Imbody asked. When told that they wanted her to be a reporter, all Imbody could think was, "Typecast-ing all the way."

Whitmire had been writing stories about the making of the film for the *Mansfield News Journal*. One day, somebody in the company asked her, "You want to be in a movie?" Both Whitmire and Imbody appear in the scene where the 1966 district attorney (Charlie Kearns) arrives at Shawshank and informs Clancy Brown's character, Byron Hadley, that

Extra Steve Oster, center, playing a guard, poses between Jane Imbody and Lou Whitmire, reporters playing reporters in *The Shawshank Redemption*.
PHOTO COURTESY OF LOU WHITMIRE

he's under arrest. They're easy to spot in the film. They're both blondes with big hair. Whitmire is the one with the bouffant hairdo and the distinctive spotted brown coat. Imbody is in a tan dress and holding a microphone.

"Your hair had to be done up in curlers the night before, and they specified magnetic rollers," Imbody said. At 6:00 a.m. the next morning the extras were bused out to the prison and were prepped for their scenes. "I had long hair, and they teased it so tall, you could feel the sweat running under your hair," she said. "It was so hot. But I didn't want to say anything, because they might give the part to somebody else."

Then came the call for "action," with the two reporters being told how to act like reporters.

"They had some reporters on one side of the drive and some on the other side," Imbody said. "But when the police officers got out of the car, they had instructed the people playing the reporters on the other side of

Mansfield reporters Lou Whitmire and Jane Imbody prepare to play reporters for the scene where the district attorney comes to arrest Byron Hadley and Warden Norton.

PHOTO COURTESY OF JANE IMBODY

the drive from us to follow them. And I thought, 'Well, heck, no! You want realism? I'm a reporter. You're not keeping me away.' So I just ran with the rest, and nobody said anything. They hired me to play a reporter, so I was going to act like a reporter."

The scene shifts to the warden looking out the window of his office, observing the arrest of Hadley.

"You can see Lou really well in that shot where Hadley is arrested," Imbody said. "When the warden is looking out of the window and they're leading Clancy away, I'm following, in a tan dress and with the microphone. So I'm easy to spot in that scene. It was such a kick. You know, living and working in the middle of Ohio, you never think you're going to be in a movie. And my friend who played a juror and I was so jealous of in June, well, you barely see her in the film, and who would have guessed that I'd end up with the better part?"

Imbody was called back for a second scene requiring reporters. Also filmed in front of the main OSR building, this was the one where the warden announces to the press his "Inside-Out program." The scene was set a few years earlier than the arrest of Hadley, but, if you look sharp as the camera tracks over the reporters toward Norton, you'll see Imbody wearing the same dress.

"And I thought, 'Well, of course, reporters don't make a lot of money," Imbody said. "She's wearing the same dress."

Because she was on local television back then, Imbody often was recognized by people in Mansfield. One afternoon, she was with her mother, getting a sandwich at the Coney Island restaurant, not far from the building where they were shooting Red's pawn shop scene.

"They were filming the scene where Red sees the compass in the pawn shop window," Imbody said. "Morgan Freeman was walking around Central Park, just outside the Coney Island. People in the restaurant recognized me from television and were asking me for my autograph. I said, 'Guys, Morgan Freeman is walking around outside. He's outside.' My mom got the biggest kick out of that. A big star a few feet away and everyone is asking for my autograph."

———

Also reporting for work on the day of the Hadley arrest and the warden's suicide was Steve Oster, cast as a guard. He very much wanted to be in the film when he heard about auditions on local radio station Mix 106 FM, but believed he missed his chance. Oster, who had done local theater and some modeling, was living in Mansfield and working at the Ohio Department of Developmental Disabilities in Columbus, about an hour's drive away.

Oster was cast as a security guard and recalled, "I was there the day the warden shot himself in his office. It took three takes. The first time, the window blew out. The second time, the window cracked, but it basically just cracked down. The third take, is the one you see in the movie."

During a break, he posed for pictures with Whitmire, Imbody, and other extras playing reporters. Today, Oster is the superintendent of the Coshocton and Knox County Boards of Developmental Disabilities in Ohio. He gets to catch up with Imbody every so often because she is now the director of community relations for Richland Newhope (the Richland County Board of Developmental Disabilities). Whitmire still is a reporter at the *Mansfield News Journal*.

"I will be somewhere with people I know and out of the blue they will tell someone, 'Steve was an extra in *The Shawshank Redemption*,'" Oster said. "It makes me laugh, but, I must say, it is one of my most treasured memories."

Also cast as extras in the Hadley arrest scene were Ben and Amber Bissman, who had provided everything from signs to beer bottles (yes, *those* beer bottles) for the film. They also arranged for Ben's father to be with them for the scene.

"We were kind of a go-to couple for many of the people on the film, so we got to know a lot of people on the film," Ben Bissman said. "Amber is the blonde standing near the police car. I'm standing in the back. And my dad kind of got cut off at the waist. We were spectators, like, 'Ooo, something is going on at the prison.' We shot it like eight or nine times."

Between one of the takes, Amber impishly triple-dared Ben to lock the police car door so it wouldn't open on the next take. He did and the door didn't.

"And it was a big stink," he said. "They got so mad and told everybody that it cost them like nine hundred dollars a minute to film. I sweated the next two or three times they did it. But they never found out who had locked the door."

Brian Connell, who was living in Galion, Ohio, about fifteen miles from Mansfield, went to audition with two members of the band he was in, as well as a coworker. Connell was told that he would need to get a 1940s style haircut, and that's when he decided he really didn't want to be in the film, after all. A few days later, he got a call from Ivy Weiss, in charge of extras casting. Because they needed extras to play convicts for the entire summer, they had no shortage of young men out of high school and older men who were retired. She needed more extras in the middle range. Would he reconsider? He reversed course, agreed to a haircut, and arranged for a three-month leave of absence from his job. His boss observed with a laugh, "They had to clean you up to play a convict!"

Connell became a member of the Core Con. Connell's band's bass player, Jeff Gledhill, was cast as one of the "new fish" who arrive on the prison bus with Andy.

On the bus ride over to Upper Sandusky for the woodshop scenes, Connell and other members of the Core Con asked executive producer David Lester if the movie was going to be any good. Lester told them that they were part of something really special. He said that the movie was not only good, it would be nominated for major awards.

"I thought he was blowing smoke, but, as it turns out, he was correct," Connell said.

Lester's estimation spread fast. "Rumor on the set one week was this could be an Oscar quality movie in the making," extra Bob Cassity said. "The principal actors were that good early on."

Although extra Brian Connell played a convict in *The Shawshank Redemption*, he has held on to these two patches used on guard uniforms.
PHOTOS COURTESY OF BRIAN CONNELL

Being part of the Core Con came with instructions, guidelines, and ongoing suggestions. For instance?

"We were told to keep out of the sun, because too many were showing up with sunburn and suntans," Connell said. "After that, we got sunscreen every day, because there were not supposed to be tanned cons. Nor any jewelry or glasses. So at the beginning of a shoot we all would put our glasses in our pockets and wander around blindly until, 'Cut . . . Back to one' was heard, then the glasses would all pop back out."

During one mess-hall shoot, one of the extras playing a con ate all of the food on his tray and then asked for more.

"Then we had to be told to act like we were eating the food, but DON'T EAT IT," Connell said.

Max Gerber experienced the film as both a stand-in and an extra.

"I was a farmer, farming with my father," Gerber said. "I was a little leery at first. I started out as a utility stand-in, standing in for Clancy or the guy who played Bogs [Mark Rolston]. They had me stand in for Bogs as they lit the scene where he's in 'The Hole.' And I kept falling asleep in there. Roger Deakins was so nice, because the producers didn't like you falling asleep. He kept whispering to me: 'Max, Max, wake up, wake up.' I liked being a stand-in. You got treated much better as a stand-in than as an extra."

Perhaps, but you didn't end up on screen if you were a stand-in. You might end up in a scene or two if you're an extra, and few extras can be spotted in more scenes than Gerber.

"I got good at strategizing," said Gerber, who received an on-screen credit for his work as a lighting stand-in. "I ended up in a lot of scenes. I'd anticipate where I'd need to stand in order to be seen, and I'd position myself in the right place. When they're throwing the ball, I'm behind one actor in one shot, then behind another actor in another shot. I got very good at it. I wore my gear every day so I'd be ready to be in any shot."

So good, in fact, that when Andy is playing *The Marriage of Figaro* over the public address system, Gerber is standing in the prison yard (he's the one holding the football) *and* in the woodshop. Music can transport you? Well, this particular convict is in two places at the same time. Still, he's much less noticeable in the woodshop, and that's because Darabont noticed how prominently Gerber had positioned himself, standing right next to Freeman.

"Max, we've seen a bit much of you," Darabont told him. "Why don't you slide back in the corner a bit?"

When the convicts are chanting "fresh fish," Gerber is in the mix. When the prisoners are signing up for the roof detail, he's near the end of the table. And, although you can't see him, he was one of the prisoners in the cellblock when Byron Hadley is beating Fat Ass.

"I'm lying there in one of the cells in the warehouse, and Clancy is just beating the living hell out of what sounded like a mattress," Gerber said. "It sounds real, and he's just f-bombing this and that, and I'm a little farm kid from Ohio thinking to himself, 'My mom is going to kill me. What have I gotten myself into?'"

He had gotten himself into a lot of scenes in a great movie, although one scene did put him out of action for a couple of days. They shot a night scene and condensation had made the steps on the aluminum ladders deceptively slick. Gerber slipped on one of those steps and landed in the ER with an injured back. He bounced back quickly, though, and added it to his store of *Shawshank* memories.

There's a scene in the movie where Andy offers to teach Red how to play chess. Another extra actually made that offer to Gerber.

"I never played chess in my life, but we had so much down time," he said. "And I kept getting better and better. He was a good teacher. I was playing chess with Morgan's stand-in at one point, and his stand-in got called away, so Morgan plopped down in his seat and kept playing. Morgan knew how to play. I ended up beating him, and Morgan said, 'I want a rematch.' We never got a chance for the rest of the movie."

Dick Jourdan, who ran a truck driving school in Columbus, saw the notice about auditions in the local newspaper. You can't spot him in nearly as many scenes as Gerber, but he has the distinction of play-

Extra and stand-in Max Gerber recalls his good times on *The Shawshank Redemption* (and how he got good at getting into shots).

PHOTO BY BECKY DAWIDZIAK

ing both a prisoner and a member of a parole board in *The Shawshank Redemption*. For an extra, that's mighty impressive range.

"They asked me if I'd mind being naked in the shower scene, and I wasn't crazy about that," Jourdan said. "But they used me for some of the prison-yard scenes. At one point, I was in the bleachers with several other people playing prisoners, and four of them were actual ex-convicts. They had some stories to tell, believe me. We were there for the day Morgan Freeman kept throwing the baseball for nine hours."

Near the end of the shoot, Jourdan was asked to be on the last of the three parole boards. You can spot him seated on the left.

"When they sent me to the makeup trailer for the parole board scene, I sat down in a chair, and sitting right next to me, reading a newspaper, was Morgan Freeman," Jourdan said. "He looked over at me and started chatting and telling me how nice everyone was being to him. Then he gave me that big smile and said, 'I guess we'll be working together today.' Couldn't have been nicer."

———

David Lessig was actually working at the lumberyard in Upper Sandusky at the time, so he was a natural for extra work in the woodshop scenes.

"I sort of got grandfathered into the film and didn't have to audition," Lessig says. "We had an eleven-hour day here at the woodshop. There were thousands upon thousands of feet of cable everywhere for all of the equipment, and it was in the low nineties that day. So they brought in a big air-conditioning unit and ran it in through two big pipes. Then, when the director said quiet, he meant quiet. The police even stopped the traffic on the street in both directions so there would be no noise. It was amazing to us to see how you go through all of that for a few seconds of film."

———

Doug Wertz showed up for auditions with some acting experience and a strong desire to be in the movie. He'd been in a film before *The Shawshank Redemption*, and he'd had the lead role in *The Men in Black* (a low-budget 1992 movie filmed in Mansfield, not to be confused with the 1997 blockbuster starring Tommy Lee Jones and Will Smith).

Then came the newspaper notice about Castle Rock holding auditions.

"I reached out to my representing agent but with no luck, as they were not looking to go through an agency," Wertz said. "So I tried the next best thing: attending a cattle call. Interestingly enough, I was turned down the first time with the comment that 'we have enough of your type.' Disappointed, I walked away."

A couple of weeks later, he attended a second cattle-call audition, only to be turned away again. He'd given up, but then there was a message on his answering machine from Weiss. Would he like to be a member of the Core Con?

"As zealous as I was, I also realized that I would probably never be seen, heard, or recognized," Wertz said.

This time, he turned them down, thanking Weiss for getting in touch and figuring he wasn't destined to be in the film. The next day, Weiss called back and offered him the role of "The Tower Guard." This didn't sound like much of an opportunity, either. He'd probably be unrecognizable and filmed at a great distance. So he turned them down again. For those of you keeping score at home, this was twice he'd been rejected and twice he rejected them. So how did Wertz end up in the film?

"Another day passed and a third phone call came in," Wertz said. "It almost became a sales job as Ivy started to tell me that Frank Darabont saw my resume and wanted me to take part. No lines to be spoken but she mentioned the specific 'Tower Guard' role would have a close-up shot. I had no idea who the hell Mr. Darabont was, but I was intrigued to get in front of the camera one more time, even if it meant I may have a cameo, so I accepted."

Being around the film, talking with the actors and crewmembers, turned out to be the big experience he had been looking for when he first auditioned. He got to pal around with Brown, Sadler, Whitmore, and Freeman, while also feeling like part of the big family during filming.

"I ended up spending the entire time the crew was in Mansfield assisting with things like setting up new cast with props, taking them to wardrobe, or whatever else I could do to help," Wertz said. "My experience was turning into exactly what I had hoped for, to be part of the cast and honorary—non-credited—crew."

And his shot as "The Tower Guard"? It made the national promotional trailer for the film. You also can spot Wertz in several other scenes, normally dressed as a guard. For instance, he's on the opposite side of the table when Red and the others are signing up for roof detail.

"Dressed in civilian clothing, I can be seen just beyond the doorway during one of the tax consulting scenes with Andy as I am leaning into the shot looking at my paperwork," Wertz said. "Funny thing, several years later, 'The Tower Guard' was immortalized in animation through *Family Guy*, during their satirical version of a Stephen King trilogy."

Tracy Love was studying criminal justice in college when he read about auditions at the Upper Sandusky High School. He ended up being cast both as a spectator in the courtroom scene and a prisoner. "I would have done it for free, just to observe how they make movies," Love said. "Everything about it was incredibly fascinating. Coming from rural Ohio, you can't begin to realize how big a kick this was."

Mike Thatcher was a traveling salesman working for a company that made eyeglasses. He found out about the film during a visit to an optometrist in Ashland. After considering him for a part in civilian clothes (three-piece suit, winged-tip shoes), Weiss and her team cast Thatcher as a guard. He and three other extras playing guards reported for work on the scene where Andy is dragged off to solitary after calling the warden obtuse. Two of them were actual prison guards hired as extras. Two of them were salesmen playing guards. They ran through the scene with a producer standing in for Robbins. In the first run-through, the real guards were used. The thinking was that they'd know how to handle a struggling prisoner. They did. After the run-through, the producer took Thatcher and the other salesman outside of the room being used for the warden's office. "You're going to be in the scene," he told them. "The real guards just about ripped my arms off, and we can't afford them hurting Tim."

On the first take, Robbins got up out of the chair awkwardly, causing Thatcher to stumble and bump into a camera. Someone yelled, "Cut! Where did we get these Keystone Kops from?" They tried it again, and, this time, Robbins accidentally stomped on Thatcher's ankle. But he managed to keep from hitting the camera this time.

"He felt bad, because my ankle was bleeding, but we kept trying to get it," Thatcher said. "We kept filming it over and over, and always something was wrong. We kept going, all the way to lunch. Great lunch of turkey, dressing, and green beans. Then we came back and did it over and over again. They finally had what they needed and I had a sore ankle."

Many extras hired for the film wound up looking in vain for a glimpse of themselves on screen. One of these was Brenda Kelly, a department store clerk hired to play a pedestrian as Brooks tries to cross a busy street. She missed getting in the shot by a few feet.

One extra whose scene wasn't cut was Janet Kelly Irey, who gets a gorgeous full-screen shot as the passenger in the light brown dress sitting in front of Red on the bus taking him away from Shawshank and into town. The shot begins with the lifelong Mansfield resident in full frame, then moves in more and more on Freeman.

"It's a wonderful full-blown close-up, right on her face," said her daughter, Marilyn Irey Burchett. "It takes up the whole screen. When she heard about the auditions, she went down to the Renaissance Theatre and stood in line. She just wanted to see what it was all about. She had no expectations. When she showed up to do her scene, they did her hair and tried several dresses before settling on the light brown one. She truly felt like a movie star. In her words, it was one of the highlights of her life to be chosen to be in this film."

She ended up working two days on the film. The first day, they didn't get to her scene. The second day they captured the bus scene, with all the doubt and anxiety apparent on Red's face. It contrasts beautifully with the later scene of Red on the Trailways Bus, heading for Fort Hancock, Texas, his face full of optimism and hope.

"She always was being recognized around town for being in this film," Marilyn Irey Burchett said of her mother, who died in 2014. "When a cable station would show the movie, people would stop her in the store the next day and say, 'I saw you on TV last night, Janet.' And she went to the screening of the movie at the Renaissance for the reunion in 2013. There was a line of people waiting to talk to her, and, when her scene came up, everybody applauded. It was a special night."

Special, yes, and truly something extra.

TWENTY-FIVE SCENES NEVER FILMED

There were scenes in Frank Darabont's screenplay that never got filmed, either because of time or because they were deemed non-crucial to the narrative. They included:

1. **Andy's First Interaction with Byron Hadley:** When Andy gets off the prison bus, he stumbles and is rewarded with a sharp blow in the back from Byron Hadley's baton. Darabont deemed the scene excessive, especially with the batting of Fat Ass just around the Shawshank corner.

2. **Andy's Introduction to Shawshank:** When Andy and the new fish arrive, after being deloused and before being marched into the cellblock, there are stops at the infirmary for the doctor's cursory examination and the chapel for some words of "comfort" from the chaplain. Darabont has said that it's just as well that these moments weren't filmed since they undoubtedly would have been excised in the editing process.

3. **The New Fish:** Before the cons go "fishing" with the new prisoners spending their first night in Shawshank, there are glimpses of the "new fish" in their cells—pacing, weeping, dry-heaving. There wasn't enough time to catch these shots.

4. **A Thank-You Note:** After Brooks delivers the rock hammer to Andy in his cell, Andy gives him a thank-you note to take back to Red. It was deemed too awkward and time-consuming to send Brooks and his library cart of books back to Red's cell.

5. **The Beer Run:** Darabont had included a scene of the bucket of beer, ice and all, being hauled up to the roof of the license-plate factory. This was never filmed, since it seemed better to switch directly from Andy requesting the beer to the convicts drinking the beer.

6. **Bogs's Beating:** The beating of Bogs is a much more extensive sequence in Darabont's script. There are reaction shots of Red, sitting in his cell, hearing the horrific trouncing above him, and there's a sickening fall, with Bogs thrown over the cellblock railing and landing on a mop cart. Byron Hadley (Clancy Brown) concludes that Bogs must have tripped. Darabont calculated that he would have needed three full days at the cellblock set to get everything needed for this ambitious run of scenes. Not able to spare the time, he ended the scene with the chilling glimpse of Bogs being dragged back into his cell, then cutting to him being loaded into the ambulance.

7. **First Glimpse of Rita Hayworth:** When Andy gets out of the infirmary and discovers the collected rocks and the waiting poster of Rita Hayworth, there is a morning lineup scene of Andy nodding thanks to Red, followed by Red walking past Andy's cell and seeing the poster.

8. **Intramural Prison Baseball:** A scene of an intramural baseball game with the prison guards was dropped from the montage about Andy's growing popularity as a financial adviser, particularly at tax time.

9. **Andy's Chess Set:** A scene of Andy in his cell, polishing the crafted chess pieces, wasn't filmed because Darabont felt it would slow down the action.

10. **The Rising Sun:** After Red explains how prisoners become institutionalized, there is a sunrise scene, followed by another glimpse of the Rita Hayworth poster. These were judged expendable.

11. **Airplane Scene:** When Brooks is walking toward the Brewer Hotel, he sees a prop-driven airliner streaking across the sky. Darabont said he knew this scene would never be shot, even as he was writing it.

12. **Jake's Funeral:** After they learn that Brooks has killed himself, the friends discover Jake the Crow's body in the prison and decide to give Jake a funeral. There wasn't time to film this sequence, and Darabont admitted to mixed feelings about it. As a writer, he counted this among his favorite scenes. As a director, he saw that it wasn't necessary to the narrative.

13. **Reporting on the Inside-Out Program:** After Warden Norton announces his Inside-Out program, there's a scene of a bossy reporter demanding that Heywood and the rest of a road gang grading a culvert pose for her photographer. When she threatens to report them to the warden, Heywood exacts his revenge. She turns to see them posing, pants unzipped. He encourages her to take the picture, since they are "showin' our tools and grinnin' like fools." The sequence ends with Heywood sighing, sitting in solitary. It's another scene that Darabont the writer loved but Darabont the director knew was unnecessary.

14. **The Pie:** After the warden gives Andy the rest of the pie and before Andy explains the Randall Stevens scam to Red, there is a scene of Andy walking down the corridor with the pie. It wasn't necessary and wasn't shot.

15. **Tommy's Arrival at Shawshank:** Tommy's arrival, like Andy's, includes the fresh-fish taunting and the naked walk into the cell-block after delousing. Not only needless, they would have been time-consuming to shoot.

16. **Tommy Sees His Wife:** A scene Darabont wished there had been time to shoot was a visitors' day encounter between Tommy and his wife, Beth. It helped explain why Tommy was motivated to better himself. Darabont also had selected the actress, Tracey Needham, to play Beth, and he was sure she'd be wonderful. Needham had played Paige on the ABC drama *Life Goes On*.

17. **"The Raven":** Three scenes were cut from the sequence showing Andy teaching Tommy, including one where Andy reaches the final

Gil Bellows as Tommy Williams, the young thief who finds brains he didn't know he had

verse of Poe's "The Raven" and Tommy wonders why the narrator doesn't just dust the talkative bird with a twelve-gauge shotgun.

18. **Registering the Killer:** When Tommy realizes he knows who killed Andy's wife and lover, he registers his shock with a line and by dropping the Coke he's holding. This was deemed too melodramatic and was never shot.

19. **A Second Visit from Tommy's Wife:** A second scene with Tommy's wife is in the screenplay but was never shot. He shows Beth his high school diploma.

20. **Revealing Tommy's Death:** Scenes of Andy emerging from solitary and being led to Norton's office after Tommy's shooting were made unnecessary when Robbins shifted the conversation between Andy and the warden to "The Hole." Since the scene finds Andy

at his lowest point, Robbins said, it should take place in solitary. Darabont saw the great wisdom in this and made the change.

21. **Empty Cell:** When the guard goes to investigate why Andy hasn't emerged from his cell, there is a scene showing the empty cell. Darabont knew it would be more effective to cut from the guard's face to the warden opening the shoebox.

22. **The Sewer Scene:** The scene of Andy climbing down to the sewer pipe, rats and all, was greatly condensed, with much of the action eliminated. Also, in the screenplay, Andy uses his rock hammer to break into the sewer pipe. Obviously too small to accomplish the feat, it was jettisoned in favor of the concrete Andy uses, leading to two of the most argued-about elements in the film. Would it be possible for Andy to time the strikes against the pipe with the bursts of thunder? And, without any kind of pump or some such device, why would there be a geyser-like eruption when Andy finally smashes through the pipe? A meteorologist, an engineer, and a plumber might take issue with these scenes, but, come on, they sure look and sound fantastic.

23. **Norton's Suicide:** The screenplay calls for Norton to shoot himself after the district attorney and the trooper get through the door. We would see their horrified reactions. To save time when filming, it was decided to have Norton commit suicide before they got through the door.

24. **Red's Dream:** After the scene in the cemetery that concludes with Red saying he misses his friend, there is a dream sequence with Red being sucked into the tunnel behind a Rita Hayworth poster. He finds himself in a warm place with no memory, but is terrified by how blue and sunny and big everything is, and he can't find his way home. Of all the scenes that didn't get filmed, this is the one Darabont most regrets sacrificing.

25. **Red's Home at the Halfway House:** A scene with the 1967 land-lady climbing the stairs with Red was never filmed.

THE CANINE REDEMPTION

THE DOGS KEPT A WARY EYE ON THE FILMING OF *THE SHAWSHANK Redemption*, continuing to maintain a cautious distance from the actors, extras, and crewmembers. You'd see them running around at the very edges of the production, getting close but not too close. There were two of them, both on the small side, both in obvious need of a bath and a good meal. Occasionally during the early days of that hot, humid shoot, someone would try coaxing the homeless pooches with food or kind words. They'd invariably bolt, only to be spotted the next day scampering through a field near the Ohio State Reformatory.

The Shawshank Redemption is a movie about men locked behind walls, dreaming of escape. Here were two four-legged refugees on the run, refusing to get near those walls. And it may have continued this way for the entire three-month production if it had not been for a fellow named Jodiviah "Joe" Stepp. The twenty-seven-year-old Stepp had been hired to play the "fresh fish" new convict marched into Shawshank State Prison in front of Andy Dufresne (Tim Robbins). You can see him on the convict bus taking Andy to the prison. You can see him walking in the prison yard with the chained line of prisoners. You can see him in the group of "convicted felons" Warden Norton (Bob Gunton) welcomes to Shawshank. You can see him, briefly, in the delousing scene.

"These two dogs were just running loose and wouldn't get near anyone," Stepp recalled twenty-five years after filming on *Shawshank* wrapped up in Mansfield. "They were malnourished and mangy, and one day I went off by myself to have lunch. For some reason, they took a liking to me, and I gave them my lunch. I started to look after them and feed them. We gradually became friends over the summer, and the director, Frank Darabont, noticed this."

There's a moment in *The Shawshank Redemption* where Red says to Andy, "We're getting to be kind of friends, aren't we?" Andy replies, "Yeah, I guess." It might have been an exchange between Stepp and the increasingly friendly hounds of Shawshank.

Near the end of shooting, Darabont assembled cast and crew, and an assistant summoned Stepp. As Stepp approached Darabont, he noticed that the writer-director had two dogs on leashes. At first, Stepp didn't recognize them.

"Frank had sent them to a vet and a groomer, so they didn't look like the same dogs," Stepp said. "They had been given complete checkups and grooming. I finally realized that these were the dogs I had befriended and

Hayworth, left, and Rita, right before director Frank Darabont presented Rita to Jodiviah "Joe" Stepp

took care of that summer. So Frank calls me up in front of all of these people, hands me the leash for one of the dogs, and says, 'I understand you two have gotten to be friends.' And he gave me the dog. They were named Rita and Hayworth because, at that time, the film still was titled *Rita Hayworth and Shawshank Redemption.* I got Rita and another extra took Hayworth."

End of story? No, just the beginning of a beautiful friendship. Stepp really didn't know how old Rita was or how long he'd have her. He didn't even know if he'd be allowed to keep her in his apartment.

"But there was no way I was going to say no to Frank Darabont," Stepp said.

Mighty good thing, too. It was a match made in . . . well, Shawshank, of course, but it was a heavenly match nonetheless.

"I ended up having Rita for about nine or ten years," Stepp said. "She literally became my best friend. She went everywhere with me. She became attached to me at the hip. Just a wonderful dog."

The symbolism is not lost on Stepp or anyone who hears his heart-warming story. *The Shawshank Redemption* is a film about hope, redemption, and finding friendship in the shadow of a Gothic prison. In this setting, Rita took a chance on Stepp. Stepp took a chance on Rita. Both were rewarded beyond measure. The old saying about a dog being "man's best friend" was given a howling good endorsement during the filming of *The Shawshank Redemption.*

So, now end of story? Not quite. Like Red and Andy in *The Shawshank Redemption,* Joe and Rita have inspired others looking for a life-affirming bit of hope and friendship.

"My taking in Rita inspired several of my friends to give homeless dogs a chance," Stepp said. "And then the book came out and even more people were inspired to rescue homeless dogs."

The book he's referencing is *Rita the Shawshank Dog,* written by another extra hired to play a new fish on the bus, Brad Mavis. A writer, artist, and independent film director, Mavis met and befriended Stepp during the filming of *The Shawshank Redemption.* Inspired by Stepp's kindness toward the two homeless dogs, he decided to tell the story in a 2014 paperback book that features his pen-and-ink illustrations. The book also inspired Mavis to help homeless animals as a volunteer at the Capital Area Humane Society near Columbus, Ohio. Stepp shares the story of Rita (and lots of pictures) at his website, shawshankdog.com.

"The dog is a gentleman," observed Mark Twain, a cat lover always happy to give dogs their due. "I hope to go to his heaven, not man's." You've got to know that another superstar American writer, one named King, agrees with and approves of that statement. And you have to know that, somewhere in that heaven, a Shawshank dog named Rita is wagging her tail in agreement and approval and, yes, friendship.

III.

POSTPRODUCTION, RELEASE, REVIEWS, DISCOVERY

You know how a great song doesn't age, no matter how much time goes by? Like a Beatles song. No matter when you hear it, it never loses its resonance. Great music never goes out of style. That's Shawshank. It's never gone out of style, and it never will.

—JANE IMBODY
ANCHOR-REPORTER CAST AS A REPORTER
IN *THE SHAWSHANK REDEMPTION*

POSTPRODUCTION

FILMING ON WHAT WAS STILL BEING CALLED *RITA HAYWORTH AND SHAW-shank Redemption* wrapped about a year before the film was released. The raw material had been mined and collected in Ohio and St. Croix. It was now time to assemble, mold, shape, polish, fine tune, and package the mountain of footage into something spellbinding. The fate of a movie isn't just decided by what happens when the cameras are rolling. Far from it. A film can be rescued or completely undone in the editing process. It can be magnificently amplified or miserably doomed by the music (imagine, say, *Jaws*, without that ingenious John Williams score providing the proper mood and tension and general sense of unease). It can be rendered pitch perfect or tone deaf by the quality of its sound effects. The work of the actors, except for some dubbing and narration work, is done. They've worked their magic. The process now belongs to the cinematic wizards known as editors, composers, Foley artists, sound editors—unsung and underappreciated artists being guided and overseen by the director and producers.

Without these magicians, Harry Potter and his Hogwarts friends couldn't work a lick of magic on the screen. And while you might take notice of the music and cinematography, you are likely to give little attention to such things as editing and sound. That's a good thing, by the way. The more exceptional the editing and sound aspects of a film are, the less the casual filmgoer is supposed to notice. Indeed, you tend to notice such things when they are bad. Yet they are crucial to a film's ultimate success. That's why they give out Academy Awards for sound and editing (but, come on, you probably don't notice those, either).

Darabont, for instance, credited the sound team on his film with making the "first night in Shawshank" sequence so effective. And that's because of much of what you hear and think you see in these cellblock scenes. The scene was shot with a few dozen extras on the cellblock set built by production designer Terence Marsh's team in the old Westinghouse warehouse. Extra Max Gerber was sitting in one of those cells, and he was listening to what was going on as the action built to Byron Hadley (Clancy Brown) clubbing Fat Ass (Frank Medrano). That's right, listening, and not joining in with all of the "fresh fish" chanting and taunting you hear. Most of the voices were added in the postproduction phase. So think of all the sound elements in this section of the movie. There's Red's voiceover narration, which had been prerecorded. There are various sound effects. And there is enough yelling and jeering to convince you that you're trapped in that Shawshank cellblock with maybe two hundred yelling convicts. Darabont took pains to credit ADR (Automated Dialogue Replacement) voice casting supervisor Barbara Harris and her "loop group" troupe of actors who did most of the yelling and taunting. Then supervising sound editor John M. Stacy and his team put all of those elements together. Then re-recording and dialogue mixer Robert J. "Bob" Litt brought it all home with what Darabont described in his screenplay notes as "the precision of a brain surgeon."

He also gave a hearty shout-out to David J. Schow for helping with all the shouting. If you don't know Schow's work, you should. Working primarily in the horror field, the gifted writer has penned novels, short stories, and screenplays, as well as insightful and influential nonfiction works about the genre. His uncredited contribution? As a favor to his frazzled pal Darabont, he wrote several pages of cellblock lines to be shouted offscreen in postproduction.

Before the postproduction process geared up in Los Angeles, however, there were still matters to be attended to in Mansfield. To defray some production costs and to give locals a chance to own a piece (or pieces) of the film, an auction was held on September 15 to sell off the costume pieces, props, equipment, and other items being left behind in Ohio.

Many extras in the movie showed up to purchase a guard's uniform, a mess-hall tray, or one of the prison mugs used during filming. Many more regret that they didn't. Think of what the *Shawshank* fans of today would give for this opportunity. With a little research and a time machine, they could be in possession of a small warehouse full of cherished memorabilia. Priceless stuff today, but, in 1993, most were unaware of the film. And those that knew of it didn't know if it would be any good.

Speaking of warehouses, both contractually and for safety reasons, Marsh's magnificent cellblock set had to be torn down, and the downtown Mansfield warehouse that housed it had to be restored so that this section of the building could resume its former duties.

"There was no trace of it when they got done," Destination Mansfield president Lee Tasseff said. "It went back to being a warehouse, and the only remnant of the cellblock set was a cement floor they'd put down. Otherwise, you'd never know it had been there and how intricate it had been."

The property with the alfalfa field and the oak tree also had to be put back as it was, and that meant removing the rock wall where Andy leaves the buried letter and money for Red.

A year before the film was released, there was an auction of set pieces, props, and costumes, among other things.

PHOTO COURTESY OF BRIAN CONNELL

"When you build something like that on location, you almost always have to remove it," location manager and production supervisor Kokayi Ampah said. "In this case, we were renting property that already had a use. But even if that hadn't been the case, you tear it down for legal and liability issues. If someone gets hurt on a set you've left behind, they can sue the production company. So, for the sake of safety, you get rid of it and sell off what you can for scrap and salvage. That's pretty standard."

Try telling that to the legions of *Shawshank* fans who go out to Malabar Farm looking for that wall.

Darabont managed a cameo of sorts in the postproduction phase. The glimpse of a drunken Andy loading the gun while sitting in his car was one of only four insert shots grabbed in postproduction at a small stage near Darabont's cutting room at Warner Hollywood Studios. So the hands loading the gun belong to Darabont, not Tim Robbins.

King recalled that Darabont worked obsessively in postproduction all the way to the film's release. Watching the last scene in the movie with King, Darabont griped about the makeup used on Robbins. King, knowing what Darabont had accomplished, told him not to worry about the makeup. They won't notice at this point, King said, because they'll be too busy crying.

As they were wiping away tears and the final credits started rolling over the Zihuatanejo reunion of Andy and Red, the first words you see are a dedication: "In Memory of Allen Greene." Darabont's agent and close friend, Greene had died of AIDS at thirty-six in 1989. He had taken Darabont on as a client when many other agents wouldn't have considered him, due to his lack of experience and credits.

"Allen was a wonderful guy," said first assistant director John R. Woodward. "Allen and I went to USC film school at the same time, so Allen also was a good friend of mine. I hadn't seen him in a long time, and, years later, I found out that he's not only an agent, he's Frank's agent. The film being dedicated to him is just a beautiful touch, and it's beautifully timed in the film."

It appears with an emotional swell of music, thanks to composer Thomas Newman's splendid score. Excerpts from only five previous recordings were used in *The Shawshank Redemption*: the Ink Spots singing

"If I Didn't Care" for the opening; the Deutsche Oper Berlin rendition of "Duettino—Sull 'Aria" from Wolfgang Amadeus Mozart's *The Marriage of Figaro*; a couple of bars of "Put the Blame on Mame" (listen closely in the first clip from *Gilda*); "Lovesick Blues" by Hank Williams (accompanied by Heywood in the prison library); and, to introduce Tommy's arrival at Shawshank, the Johnny Otis 1958 single "Willie and the Hand Jive" (inspired, appropriately enough, by a chain gang Otis heard singing while touring). All of the rest of the wonderful music in *Shawshank* is by Newman, one of many celebrated members of Hollywood's dynastic family of film scorers (which includes his father, Alfred Newman, brother David, sister Marie, uncles Lionel and Emil, and cousin Randy). He reported to work on *Shawshank* after having worked on such films as *Fried Green Tomatoes* (1991), *The Player* (1992), and *Scent of a Woman* (1992).

Newman's acclaimed score for the film included such haunting and memorable compositions as the "Shawshank Prison" theme, "Brooks Was Here," "So Was Red," and "Shawshank Redemption." Newman has said that his goal in tackling this assignment was to enhance the story's powerful emotions without distracting from them. Some of this was accomplished with input from Darabont and others. Darabont asked that the three-note motif for Andy's escape, "Shawshank Redemption," be less grandiose and taken down to a one-note motif. He also was convinced to add a harmonica to "So Was Red," originally intended to be a solo for oboe. The harmonica is supposed to recall Andy's gift (of music) to his friend, and does it ever. The challenge was a formidable one for Newman, but his sublime efforts resulted in a musical journey that's everything Darabont (and *Shawshank* fans) could ask for, and more (as several reviews properly noted). The soundtrack, complete with the four recordings mentioned above, was released by Sony BMG in September 1994.

Back in Mansfield, those associated with the film were starting to speculate about what would end up on the screen.

"Nobody knew whether it would be any good," Tasseff said. "There was no way to tell. But one of the first inklings we got that it was something special was from Eve Lapolla. I'll never forget the day she called us from Columbus with news. She told us that her contacts at Castle Rock said that, when Rob Reiner saw it, he said, 'Oh, my. This is the best thing we've ever done.' That's when we started to get excited about this film that had been shot in our town."

Out in California, Frank Medrano also was starting to get hints that perhaps he was part of something momentous.

"There had been industry screenings, and some friends of mine, like agents and producers, had seen it," said the actor cast as Fat Ass. "So I was getting a lot of calls, telling me how great the movie was and how good my performance was, which was humbling, because it wasn't that big a role. But I guess it's impactful. When I finally saw it, I was overwhelmed. I was relatively green as an actor, so to be in a movie that created so much buzz, was incredible."

Not holding back tears got Medrano the part. Now, finally watching the film, he found himself fighting to hold back those tears. He was not successful.

"I cried when Andy played the music over the public address system," Medrano said. "And then at the end, when Red and Andy are on the beach, I cried again. I'm tearing up right now thinking about it."

For Robbins and Freeman, the intensity of the shoot had robbed them of perspective and expectations. They knew Darabont had handed them great roles and a spectacular screenplay. But they also knew this was a director tackling his first feature film and that so many things needed to go right for the movie magic to work. So when did they know just how incredible the film was?

"Let's say that happened when we saw it," Robbins said. "I think staying emotionally true to the source material is the key, but there are so many other factors. Is it cast well? Are the scenes chosen well? What is being left out? And even when you get all of that right, it still might add up wrong. It's one of the great mysteries of this business. But once in a while, everything falls into place and all of the right things add up in the right way, as it did with *Shawshank*."

ON THE CUTTING ROOM FLOOR:

TWENTY-FIVE DROPPED SCENES

SEVERAL SCENES FILMED IN OHIO DON'T APPEAR IN THE FINAL FILM, dropped because of time or because it was decided the storytelling process could do without them. How did Darabont and his ace team of editors trim the first cut from two and a half hours down to two hours and twenty-two minutes? This is how:

1. **Jury's Vote:** After the 1946 district attorney (Jeffrey DeMunn) makes his final summation, there was a tracking shot of the jurors voting. Darabont liked the shot, but the overall opening sequence was tightened as much as possible to get Andy to Shawshank as quickly as possible.

2. **Andy's Night of Insomnia:** A 1947 scene of Andy in his cell, staring into the darkness and unable to sleep after first being approached by the Sisters, was cut in postproduction.

3. **Fly Ball:** During the tossing of the baseball scene, they filmed a moment when Heywood (William Sadler) gets the attention of Jigger (Neil Giuntoli), then zings the ball directly at Andy's head. While talking to Red, Andy glimpses the ball coming toward him, whirls, catches it, and zings it back to Heywood, who drops it and rubs his stinging hand. It was right after this bit of business that Andy says to Red, "I understand you're a man who knows how to get things." It was decided in editing that Heywood's prank didn't work in the flow of the scene, so out it went.

4. **Paying for the Rock Hammer:** After Andy makes the deal for the rock hammer, there were two quick scenes showing how he paid Red for it. First, in the mess hall, Andy falls in step behind Red and slips him a tightly folded piece of paper. It was immediately followed by a scene of Red in his cell, unfolding the paper and finding the $10 bill. Red said in voiceover narration, "He was a man who adapted fast." These were cut for time, and the action went directly from Andy strolling away from Red in the prison yard to the laundry truck driver (Morgan Lund) hurrying the cons unloading the sacks from the truck bed.

5. **Andy's Stash of Money:** Cut from the sequence of scenes beginning with the laundry truck at the loading dock was Red's voiceover narration about how he later learned that Andy brought a lot more money into prison with him. A bigger point is made of this in the original novella, but since the audience was listening to Red

Red (Morgan Freeman) and Andy (Tim Robbins) meet on the prison yard—a scene that took all day to shoot and ended up being trimmed.

make one point while watching something else being played out on the screen, the narration was dropped (and with it the explanation of how Andy walked into Shawshank with $500 shoved up—way up—his ass).

6. **Blowing Kisses:** It was decided in editing to cut a brief scene showing Bogs (Mark Rolston) blowing a kiss at Andy. It not only seemed a trifle silly, it undercut the depiction of Bogs intended by King and Darabont. They wanted to make a distinction between a homosexual and a prison rapist, since the sociologists consulted said that the prison rapist seldom is a homosexual in the outside world. Bogs doesn't represent homosexuality, Darabont wrote in his notes for the screenplay, "he represents the predatory sexual violence of rape."

7. **Fighting the Sisters:** Red explains in narration that fighting back against the Sisters had one of two consequences. It either landed Andy in the infirmary or in solitary. So a scene was shot that showed a beaten Andy in "The Hole."

8. **Andy in the Infirmary:** After Bogs and the Sisters beat Andy "within an inch of his life" in the projection room, there was a scene of a badly injured Andy in the infirmary.

9. **Contraband Consequences:** When Warden Norton (Bob Gunton) is tossing the cells on his surprise inspection, there was a scene, before he gets to Andy, of a prisoner given a week in solitary for hiding a sharpened screwdriver in his mattress (and another week for blasphemy).

10. **Summoning Andy:** A scene of Andy being summoned from the laundry room to Warden Norton's office was deemed unnecessary. The moment in the film begins with Andy already in Norton's office, about to learn that he is being transferred from the laundry to the prison library.

11. **Financial Advising:** The scene where Andy offers financial advice to the guard Dekins (Brian Delate) in the prison library had more

dialogue. It was cut short, jumping to Brooks (James Whitmore) telling the others about the encounter.

12. **Rules at the Halfway House:** The landlady's stair-climbing explanation of hotel rules was cut.

13. **Special Delivery:** When the boxes of books, magazines, and records arrive at the warden's office, there was a scene of an angry Hadley summoning Andy from the prison yard. It didn't survive the editing process.

14. **Finding Mozart:** Before the playing of Mozart over the public-address system, there were scenes of Andy going through the boxes and setting up the record player. They slowed down the sequence you see in the film.

15. **Removing Andy from Warden Norton's Office:** Cut for length was a corridor shot of Norton and Hadley making their way to Andy, who has locked himself in Norton's office, as well as a scene of Andy being dragged off while the guard Wiley (Don R. McManus), locked in the bathroom, yells to be let out. A moment not in the script was Andy's response to Norton's demands that he turn off the music and open the door. Andy casually turns up the music. That bit of business came from Robbins.

16. **Additional Solitary Scenes:** Shots of solitary and Andy, serene, inside "The Hole" after treating the prison to Mozart, were eliminated for time.

17. **Orders from Above:** The prison-yard scene of the "Bullhorn Tower Guard" (first assistant director John R. Woodward) ordering Red and the other cons back to their cells.

18. **Following Andy's Tunnel:** One of the biggest cuts also was one of the funniest scenes in King's novella. Having discovered the tunnel behind the poster in Andy's cell, Norton orders a skinny guard named Rory Tremont to explore where it leads. Rory crawls his way toward the pipe, complaining the whole time how bad it smells.

He finally gets to the floor, slips, sits down in the spilled contents of the sewage pipe, and gets ill. His shouted exclamation has led fans of the novella to dub this the "oh, shit, it's shit!" scene. And Darabont, being one of the novella's biggest fans, couldn't imagine the movie without this moment. It ends with Red laughing so hard, he earns a two-week stretch in solitary. But what worked so well on the printed page just slowed down the story of Andy's escape on film. The entire sequence jumped to life when Darabont asked editor Richard Francis Bruce to cut the scenes with Rory and Red laughing. It meant that Anthony Lucero, the actor playing Rory, would be cut from the film. And it meant the audience wouldn't get to laugh along with Red.

19. **Flashbacks:** A 1962 flashback scene of Andy working on the tunnel was cut for time, as were 1965 flashback scenes of him breaking through to the shaft and seeing the sewer pipe.

20. **Tommy's Body:** When Red talks about Tommy's killing and how it led Andy to decide he'd been in Shawshank long enough, there was an image of Tommy's bullet-riddled body. It was dropped for being too jarring an image at that moment in the film.

21. **Brewer Hotel:** Red's arrival outside the Brewer Hotel was cut for length.

22. **Red's Life Outside of Prison:** Three minutes were cut from the film by eliminating a sequence that told the audience what they already knew: that Red, like Brooks, had been institutionalized and wasn't adjusting to life outside of prison. The first scenes showed Red walking through town and in the park, noticing how the world had changed, including how women were dressing.

23. **Parole Officer:** The second scene in the "institutionalized" sequence was a meeting between Red and his parole officer.

24. **Toy Gun:** The third part was in the Food-Way, with a kid pointing a toy gun at Red and pulling the trigger. Red focuses on the gun, the noise around him triggering a full-blown panic attack. He bolts

to a bathroom stall, where the closeness of the walls seem comforting. Here he feels safe.

25. **Last Words:** Darabont wisely cut the final exchange of dialogue between Andy and Red, recalling their first meeting. Andy was to tell Red that he looked like a man "who knows how to get things." And Red would respond that he was known "to locate certain things from time to time." Instead, he let Thomas Newman's soaring music carry us out for the reunion on the beach.

THE TITLE FIGHT: TO KEEP RITA OR KEEP HER OUT

WHEN FRANK DARABONT WAS DRAWN TO THE STORY OF ANDY AND Red in Stephen King's *Different Seasons*, the title of the novella was "Rita Hayworth and Shawshank Redemption." When Darabont completed the screenplay adaptation of that novella, the title on it was *Rita Hayworth and Shawshank Redemption*. When Darabont and his crew arrived in Mansfield, Ohio, to begin filming, the name of the film was *Rita Hayworth and Shawshank Redemption*. And when the remaining crewmembers left Mansfield in September 1993, the title of the film still was *Rita Hayworth and Shawshank Redemption*. But, a year later, when the Castle Rock film was distributed to theaters by Columbia Pictures, the title had become *The Shawshank Redemption*.

What happened to Rita Hayworth? Well, just as films need to be edited, so do titles, sometimes. Castle Rock had, after all, completely changed the title of the novella from *Different Seasons* that had all but created the company, switching from "The Body" to *Stand by Me*. And that hadn't turned out too badly. So what to do with the ungainly title *Rita Hayworth and Shawshank Redemption*, which worked dandy for print but seemed a marketing nightmare for a widely distributed movie. Now, before we discuss the fate of poor Rita, keep this in mind: Titles are tough, titles are killers; titles have been known to take years off an author's life. Titles and endings (and they're killers, too) are what keep writers awake, staring wide-eyed at the ceiling in the middle of the night.

To this day, those associated with the film argue over the title to a film that eventually overcame all of the possible barriers to its popularity (at least, those raised at the time of its release): a running time well past two hours, the deliberate pacing, the dreary setting, and, yes, its title.

Few connected with the film would contend that they'd settled on the ideal title when they excised Rita Hayworth and let it stand as just *The Shawshank Redemption*. Morgan Freeman has said, and said often, that he thought the original title should have been kept. Too long to fit on a marquee, it was argued.

"So what?" Freeman countered. Just put *Rita Hayworth* on the marquee. People will recognize that. They'll remember that. There's a one-sheet poster that will tell them the rest of it. "Don't choose *Shawshank Redemption* when you've got Rita Hayworth," Freeman told Seth Meyers during an appearance on his NBC talk show.

Freeman complained about the changed title at the time. He remains convinced that the title they settled on hurt the film in its initial release.

"Word of mouth is the marketing tool," Freeman said during an interview on CNBC. "I don't care what you spend. If word of mouth doesn't catch you, you ain't going anywhere. Right? So, imagine going to see a movie, then going to your friends and saying, 'I just saw one of the most terrific movies. It's called . . . um . . .uh . . . *Shipshank . . . Shemp . . .* uh . . .'."

Freeman and Tim Robbins both say that, in the year that followed the film's release, people would tell them how much they loved . . . and they'd invariably struggle for the title. The costars will lapse happily into a bit of vaudeville routine, alternating favorite wrong titles, one after the other.

"The Scrimshaw Reduction."

"The Hudsucker Reaction."

"Shimshank."

"Shipshape."

"Shanksham."

"Shinkshonk."

Time and devotion have taken care of this problem. Fans remember the title.

"They do now," Freeman told Meyers.

It was a title fight in 1994, but time healed all of the *Shawshank* objections.

RELEASE AND BOX OFFICE

If you look closely at the various posters used to herald the release of *The Shawshank Redemption*, you may notice something that's quite unusual for a Stephen King film. Most posters for movies based on King's works get the writer's name out there as prominently and dramatically as possible. And why not? He's a household name, and not many writers can claim that distinction. There are major marketing points to be gained by adding the name of STEPHEN KING to almost anything.

But test screenings of *The Shawshank Redemption* went so amazingly well, it was decided to bury King's name among the credits at the bottom of the poster. It also was decided not to make anything of the King connection in advertising and promotional material. There were a couple of reasons for this. First, they didn't want moviegoers showing up expecting a supernatural horror film in the bloody vein of *Carrie, Creepshow, Christine,* and *Cujo*. Second, they did want to attract moviegoers in the mood for a thoughtfully crafted adult drama that very well could be the type of Oscar-bait release you see after the lighter summer fare. The thought was that, if this was advertised as a Stephen King story, it could prove to be the marketing equivalent of a double-edged sword: horror fans would be perplexed, disappointed, and even angry, while moviegoers with a taste for mature prestige films simply wouldn't show up. So you really have to look for King's name on those posters, somewhere in all that print underneath the familiar and inspiring image of Andy Dufresne, hands outstretched, looking toward the light and the words, "Fear can hold you prisoner, Hope can set you free."

It was a great iconic poster for a great movie. It struck the proper tone. It sent the right message. And as to downplaying King's involvement, we'll never know whether or not that was a major marketing mis-calculation. It's the same type of what-if discussion as the title question. And the debate ends the same way: We'll never know. What we do know is that the film had two premiere screenings before it began a limited North American release on September 23, 1994. The first was on September 10 at the Toronto International Film Festival. Among the other films selected for gala presentations during the September 8–17 event were *The Secret of Roan Inish*, from writer-director John Sayles, Tunisian writer-director Moufida Tlatli's *The Silences of the Palaces*, director and coauthor Peter Jackson's *Heavenly Creatures*, writer-director Kevin Smith's *Clerks*, Woody Allen's *Bullets Over Broadway*, and *Wes Craven's New Nightmare* (from, of all people, writer-director Wes Craven).

Three days later, Mansfield got its premiere event, complete with parties, press conferences, and spotlights in front of the downtown Renaissance Theatre, where the film was shown to a wildly enthusiastic audience. Darabont and Niki Marvin came back to Mansfield to screen the movie and renew acquaintances with *Shawshank* friends they hadn't seen for about a year.

Local reporter-anchor Jane Imbody, who appeared in the film as a reporter and covered the making of the movie for her TV station, attended the press conference at the Holiday Inn (where so many crew-members and actors had stayed). Passing Darabont before the press conference started, Imbody asked him if he remembered her.

"Yeah, you played a reporter," he said.

That experience was repeated again and again as Darabont and Marvin posed for pictures at the Holiday Inn, at a party up at OSR, and then at the Renaissance. They posed with the Mansfield mayor, Lydia Reid, who had done so much to smooth the *Shawshank* path to Ohio. They posed with extras who played guards and prisoners. And they brought posters and an endless supply of smiles. *Shawshank* was about to be shared with the world. For one giddy evening, it belonged to Mansfield—a thank-you gift of sorts from Darabont and Marvin to the town and the people who had made the film possible.

"We went to the premiere in Mansfield and the pre-festivities at the prison beforehand," said Brian Connell, part of the director's Core Con group. "I asked Frank and Niki Marvin if I could possibly get a movie poster and press kit before they left. Frank made sure I got both. Super down-to-carth people."

Buses transported people out to the prison on this sunny and pleasant Tuesday evening. Then it was over to the Renaissance, the 1,402-seat movie palace opened in January 1928 as the Ohio Theatre.

"With those big spotlights outside, it felt like a big Hollywood premiere," said Jodie Snavely, the group tour and media director at Destination Mansfield. "The audience was packed with people who had been in the film and the friends and relatives of the people who had been in the film. So there was a great deal of cheering and clapping and hollering when someone they recognized appeared on screen. That happened a lot."

"And it's not a movie where there's supposed to be a lot of cheering," Destination Mansfield president Lee Tasseff chimed in.

Director-screenwriter Frank Darabont and producer Niki Marvin greet friends outside the Renaissance Theatre before the Mansfield premiere of *The Shawshank Redemption.*

PHOTO COURTESY OF BRIAN CONNELL

"Not at all," Snavely continued. "So it was a great time, but not the best way to experience the film for the first time. It was not the best way to appreciate the magic of the movie. I got caught up with how much I recognized and how many people I recognized on the screen. I kept thinking, 'I can't believe this is our Mansfield on the big screen.'"

Tasseff had more on his mind than just the premiere. He was getting married later that week.

"So I had a lot going on," said Tasseff, indulging in a bit of under-statement. "I was focused on the premiere. I had to focus on that. I'm not focused on my own wedding that much. We had the big set-up at the reformatory for a fundraiser. And we had people transported downtown by prison buses. So there are a lot of moving parts. I'm nervous. And I've got divided attention. I'm just watching and hoping that things go well."

Then everybody gets to the Renaissance. Before the film starts, four people are called up on the stage. Tasseff is one of them. He has no idea why, and he is in a bit of a daze. He is presented with a special signed poster and a special dose of gratitude.

"And I'm thinking, 'This is just cool,'" Tasseff recalled. "But it's also surreal. And the movie starts, and I can't really follow it, because, in my mind, I'm everywhere. Gradually, though, I get into it, and realize, 'This is really good.' And we get to the end of the credits, and there's my name on the film. That floored me more than anything. My name's on the screen. Five days later, I got married."

And there is his name, in that section of the credits for "We Wish to Thank:"

Dennis Baker, Warden of the Mansfield Correctional Institution
Richard Hall, Assistant to the Warden
Manny Centeno, Director of the U.S. Virgin Islands Film
    Commission
Eve Lapolla, Ohio Film Commission
Lee Tasseff, Mansfield Convention & Visitors Bureau
The People of Mansfield, Ohio and Richland County

It was what Darabont and Marvin had intended it to be—a special night for the people of Mansfield. It was a particularly memorable night for Ben and Amber Bissman, who had made signs for the film, provided the beer bottles, and allowed their family building to double for the Brewer Hotel and to be used as the location for the newspaper office.

"My mother was very ill at the time," Ben Bissman said. "She was, in fact, in hospice. Beautiful woman her whole life. She'd been a fashion model. So we came up with this scheme. We got a limo, and one of my sisters dressed her up. She looked like a million bucks that night. It was her last hurrah. She got to see the whole thing at the big premiere here in town, at the Renaissance, and it was just a perfect night . . . just perfect."

The film then moved on to a limited North American release on Friday, September 23. The opening weekend was encouraging all around. *The Shawshank Redemption* pulled in a total of $727,000 from thirty-three theaters, for an average of $22,040 per theater. The film moved to wide release on Friday, October 14, showing in 944 theaters. Here is where it got saddled with the tag of box-office disappointment. Pulling in just $2.4 million that weekend, its average per theater dropped to a miserable $2,545. It was the number nine film that weekend, which is all that need be said in terms of failure to get out of the gate. Writer-director Quentin Tarantino's *Pulp Fiction* opened wide that same weekend. It pulled in a walloping $9.3 million. That's heavy competition, no doubt, but *The Shawshank Redemption* couldn't even edge out the poorly reviewed BDSM-themed comedy *Exit to Eden*, which claimed the number-eight spot with a $3 million take. *The Shawshank Redemption* did manage to edge out director Robert Redford's drama about the game-show scandals, *Quiz Show*, which had a $2.1 million weekend, but, then again, it was in its fifth week of release.

After ten weeks, *The Shawshank Redemption* could manage only a $16 million total gross, falling far short of its $25 million budget (which did not include marketing and distribution costs). Those are not the kind of numbers destined to thrill studio executives. You know what kind of numbers they love? *Pulp Fiction* kind of numbers. It more than made back its $8.5 million budget on its first weekend. But what about its $10 million in marketing costs? No problem. *Pulp Fiction* pulled in $107.9

million nationally and almost doubled that with worldwide distribution, racking up a total box office of $213.9 million. *The Shawshank Redemption* looked to be as low as Andy spending a month in "The Hole" after calling Warden Norton obtuse. What were the big films of 1994? The top-five in terms of box office (and these are by no means bad films) were: Disney's *The Lion King* (with a staggering worldwide take of $763 million), *Forrest Gump, True Lies, The Mask,* and *Speed*. Way, way back in the pack was *The Shawshank Redemption*, in fifty-first place for the year.

The Shawshank Redemption did get a slight Oscar bump, receiving seven Academy Award nominations and being re-released in February and March of 1995. The final tally was $28.3 million in North America and a worldwide take of $30 million. A $58.3 million box office isn't a disaster, but it ain't *Lion King* numbers, either. Many reasons were given for the poor box-office showing of *The Shawshank Redemption*: bad timing, coming out when there was no great desire for prison pictures; the lack of lead female characters; the popularity of action thrillers like *True Lies, Clear and Present Danger, Speed*; the success of anything with Jim Carrey (*Dumb and Dumber, The Mask, Ace Ventura: Pet Detective*); the juggernaut phenomenon of the feel-good movie *Forrest Gump*; and, of course, the title.

However you estimate what was going against *The Shawshank Redemption*, 1994 clearly wasn't its year. Yet, we all know that Andy doesn't stay in that hole or in prison. There would be another day . . . and another year . . . many more years, in fact.

THE REVIEWS

THE SHAWSHANK REDEMPTION OPENED TO LARGELY POSITIVE REVIEWS, but there were some notably nasty dissenters in the critical crowd. But nowhere did director Frank Darabont's film fare better than in Chicago. Fueled by the cheering of nationally syndicated critics Gene Siskel and Roger Ebert, it was all fair breezes in the Windy City in September 1994.

Pulitzer Prize–winner Ebert wrote in the *Chicago Sun-Times*: "*The Shawshank Redemption* is a movie about time, patience and loyalty—not sexy qualities, perhaps, but they grow on you during the subterranean progress of this story, which is about how two men serving life sentences in prison become friends and find a way to fight off despair."

Siskel was even more enthusiastic. If on a scale of one-to-five, Ebert gave the film four stars, Siskel gave it five.

"Our Flick of the Week is *The Shawshank Redemption*," Siskel wrote in the *Chicago Tribune*, "and this is simply marvelous entertainment that breathes life into a genre that I thought had been dead for a decade—the prison picture. But to call *The Shawshank Redemption* a prison picture is as accurate as calling *One Flew Over the Cuckoo's Nest* a hospital picture. Those are the settings of these similar films, but they really are inspirational dramas of individuals struggling against overbearing authority."

Keying in on the essential appeal of the film, Siskel concluded, "*The Shawshank Redemption* is not a depressing story. . . . There is a lot of life and humor in it, and warmth in the friendship that builds up between Andy and Red. There is even excitement and suspense, although not when we expect it. But mostly the film is an allegory about holding onto a sense of personal worth, despite everything." Siskel and Ebert also brought their enthusiasm for the movie to the set of their syndicated television show.

Other reviews from the biggest cities were generally favorable while finding some slight nits to pick. Intriguingly, many of these nitpicks are elements that didn't end up bothering future fans at all. The deliberate pacing and length were common complaints, for instance. Few unqualified raves were found in the major markets, therefore, but there was no shortage of glowing notices. *New York Times* critic Janet Maslin weighed in with high praise for Darabont's direction.

"Without a single riot scene or horrific effect, it tells a slow, gentle story of camaraderie and growth, with an ending that abruptly finds poetic justice in what has come before," she wrote. "The writer and director, Frank Darabont, tells this tale with a surprising degree of loving care. . . . Needless to say, the heroes of such stories usually do succeed in defending themselves, at least when Hollywood is telling the fairy tale. But *The Shawshank Redemption* has its own brand of iconoclasm, with Mr. Darabont's direction as quiet, purposeful and secretive as Andy is himself."

Maslin, like many critics, also singled out Freeman's portrayal of Red for top acting honors.

"Mr. Freeman is so quietly impressive here that there's reason to wish Red's role had more range," she wrote. "As written, he spends his time observing Andy fondly and describing prison life. But Mr. Freeman's commanding presence makes him a much stronger figure than that. Mr. Freeman is especially moving when he suggests how dependent Red has become on the prison walls that give shape to his life."

Maslin believed the film had an excess of voiceover narration and inspirational music, and felt at times it had a "tendency to wax romantic." But, overall, this was a powerful endorsement from one of the most powerful film critics in the country. To raise funds for the prison library, Maslin told her readers, "Andy is steady and patient, writing weekly letters to state officials until he gets what he wants. Mr. Darabont, a screenwriter making an impressive directorial debut, works in much the same quietly persistent way. *The Shawshank Redemption* takes shape slowly and carefully, displaying an overall subtlety that's surprising in a movie of this genre. In the end, like Andy and Red, it gets to where it wanted to go."

Writing in the *New York Daily News*, Dave Kehr delivered one of the most overwhelmingly favorable reviews, correctly identifying Darabont as an expert interpreter of King's works: "*The Shawshank Redemption*, a first feature written and directed by Frank Darabont, finds the perfect cinematic equivalent to King's style. Based on the nonhorror novella "Rita Hayworth and the Shawshank Redemption," this is an engagingly simple, good-hearted film, with just enough darkness around the edges to give contrast and relief to its glowingly benign view of human nature."

Equally enthusiastic was critic Anthony Lane, writing in *The New Yorker* that Darabont's film was "sturdy and stirring—there's an old fashioned decency in the way that it exerts, and increases, its claim upon our feelings"—though Lane echoed the familiar complaint about the movie being "too long."

Rolling Stone critic Peter Travers joined the chorus of praise, giving high marks to Darabont's screenplay and direction, as well as the lead performances: "Writer Frank Darabont (*The Fly II*), in his feature-directing debut, doesn't skimp on the caged-bird clichés, sadistic and sentimental, but he plays enough hardball with the formula to evoke memories of such goodies as *Cool Hand Luke, Birdman of Alcatraz* and *Riot in Cell Block II*. . . . It's the no-bull performances that hold back the flood of banalities. Robbins and Freeman connect with the bruised souls of Andy and Red to create something undeniably powerful and moving. Instead of selling bromides, as lesser actors would do, they show the wrenching struggle required by any human being in a trap simply to keep hope alive."

Different critics put the spotlight on different aspects of the film, with Mike Clark of *USA Today* particularly impressed by the music: "Kudos go to the great Thomas Newman, whose score contributes as much as either lead to what is finally a two-character movie, though one well-performed by all."

Entertainment Weekly critic Owen Gleiberman wound up giving the film just a B minus grade, finding some aspects of the film to be overwrought. Referencing Andy's targeting by the Sisters when he gets to prison, Gleiberman wrote, "Make no mistake: Andy gets worked over—and so does the audience."

But Gleiberman conceded that a director needs "a certain craftsman-ship to traffic in twin brands of manipulation—the exploitative and the sentimental—and there's no denying that Frank Darabont . . . knows just what he's doing . . . you feel as if you could reach out and touch the prison walls. And Darabont is an accomplished button pusher. He coaches the actors so that you always know exactly who to root for and against."

It was a split decision at the *Washington Post*, which published two assessments of *The Shawshank Redemption*. Film critic Rita Kempley wrote that the director "manages to fashion an improbable new pattern from the same old material in his remarkable debut. While he deals with the grimmest aspects of prison life (sadistic guards, gang rapes and befouled food), Darabont is chiefly interested in the 20-year friendship that sustains" Andy and Red.

Kempley concluded with one of the keenest insights to be found in any of the September 1994 reviews: "Mostly, though, it reminds us that we all hold the keys to our own prisons."

Desson Howe wrote a dissenting view of *Shawshank* for the *Wash-ington Post*, calling it "a complete fairy tale, a sentimental yarn full of the darndest twists and turns since Frank Capra rolled his cameras." Howe said that the Roger Deakins cinematography was "burnished with that 'long time ago' golden glow" and that the inmates ultimately were "a bunch of cute pushovers." This review was a stinger, all right, one of the most negative the film would receive. "Speaking of jail," Howe wrote, "*Shawshank*-the-movie seems to last about half a life sentence. The story . . . becomes incarcerated in its own labyrinthine sentimentality."

Howe also took issue with the ending, which he found to be pat and manipulative: "And leave it to pandering, first-time director Frank Dara-bont to ensure no audience member leaves this film unsure of the ending. Heaven forbid a movie should end with a smidgen of mystery."

Still, Kempley's review took some of the sting out of Howe's eviscer-ation, at least as far as the response from the nation's capital went. Where Darabont's movie really hit the opening-month wall was in his home-town, Los Angeles. The director would blame *Los Angeles Times* film critic Kenneth Turan's extremely negative review with hurting the box-office chances for a movie that was a challenge to market. Still, just as the most positive reviews tended to have a quibble or two, the most negative ones found aspects to praise (usually the lead performances). And Turan was no exception there, writing that Freeman's narration was "one of the film's strongest points." He also observed that "it's nice to see the chaste though loving relationship between Andy and Red develop over 20 years." Not bad, but, even here, the praise sounds qualified and a compliment comes across as conditional. Freeman's contribution, he wrote, was "the closest thing to credibility" the film could manage. And as for the portrayal of Andy: "Though Tim Robbins always seems to be playing a part, he is good at it." Even James Whitmore's "nice" performance is arraigned for "being overly familiar."

Many other aspects of the film came in for sharp criticism from Turan, who wrote that, despite its moments of brutality and "unappetizing violence," *The Shawshank Redemption* was "a big glob of cotton candy" and the convicts were "a blubbery Boys Club." The *Los Angeles Times* critic also went after King's original story, saying the situations felt "like thin doodles blown up to big-screen size." Turan concluded, "Paradoxically, it is *Shawshank*'s zealousness in trying to cast a rosy glow over the prison experience that makes us feel we're doing harder time than the folks inside." File the Howe and Turan reviews under "O" for ouch.

These are reminders that no film, no matter how popular, is universally loved. *Forrest Gump*, released the same year, came in for its share of negative reviews, as well. A quick cruise around the Internet will yield contemporary views of *Forrest Gump* and *The Shawshank Redemption* that are equally harsh. It's also a reminder that, when someone says "the critics loved this movie," it's important to specify what critics. The weight of opinion might lean one way or the other, but it's never monolithic.

The two major trade publications, *Variety* and the *Hollywood Reporter*, both had praise for *The Shawshank Redemption* but warned it would be a tough sell in theaters. Since the film was from Castle Rock and the story was from the same book as *Stand by Me*, the trades compared its box-office potential to that earlier King adaptation—unfavorably. "While it seems unlikely that this well-wrought film about hope and friendship in a maximum security prison will do *Stand by Me*-level business, *The Shawshank Redemption* should appeal to a mature audience," Duane

Byrge wrote in the *Hollywood Reporter*. "The marketing challenge will be to lure a mainstream audience to this dark drama starring Tim Robbins and Morgan Freeman with, to boot, an enigmatic title."

Despite the many things he admired about the film, including Darabont's crisp writing and direction, he concluded that *Shawshank* was "a tough watch and audiences could use some time cut from its 142 minutes."

Variety reviewer Leonard Klady was more effusive in his praise, saying that Darabont had adapted "his source material with sly acuity." The screenplay, he wrote, was "a fiendishly clever construct in which seemingly oblique words or incidents prove to have fierce resonance."

Among the many things Klady found to champion were the strong supporting performances, mentioning the studies in villainy by Bob Gunton and Clancy Brown, as well as the cinematography of Roger Deakins, Thomas Newman's score ("providing just the right balance between the somber and the absurd"), and Terence Marsh's sets. His quibble was that Darabont erred by digressing "too long on a supporting character or embellishes a secondary story." His conclusion, though, was, befitting the film, uplifting. "A testament to the human spirit, the film is a rough diamond," Klady wrote. "Its languors are small quibbles in an otherwise estimable and haunting entertainment."

Still, Darabont believed that the *Los Angeles Times* review had done its damage. As the reviews rolled in from around the United States and Canada, there was no shortage of rave reviews awarding *The Shawshank Redemption* top grades. Some of the highest rating reviews came from *Desert News, Toronto Sun, Satellite News Network, The Oregonian, Ottawa Citizen, Buffalo News, San Diego Union Tribune, Orlando Sentinel,* and the *Fort Lauderdale Sun-Sentinel.*

And, perhaps the most prescient evaluation of all, since it unknowingly anticipates the film's success after its theatrical release:

Bob Fenster, *The Arizona Republic* (four out of four stars): "We can always use a movie that offers us a moment of redemption. It will affect some people profoundly."

One of the earliest reviews of *The Shawshank Redemption,* running well before its national release, appeared in the Saturday, September 10, edition of the *Mansfield News Journal.* The newspaper printed a special supplement section that day. It looked back on the making of the film, and it contained a "special to the *News Journal*" review by Mark Cappelletty. To avoid any hint of home rooting, Cappelletty started his advance review by pointing out that he was not from Mansfield and that he had absolutely nothing to do with the film. He was, in fact, a film student living in Los Angeles, where he had been invited to attend the screening for the cast and crew in early September.

"But if you are from Mansfield," Cappelletty wrote, "consider yourself lucky. *The Shawshank Redemption,* filmed in Mansfield last summer, is a haunting, deeply-moving tale of hope and human dignity, a brilliantly drawn character study of men whose desperation is matched only by their ability to survive."

He concluded by observing that *The Shawshank Redemption* was so good, it was difficult to imagine it was the director's first theatrical feature: "Darabont not only carefully transforms what could have been an ordinary tale of survival of the fittest into something greater, but spins a story about the human condition which preserves the idea of hope, something seemingly lost in the cynicism of the films, and the society, of today. This is a brilliant film."

AWARDS SEASON

The Shawshank Redemption was far from ignored during the film industry's November-to-February awards season, at least as far as nominations go. If you're a proponent of the "it's an honor to be nominated" school (and no one in Hollywood really is), then *Shawshank* did fairly well by that metric. There were two Golden Globe nominations, for best actor in a drama (Morgan Freeman) and best screenplay (Frank Darabont). It lost in both categories, Tom Hanks (*Forrest Gump*) winning for best actor and Quentin Tarantino (*Pulp Fiction*) winning for best screenplay. A harbinger of things to come? You bet it was. The immensely popular *Forrest Gump* would prove to be just as much a juggernaut at the awards bashes as it had been at the box office. The Golden Globes didn't even see clear to nominate *The Shawshank Redemption* as best drama (although *Nell, Quiz Show,* and *Legends of the Fall* were, along with *Pulp Fiction* and category winner, you guessed it, *Forrest Gump*).

That was the first year for the Screen Actors Guild awards, and both Freeman and Tim Robbins were nominated for outstanding performance by a male actor in a leading film role, but they lost to, yes, Hanks. It was getting so that, contrary to what Forrest's mother told him, life wasn't at all like a box of chocolates. We knew very well what we were going to get at these awards shows. And that's not taking anything away from *Forrest Gump*, Hanks, and director Robert Zemeckis.

The Shawshank Redemption did pull off a rare victory when Roger Deakins was honored by the American Society of Cinematographers. At least one key member of the *Shawshank* team walked away with a chunk of hardware. But despite the strong support of film critics Gene Siskel and Roger Ebert, *Shawshank* was shut out at the Chicago Film Critics Association Awards. Deakins did get the best cinematography nod from the Dallas–Fort Worth Film Critics Association. The National Society of Film Critics didn't nominate *The Shawshank Redemption* for a single award.

The Directors Guild of America nominated Darabont, but the award went to Zemeckis. But Darabont did win a Humanitas Prize and a PEN Center USA West Literary Award that year. Niki Marvin was nominated for a Golden Laurel Award by the Producers Guild of America.

When director Arthur Hiller and actress Angela Bassett announced the nominees for the 67th Academy Awards on February 14, 1995, *The Shawshank Redemption* was at least in the conversation with seven nominations: for best picture, best actor (Freeman), screenplay based on previously published or produced material, cinematography, original score (Thomas Newman), sound, and editing. The early favorite, of course, was *Forrest Gump* with thirteen nominations.

Oscar night, March 27, 1995, found *The Shawshank Redemption* being shut out, and I don't really need to tell you what the big winner was. *Shawshank* lost in every category: best picture (to *Forrest Gump*), actor (to Hanks and *Forrest Gump*), screenplay (to *Forrest Gump*), cinematography (to *Legends of the Fall*), score (to *The Lion King*), sound (to *Speed*), and editing (to, just for a change, *Forrest Gump*).

Oscars past and present, nominations and winners, are prime debate fodder for film fans. An argument certainly could be made that Bob Gunton deserved a nod for best supporting actor. It also could be argued that Darabont was unfairly snubbed in the nominations for best director. But one member of the creative team that Darabont felt was shamefully overlooked was production designer Terence Marsh. Darabont believed that Marsh's ingenious cellblock set was so authentic, few critics or Academy members would realize it wasn't an actual prison. This is borne out by Leonard Klady's favorable review in *Variety*. Klady wrote, "Terence Marsh's sets—on an actual prison location—capture the mustiness and permanence of the environment with aplomb." In a way, it was the supreme compliment to Marsh's art. The assumption was, as Darabont suggested, that the cellblock set was a redressed prison. "His work was simply too *seamless* to be noticed," Darabont said.

So, to recap: the box office belonged to *Forrest Gump* and the awards season belonged to *Forrest Gump*. That was undeniable and not undeserved, but the future belonged to *The Shawshank Redemption*.

HOPE NEVER DIES: AMERICA DISCOVERS *SHAWSHANK*

SOME MOVIES ARE LIGHTNING-FAST SPRINTERS, GETTING OUT TO QUICK starts at the box office and posting blockbuster numbers during their initial releases. That was true for three of the 1994 films that stole much of the box office and awards thunder: *Forrest Gump*, *Pulp Fiction*, and *The Lion King*.

"I was shocked," Bob Gunton said of the film's theatrical release and dismal showing at various awards ceremonies. "I think all of us were shocked. I mean, it's not the first time that an exceptional movie does not break down the doors when it's initially released. And then, over time, people begin to appreciate its nuances. You know, it wasn't written for critics. It was written for people for whom hope is a precious commodity."

So, it's certainly fair to say that *The Shawshank Redemption* was no great shakes as a sprinter. Indeed, it stumbled badly at the starting gate. After the disappointing box office and the shutout at the Oscars, *The Shawshank Redemption* might very well have gradually faded from memory, cherished only by a small but devoted group of admirers. Other films, however, as Gunton suggests, are long distance runners, finding their audience over the long haul and able to build a following year after year. Certainly no movie in Hollywood history has proven to be a more durable long distance runner than *The Shawshank Redemption*.

Another beloved film that fits this description is one Frank Darabont has mentioned as an all-time favorite, director Frank Capra's *It's a Wonderful Life*. Released in late December 1946, it received mixed reviews and placed an unremarkable twenty-seventh among the top-grossing films of 1947. It was nominated for six Academy Awards, including best picture, actor, and director. It managed only one technical achievement award. Until the early 1970s, Capra's reputation as a great director rested solidly on other films, particularly the common-man trilogy of *Mr. Deeds Goes to Town, Mr. Smith Goes to Washington,* and *Meet John Doe.* Most forgot that he'd even made a movie called *It's a Wonderful Life* . . . until it started showing up again and again on television. And thanks to television, it was rediscovered and on its way to becoming a highly venerated American classic.

"Many of our most beloved films found their audiences on television," said Maura Grady, coauthor of *The Shawshank Experience: Tracking the History of the World's Favorite Movie.* "That's true of *The Wizard of Oz, A Christmas Story, It's a Wonderful Life, Shawshank.* Most of them didn't do gangbusters at the box office when they first came out, but repeated viewings on television endeared them to audiences. And *Shawshank* is the kind of film you can watch many times and have a different experience each time. Part of that is the quality of the screenplay, where Darabont plants very subtle clues about what's going to happen, and you catch that in later viewings. That made it ideal for repeat viewings on television."

The Shawshank Redemption didn't have to wait nearly as long as *It's a Wonderful Life* for its rediscovery. Compared to Capra's classic, it was hardly any time at all. The same could be said of *A Christmas Story* (1983), another box-office disappointment. All three films were rescued by television. But *The Shawshank Redemption* and *A Christmas Story* had an advantage over *It's a Wonderful Life*—a little thing called home video. Even before Turner Broadcasting System had acquired the broadcast rights to *The Shawshank Redemption,* the rediscovery (if you wish to call it that) was well underway, thanks to an extraordinary show of faith by Warner Home Video. Although *The Shawshank Redemption* had fared poorly at the box office, Warner shipped an astounding 320,000 VHS copies in the United States alone. The word-of-mouth buzz that failed to materialize in the theater quickly built on the home-video front. The award nominations didn't hurt, and Darabont has said the frequent mentions of the film on the Academy Awards telecast significantly boosted its profile. But the numbers behind its success on home video suggested that there was an actual phenomenon in the making. And there was.

On home video and cable, a rapidly growing number of fans kept going back to Shawshank State Prison to spend time with Red and Andy.
PHOTOFEST

In those pre-streaming days when there were such things as video stores around most corners, the rental figures showed customers came back for repeat viewings. These video store metrics also showed that *The Shawshank Redemption* was equally popular with male and female customers. In fact, its appeal was cutting across all adult demographics. Runaway word of mouth, incredibly wide appeal, and repeat viewings made *The Shawshank Redemption* one of the top-rented films of 1995. Here, on home video, was the success formula that would be duplicated on an even bigger scale when it jumped to television.

"I used to be surprised that women loved this movie," Gunton said during a 2013 visit to Upper Sandusky. "It's a prison movie. But then I thought, you know, there are a lot of women who are in what seem like hopeless positions: in bad marriages, in jobs where they are the superior employee and they've hit that glass ceiling, problems with children, and just problems with being a woman in this world. You've got to have hope. And also, I think a lot of women understand, as men don't always do, the

176

transforming power of friendship. Andy and Red save each other . . . each of them brings out the best in the other."

Think of the theatrical release for *Shawshank* as a swing and a miss. The second swing was a home-video home run. Instead of gradually fading, *The Shawshank Redemption* came roaring back, gradually increasing its following, year after year, thanks first to home video, then to cable. Ted Turner had purchased Castle Rock in 1993. In 1996, Time Warner and the Turner Broadcasting System merged, transferring the rights to *The Shawshank Redemption* to Warner Bros. Turner, therefore, had the inside track to securing the television rights to *The Shawshank Redemption*. The film began regular TNT airings in 1997, showing the same durability and appeal as it had on home video. Encouraged, TNT started airing it more and more. Another film might have burned out after a few months of this. Instead, the *Shawshank* phenomenon kept building. It spread to other cable channels, including those aimed at men (Spike) and women (Oprah Winfrey's OWN). It was given another home video boost on DVD. And by this time, it had long shed the label of financial loser. In May 2014, the *Wall Street Journal* ran an article charting the film's long-term success. Written by Russell Adams and titled "The Shawshank Residuals: How One of Hollywood's Great Second Acts Keeps Making Money," the story reported that the film's combined box office, home video sales, and television licensing amounted to $100 million. Jeff Baker, then executive vice president and general manager of Warner Bros. Home Entertainment, told Adams that the film's home video sales stood at about $80 million. That same year, *Business Insider* reported that *The Shawshank Redemption* was one of the most valued titles in the Warner Bros. library.

And all during this time, *The Shawshank Redemption* kept rising on lists of favorite movies, until it hit that number-one spot at IMDb. The phenomenon was not confined to the United States. A 2008 vote conducted by the British film magazine *Empire* placed *The Shawshank Redemption* in fourth place on a list of five hundred greatest films of all time. Three years later, it claimed the top spot in a BBC Radio poll.

Or as Gunton put it in a monumentally understated way to a room full of like-minded fans in 2013, "The movie seems to be holding up pretty well."

IV.

THE *SHAWSHANK* INTERPRETATION, AFTERLIFE, AND LEGACY

If you're a horror writer and you're going to give evil its innings, you should give good its innings, too.

—STEPHEN KING
INTERVIEW WITH THE AUTHOR

REDEMPTION

ALL RIGHT, IT'S ALL ABOUT REDEMPTION. THAT SOUNDS SIMPLE enough, and yet, Andy's path to redemption is anything but simple. It's a nineteen-year journey full of torturous twists and turns. But the worst thing that happens to Andy brings out the best of him, which speaks of redemption long before he actually gets out of Shawshank.

"There is something about the role of suffering in this movie that, for the lack of a better phrase, I'd call Christian, slash, Catholic," said Anthony Magistrale, author of *Hollywood's Stephen King* and coauthor of *The Shawshank Experience*. "Andy has to suffer in order to come to the realization that he is in some way responsible for the death of his wife. It personalizes what happens to Andy during his time there. It would be so easy for him to withdraw when he goes to Shawshank. He tells Red that his wife always said he was closed off. Instead, he opens himself up to everybody. He's doing penance. In this way, he's acting out a Christian ethic but he's not really a Christ-like figure."

Andy isn't taking on the sins of others, in other words, he's working toward redemption by recognizing and coping with his own failings, shortcomings, and, well, sins, if you will. Near the end of the film, when he "confesses" to Red that he was in some way guilty of his wife's death, Andy also says that "whatever mistakes I made I've paid for them and then some." It hasn't been an easy path. Christian theology teaches that all have sinned and all fall short, and the only thing necessary for salvation is an acceptance of Christ. For those looking to put too strict a religious interpretation on *The Shawshank Redemption*, keep in mind that it suggests redemption is to be earned. It's more than a gift. It's a responsibility to yourself and others.

This is accomplished in Darabont's movie by Andy relying on his gifts and strengths, rather than succumbing to despair and defeat. As Magistrale wrote in *Hollywood's Stephen King*, "We learn in the course of the film that Andy is simultaneously the representative of change and liberation as well as a symbol of rock-hard determination and endurance."

Claire Slemmer, who plays the bank teller in *The Shawshank Redemption*, adds to this the incredibly appealing notion of the little guy beating the evil forces that have him in its power. "He beats the system," she said. "He wins out over a corrupt system. It's also not a hurried film. It's a perfectly paced film. And it feels real."

Robbins believes in the film's message of holding on to hope, but he also likes another aspect of Andy's story that sometimes gets lost.

"The film speaks eloquently to the power of engagement," said Robbins, whose experiences on such acclaimed movies as *The Shawshank Redemption* and *Dead Man Walking* led him to become an outspoken advocate for prison reform. "The film reminds us that part of the path towards hope is engagement—engagement with others, engagement with your mind, educating yourself. There's that whole subplot about Andy's persistence with building the library. There's this emphasis on exposure to art. There's that wonderful scene where Andy plays the passage from the Mozart opera to the prisoners in the yard. I think that's part of it, too. It says, 'Hold on, yes, hold on, but while you're holding on, illuminate yourself with learning and new insights and fewer prejudices.'"

Robbins has put his engagement where his mouth is. He has taken his Actor's Gang theater workshop into California prisons, and participation in the program appears to cut the recidivism rate in half. There's engagement, and there's exposure to the arts.

Harold Cope, a one-time Ohio State Reformatory guard who plays a guard in the movie, finds both good advice and good sense in the scenes where Andy offers books as a literal and spiritual way out of Shawshank. "I love that idea, and I used to encourage the prisoners to read," he said. "I'd always tell them to read books. I'd tell them, 'It can get you out of here. You can escape into a book. It will take you out of this place. It will take you anywhere you want to go.'"

"I really like that the film sort of celebrates the redemptive nature of art," said *Shawshank* actor Scott Mann, a visual artist and photographer. "Reading, music, the movies—all of these help Andy to get where he's going."

Music, too, plays a strong role in the passage to redemption. Andy extols the power of music every bit as forcefully as he does reading and education. When he plays *The Marriage of Figaro* over the prison PA system, it's a transformative moment. Everyone stops, transfixed, and listens. Realistic? Perhaps not, but this sequence is about magic, specifically the magical power of music. And magic can never be fully explained.

Red tells us some things are best left unsaid. He wants to think that the two women were singing about something so beautiful, it couldn't be expressed in words. That's magic. And the music, Red says, had the power to make the gray walls of Shawshank dissolve away, and, for a few seconds, every prisoner "felt free." Later, Andy tells them that the two weeks in solitary for that stunt was easy time because he had Mozart's music to keep him company. The music was in his head, a place no warden and no guard could touch. We need music, he tells them, so we don't lose hope.

Later, Andy gives Red a harmonica—a literal gift of music and a symbol of what Andy calls "the best of things," hope. "Grief can take care of itself," Mark Twain advised, "but to get the full value of joy you must have somebody to divide it with." Andy, closed off when he is sent to Shawshank State Prison, opens up behind bars, sharing the gifts and realizing that this is the true path to redemption, for himself and others.

HOPE

ONE OF THE MOST-QUOTED LINES IN A MUCH-QUOTED MOVIE IS FOUND in the letter Andy leaves for Red. Andy writes, "Remember, Red, hope is a good thing, maybe the best of things, and no good thing ever dies."

Again, we're grappling with a concept that sounds easy. But we're not about to reduce this sentiment to a couple of lines inside a Hallmark card. After all, we've just sat through about two hours that in no way suggests it's easy to keep hope alive. The film doesn't say that's easy. It says that it's necessary. And for that challenge to work, we must relate to the central characters. We must identify with them.

The identification is not only there, it's strong and enduring. It lingers long after the final scene and it draws us back for those repeat viewings.

"We've all been in situations where we wish we could get out and there doesn't seem to be a way out—jobs they hate, drug addictions, bad marriages, connections to the past we can't escape, medical problems, abusive relationships," Magistrale said. "On some level, almost anyone can connect to Andy's dead-end situation. And yet, there is hope. If Andy can get out of Shawshank, maybe there's a way out for me."

We identify with Andy and Red precisely because the roads they take to hope are so difficult, not because they are in any way smooth and pleasant. Both characters are brought to the brink of despair before making the choice to "get busy living." This is Andy's story. It's Red's story. But we should never forget that this is also the story of Brooks, a con yanked out of the prison routine and set adrift in an unfamiliar world without an emotional roadmap of any kind.

Magistrale believes that Brooks represents the road that ends in despair. Andy represents the road that leads to hope. And Red is in the middle, having been the recipient of Andy's definition of the basic choice: "Get busy living or get busy dying." Is he going to go down the road Brooks took? Or is he going to go down Andy's road? That's the question he's facing when he finally gets out of Shawshank and is sitting in that same hotel room where the road Brooks took ended.

There is marvelous symbolism in the scene where a paroled Red stands at the pawn shop window, staring. Like Brooks, he's thought about breaking his parole so they'll send him back to where things make sense. Our immediate attention is on the row of guns in the window. But, toward the top of the frame, is a compass. Just the thing for helping you to find the right direction and the right road. Gun or compass? We soon find out, he chose the compass. The compass will help guide him to the wall and the tree and Andy's letter, which, in turn, will lead to a reunion with his friend on the beach of Zihuatanejo.

Eve Lapolla, the former manager of the Ohio Film Commission, believes the film has attracted more fans because there's more need to spend time in the company of Andy and Red. "It is redeeming," she said. "And, in this day and age, we need all of that we can get. A lot of people are scared today, and this movie offers reassurance."

———

For Bob Gunton, the identification almost has a "spiritual pull" because hope must be kept alive under the worst possible conditions, and, finally, after all of that, "Andy is crawling through five hundred yards of sewage to his emancipation, after twenty years."

It's yet another aspect of the film that draws us back for repeat viewings. You simply can't hear this message too many times. It never loses its potency and its relevance. If anything, its message is more needed and necessary twenty-five years after its release.

"I have different theories for that, and I think they all have some validity," Robbins said. "It has been said, and I think this is right, that the movie obviously offers a message of hope at a time when things seem to be more and more uncertain on so many levels. I mean, there are movies that offer hope, but it's often hope that's not really earned, and maybe it's not earned because people are afraid to go to the darkness, in order to get past the darkness and get to hope. *Shawshank* takes a difficult road to get to where it gets."

King and Darabont understand that you must fully embrace the darkness for the light to be fully appreciated and cherished.

"And I think the film powerfully speaks to what freedom is and what enslavement is—or incarceration," Robbins said. "I don't think you have to be in jail to be in prison. There are people imprisoned by lifestyle choices or relationships or unhappy jobs. There are people, like Andy, imprisoned because of things that are not of their own choosing. Ultimately, metaphorically, this movie offers hope to everyone that there is a beach in Zihuatanejo for everybody. And if my character can get there, then anyone can."

FRIENDSHIP

THERE IS ONE OTHER MAJOR ELEMENT THAT PROVIDES THE EMOTIONAL fuel for all this talk about redemption and hope. That's friendship. It provides the framework for the film. It's the unbreakable bond that holds everything together. Andy and Red are the heart and soul of *The Shawshank Redemption*, and their friendship is what connects the heart with the soul. "Above all else, *Shawshank* is a paean to friendship and love," King scholar Tony Magistrale wrote in *Hollywood's Stephen King*. "After all, if love and friendship can survive in an environment such as Shawshank prison, then is it so inconceivable that these elements might also transcend the conventional restrictions of race and class?"

This also figures prominently in any estimation of why the film has remained so popular. It's not the friendship between two lead male characters that was rare, then or now, in Hollywood. It's the depiction of that friendship that was and is rare in a mainstream movie.

"It's a portrait of a close, trusting male friendship," said Magistrale's *The Shawshank Experience* coauthor Maura Grady. "You don't see a slow, steady, developing friendship depicted over a number of years. You see buddy films and action films. This film doesn't have much of that. It does have a deep bond between two men who trust each other."

When you see a friendship between two men in a typical Hollywood movie, it's probably going to be served up with explosions, car chases, gun battles, and snarky quips traded back and forth. There's nothing flippant about the friendship we see develop between Andy and Red. It never seems like a cookie-cutter movie construct. It doesn't feel like anything we've seen before. It seems real.

The friendship between Andy (Tim Robbins) and Red (Morgan Freeman) becomes the unbreakable bond that holds the story together.

"Well, I think that's another reason it resonates with so many people," Tim Robbins said. "You know, particularly with men, there aren't a lot of stories out there about the friendship and love between two men, and it isn't sexual in any way or involves a car chase. They make those buddy comedies and buddy action films all the time, but those are kind of like relationships that are more based in masculine posing than in humanity."

In fact, the film made at the Ohio State Reformatory before *The Shawshank Redemption, Tango & Cash*, fits that description to a T—or, in this case, a TNT. It's a buddy film with plenty of explosions and banter.

The Shawshank Redemption not only presented a mature study of a friendship between two men, but a friendship with men from different worlds. Red's reality growing up was nothing like Andy's, the banker with a bright white-collar future, a home, and investments. Red knew a different reality, closer to the mean streets and farther away from the American Dream. And yet, they find common ground.

This, of course, all goes back to the casting of Freeman in a role that started out as a white Irish-American. It added a dimension to the friendship that, without a trace of explicit commentary, suggested hopeful possibilities for all of us: trust, respect, mutual reliance, affection, cooperation, understanding, empathy, esteem. These are the gifts of friendship.

The Shawshank Redemption has invited comparisons with another towering work of literature, Mark Twain's *Adventures of Huckleberry Finn*. Racial tensions were running high in Los Angeles in 1992, the year that Castle Rock agreed to turn Darabont's screenplay into a movie. Riots and civil disturbances sparked by the police beating of Rodney King rocked the city in April and May of that year. In the film's quiet depiction of how Andy and Red accept each other, then rely on each other, there is a glimmer of hope. It's more of hope than a reflection of a reality, some might argue, but this is an entire movie built on hope. Why not the hope of having a friend, as well?

When Red says that he and Andy are "getting to be kind of friends," he's not just talking about the two of them. We're sharing in that friendship, too. You may find yourself nodding in agreement when Red speaks these words, because we are getting to be kind of friends. And we care so deeply because they care so deeply. This is holy ground we're treading on, privileged to be let in on the rite of friendship.

"Without the friendship, there is no hope," said Jane Imbody, the reporter-anchor who plays a reporter in *The Shawshank Redemption*. "People, all kinds of people, responded to the friendship. It's what makes this such an incredibly real and incredibly human film."

When Andy escapes, Red is happy because "some birds aren't meant to be caged," and the part of you rejoices. It's the part that recognizes it was a sin to lock them up . . . but, still, what they've left behind is all the more dreary, drab, and empty. The reason is obvious to Red and to us: "I guess I just miss my friend."

"This really is a male love story in a lot of ways," first assistant director John R. Woodward said. "Obviously, there's nothing sexual about it, but there's great love between these guys. You feel it. All of the things that this film is about—hope, redemption, salvation—all of it is made possible by this love we call friendship."

SYMBOLISM IN THE FILM: DISCOVERING TWELVE

DISCIPLES ON THE ROOF

IF YOU GO LOOKING FOR SYMBOLISM IN *THE SHAWSHANK REDEMPTION*, you're going to find it. You'll find it inside and outside of the walls of Shawshank State Prison. You'll find it in Andy's cell and on the prison yard. You'll find it in that grim halfway-house hotel and on the sun-drenched beach of Zihuatanejo. You'll find it in lines of dialogue and the expressions on a character's face. You'll find it in the way a scene is shot and how music is used at a certain moment.

Now, good luck getting Frank Darabont to confirm the intentions behind all this symbolism or how much of it was intentional or even touching on the overall messages of the film. Like most writers and directors, he prefers that the work speak for itself. When asked about the movie's themes during a 2004 PBS interview, Darabont replied that it's best for each member of the audience to decide what it all means. Thank goodness.

Almost every story invites analysis, explication, and interpretation. Each provides an endless source for discussion and dissection. It's possible to look at *The Shawshank Redemption* and enjoy it as a tautly paced drama about two men who become friends in prison. *The Shawshank Redemption* works splendidly at that level, without any need to delve into the greater mysteries of metaphor, allegory, symbolism, and interpretation. But, when you go back to the story at different phases of your life, you're likely to see aspects of the character and plot that eluded you the first time. It's just one of the many things that make repeated viewings of *The Shawshank Redemption* so much intriguing fun.

Once you step back inside Shawshank State Prison, there's nothing stopping you from taking the almost irresistible next step: wondering if this or that moment in *The Shawshank Redemption* was framed in an intentionally symbolic way. Keep going down this path, and you may turn into Sherlock Holmes, doggedly stalking these characters and ferreting out clues that support all kinds of psychological, philosophical, political, societal, sexual, and religious interpretations.

And, if you're so inclined, no element seems more symbolic on so many levels than the portrayal of Andy Dufresne. On one of those levels, we are meant to relate to Andy as an unjustly incarcerated everyman character. Amazingly, on another level, he can be viewed as a Christ-like figure, descending to another world where he brings a message of hope. He shares this message with a core group of rough, hard-edged men, who, after he's gone, speak rapturously about what he said and did. He suffers humiliation and torture and metaphoric death, only to achieve a resurrection of sorts, defeating the devil (warden) and reaching a heavenly place. He leaves behind the possibility of redemption.

Both a relatable everyman and a messianic figure? Impossible? It's a difficult combination, I'll grant you, but it has been done. That description fits washed-up baseball pitcher "Long John" Willoughby, played by Gary Cooper in *Meet John Doe*, the 1941 film directed by one of Darabont's heroes, Frank Capra. It also fits former preacher Casy (John Carradine) in director John Ford's 1940 film version of John Steinbeck's *The Grapes of Wrath* (although it could be argued that Henry Fonda's Tom Joad is more the everyman figure in this adaptation of the Pulitzer Prize–winning novel). It most certainly fits Luke Jackson, Paul Newman's title character in *Cool Hand Luke*, the 1967 prison drama to which *The Shawshank Redemption* would be compared.

"Stephen King loves his everyman protagonists, and Andy, while special, is an ordinary man caught up in extraordinary circumstances," said Ashland University professor Maura Grady, coauthor of *The Shawshank Experience*, a book that, among many other things, does its share of discussing possible interpretations.

If there are messianic aspects to Andy's character and story, they never become so strong as to make it seem he exists in a realm above his fellow prisoners. He is of them, not above them. He is never less than intensely human, thanks to Stephen King, Frank Darabont, and Tim Robbins. They make sure that Andy's feet don't leave the ground.

"When we first see Andy in prison, he seems aloof and detached," said King scholar Tony Magistrale, Grady's coauthor on *The Shawshank Experience*. "In lesser hands, he could have come off as an almost super-human figure. Red's first impression of Andy is that he thinks he's better than everybody else. The more Red gets to know him, and the more we get to know him, the more we realize how wrong that first impression is. Andy seems more down to earth, not less, as the story develops."

Or, as Mark Browning wrote in his 2009 book *Stephen King on the Big Screen*, "Although he has some features of a Christ-figure (absence of hate, concern for his fellow man, even talking Brooks out of attacking Heywood), Andy reacts in a very human way to his situation."

No student of the movie has delved more deeply into its religious and philosophical imagery and language than film critic and broadcaster Mark Kermode, whose monograph on *The Shawshank Redemption* was published by the British Film Institute in 2003. Kermode examines much more than the Christian mysticism that many fans see running through the entire film, but he returns to this theme throughout his entire book. He notices that many characters make religious references, even when using profanity or threatening other characters.

"Even the most casual viewer of *The Shawshank Redemption* may be struck by the repetitively religious tone of the dialogue, in which biblical judgments are invoked at every turn, and each profanity tends more toward blasphemy than sexual vulgarity," Kermode observes.

Among the examples he cites:

Red early on tells the parole board that he's no longer a danger to society, and, "That's the God's honest truth."

Red telling us that, when Andy got out of the infirmary, he found, waiting in his cell, enough rocks "to keep him busy till Rapture."

Warden Norton, although angry and sarcastic, examines Andy's empty cell and shouts with mock religious fervor, "Lord, it's a miracle!"

There's more, of course. Lots more where that came from.

The district attorney cross-examining Andy says that witnesses heard him tell his wife, "I'll see you in Hell before I see you in Reno," meaning he'd never agree to a divorce. Innocent, he is going to be sentenced to a form of Hell on Earth. Lines from the district attorney's summation to the jury were cut, and they included a reference to the crime being committed in this year of our Lord, 1946, and a description of the jurors as "God-fearing Christian folk."

After warning the new prisoners about blasphemy, the warden famously (and infamously) tells them, "I believe in two things: discipline and the Bible. Here, you'll receive both. Put your faith in the Lord. Your ass belongs to me."

When the warden visits Andy in his cell to size him up, he's pleased that Andy is holding his Bible. He asks Andy if he has any favorite passages. Andy responds with Mark, Chapter 13, Verse 35: "Watch ye therefore, for ye know not when the master of the house cometh." The warden says he prefers John: Chapter 8, Verse 12: "I am the light of the world. He that followeth me shall not walk in darkness, but shall have the light of life." Each recognizes the other's favorite passage and correctly cites the book, chapter, and verse. Andy's quotation can be taken as a sly jest. The warden's selection is a reminder of Shakespeare's observation that, "The devil can cite Scripture for his purpose." Handing Andy back his Bible, Norton tells him, "Salvation lies within," not realizing the literal truth of what he's saying (Andy's rock hammer—the instrument of his salvation—is hidden within the Bible).

The references to judgment and salvation, Heaven and Hell, God and miracles are there, beginning to end, uttered by all sorts of characters—good and evil. Again, the more you go looking, the more you'll find.

Kermode moves beyond language, however, pointing to scenes that, to his mind, symbolically echo Christian theology. When Andy arranges for the cold beer for his twelve fellow convicts, Kermode sees powerful parallels with the Last Supper (beer instead of wine, but they could be "the lords of all creation"). When Andy refuses the offer of a beer from Heywood, Kermode believes this recalls Jesus not partaking of the wine he gives the apostles at the Last Supper.

Director of photography Roger Deakins sets up the woodshop shot of Red
(Morgan Freeman) listening to a Mozart opera played over the prison's public
address system.

PHOTO BY DENNIS BARNES, COURTESY OF BILL AND APRIL MULLEN

"Andy is very Christ-like in parts of the film," Magistrale said. "You
see him again and again ministering to others. He gets the beer for his
fellow prisoners, allowing them to feel like real men for a brief time. He
brings the gift of music to the prison, inspiring all of them, even those
sick in the infirmary, to look heavenward. He builds the library. He helps
the other prisoners study for their GED exams. All of these represent
avenues to redemption."

Still, Kermode also discusses the possible influences of other
philosophies and forces on *The Shawshank Redemption*, everything from
Nietzsche to, well, the movies. In the scene where Red and the other
inmates are watching Rita Hayworth in *Gilda*, he finds a clear symbol
of what he calls Darabont's "peculiar mix of Christian myth and cine-
literate magic." One aspect of the scene he points to is the room at the

Ohio State Reformatory where it was shot. It's referred to as "the Jesus room" and there is a large painting of Christ on one wall. It was, in fact, used as the Protestant chapel. The projection booth was set up behind that wall, so the images of Rita Hayworth, who will symbolize Andy's path to freedom and redemption, are being projected through the body of Christ, onto a movie screen (and, of course, audiences first saw this story of redemption on movie screens). It will be images from the movies—*Gilda, The Seven Year Itch,* and *One Million Years B.C.*—that will grace and hide Andy's ultimate avenue of escape. He will go through one of those images, just as the image of Rita Hayworth passed through the picture meant to inspire prisoners with thoughts of salvation. The mix perfectly captures the title King put on the story, "Rita Hayworth and Shawshank Redemption."

The Ohio State Reformatory's Protestant chapel was where Red and the other convicts watched the Rita Hayworth movie *Gilda.*

PHOTO BY BECKY DAWIDZIAK

Did Darabont know he was putting twelve "disciples" on the roof of the license-plate factory? Was he shooting for symbolism with the way he shot the scene with Red watching *Gilda*? Does it matter? Symbolism, after all, is in the eye of the beholder. Maybe when Andy gets out of that tunnel, it's just the image of a man happy to have all that shit behind him. Maybe it's a moment for him to rejoice, and for us to rejoice with him, without the weight of symbolism and metaphor weighing it all down. Sometimes a rock hammer is just a rock hammer, Mr. Freud. It ultimately doesn't matter what lens you choose to view this or any other scene. One aspect of it all is immutable. It all leads to the key word in the title, redemption, which is in there for a reason, and that reason covers all analysis and interpretation.

THE *SHAWSHANK* ATTRACTION:

THE FILM'S GROWING APPEAL

THE CAST AND CREW MOVED ON FROM MANSFIELD AND SHAWSHANK State Prison, occasionally seeing each other on future movie sets or industry events honoring the film they so brilliantly crafted from Stephen King's novella. Many of them worked again with Frank Darabont on various movies. Among the actors to get repeated calls from the writer-director were William Sadler (in the adaptations of King's *The Green Mile* and *The Mist*), James Whitmore (in *The Majestic*), Brian Libby (in *The Green Mile, The Majestic,* and *The Mist*), and Jeffrey DeMunn (in just about everything with Darabont's name on it). Darabont re-teamed with composer Thomas Newman, production designer Terence Marsh, editor Richard Francis-Bruce, and unit publicist Ernie Malik on *The Green Mile*. He again worked with casting director Deborah Aquila on *The Majestic* and *The Mist*.

Robbins went on to direct the acclaimed film *Dead Man Walking* (1995) and to win the Academy Award for best supporting actor for *Mystic River* (2003). Freeman went on to play God in the 2003 Jim Carrey comedy *Bruce Almighty* and to win the Academy Award for best supporting actor for director Clint Eastwood's *Million Dollar Baby* (2004).

About three months before *Million Dollar Baby* premiered, Freeman, Robbins, and Darabont reunited for a PBS interview celebrating the tenth anniversary of *The Shawshank Redemption*. Much of the discussion addressed the question of why a film that was such a box office disappointment had become so beloved by so many people. The answers started with the familiar points (no less valid for them being familiar):

Director-screenwriter Frank Darabont is flanked by his stars, Morgan Freeman and Tim Robbins, at a twentieth anniversary Academy event for *The Shawshank Redemption*.

the message of hope, the portrait of a friendship, the notion of redemption. Others associated with the film have added bits and pieces to the grand mosaic of reasons the fandom keeps growing and those fans keep returning to *The Shawshank Redemption*. If we were to assemble a round-table discussion to solicit views on the tantalizing subject, each participant might have a different response.

So let's start with the unpretentious and gracious man who so brilliantly portrayed the smug and hypocritical Warden Norton. He offered one idea about why the film's appeal is both (to borrow the title from the old hymn) deep and wide.

"It's a very mature piece," Gunton said. "And yet it's not a snobby, intellectual exercise."

For Scott Mann, who played doomed golf pro Glenn Quentin, a basic appeal of the film is that it manages to be both inspirational and motivational, both realistic and relatable.

"My mom used to say, 'Get over it . . . Get over it and move forward,'" he said. "It was her way of saying, 'Get busy living,' and I think everybody has something like that you can relate to in the film."

—❦—

To this mix, you can add a richness of dialogue, cinematography, music, editing, sound: the works. Going all the way back to King's original story, the power of the narrative can't be underestimated. Darabont has described this narrative as a tall tale, but it's the kind of tall tale one of his filmmaking heroes, Frank Capra, spun in such movies as *Mr. Smith Goes to Washington* and *It's a Wonderful Life*.

For Stephen King scholar Mark Browning, it's a matter of great narrative and great narration. Yes, don't forget the entrancing voiceover work by Freeman: "Usually, overt voiceover narration would be seen as too obvious but the key difference here is Morgan Freeman's acting persona and the sheer charismatic power of his oratory."

—❦—

Grady has studied the film both as a fan and from the perspective of fans. All of the reasons given for the film's popularity are pieces of the puzzle, she said, but, no matter how correctly you arrange them, they might not add up to the entire picture.

"It's difficult to define why fans love something," Grady said. "There are as many reasons that fans love something as there are fans. There are some common themes, and the message of hope is one. The melodramatic aspects of the story are very appealing—the way Stephen King can blend sweetness and bitterness. The scenes that matter the most are emotional moments, not action moments. And there weren't a lot of those kinds of movies at that time. But what we know for certain is that this film appeals on a lot of levels to a lot of people."

And it's inevitable that, as more fans share their love of *The Shawshank Redemption*, more reasons will appear. After twenty-five years, perhaps we've only begun to chart the true dimensions of Shawshank State Prison.

"Everybody is different," said Ben Bissman, who regularly welcomes people to his family's building, which doubled for the Brewer Hotel. "Everyone latches on to a different part of the movie. We ask everybody that. 'What's your favorite part of *Shawshank*?' And everybody goes to a different moment. They only have one thing in common, really. They share one thing. They all love the movie. You see it on their faces when they walk in here. You see it in their eyes as they look around. You hear it in their voices when they tell you how much this movie means to them. They just love this movie."

THE SHAWSHANK TRAIL:

PILGRIMAGES TO THE FILM LOCATIONS

WALK INTO THE SQUIRREL'S DEN CHOCOLATE FACTORY ON MAIN Street in Mansfield, and you can't help but notice a series of charming tableaus from *The Shawshank Redemption*. There's the halfway-house hotel room where first Brooks and then Red stayed after getting out of Shawshank. There's Andy's rock hammer and the rock wall with the piece of volcanic glass. There's Warden Norton staring in astonishment into Andy's escape tunnel. There's Andy welcoming Red on the beach of Zihuatanejo. The savory thing about these scenes is that they've been rendered in the store's favorite medium: chocolate. If this has whet your appetite, stroll over to one of the central tables in the Squirrel's Den and pick up a couple of Shawshank Prison Bars (chocolate bars, of course, available in a variety of Shawshank-themed wrappers).

"People come in here after touring the reformatory, and they're just delighted," said Squirrel's Den owner LaDonna Secrist. "We know a lot of people make their way to Mansfield because of the film, so this is our way of recognizing the town's association with the film."

And a sweet form of recognition it is, to be sure. If it's a particularly hot day in Mansfield, as it tended to be during the filming, and you need something to wash down the chocolate, you can purchase a bottle of Prison Break soda—Red's Strawberry or Andy's Root Beer—at the Richland Carrousel Park in the middle of town (just a couple of blocks down the hill from the Squirrel's Den).

Hungry? There's more than one restaurant in town with a *Shawshank*-themed item on the menu. They're all here for those fans eager to savor

A selection of *Shawshank* candy bars available at the Squirrel's Den in Mansfield, Ohio

PHOTO BY BECKY DAWIDZIAK

the *Shawshank* experience in the town where much of it was filmed. They're all tasty reminders of how Mansfield has embraced the *Shawshank* connections, but, fun as they are, these are merely the appetizers on the extensive menu offered to fans wanting to make meaningful contact with the movie that means so much to them. There's an entire driving tour that will guide them to fifteen area sites used in the film. They can go to the park and see where Brooks fed the birds, hoping Jake might stop by. They can saunter into the bank in Ashland where Andy cleaned out Warden Norton's account. They can go up to Shawshank State Prison itself, the Ohio State Reformatory, and sit at Warden Norton's desk or peek into his wall safe. Yes, it's quite the pilgrimage for the *Shawshank* enthusiast, but The Shawshank Trail didn't have its origins in Mansfield. To find the beginning of The Shawshank Trail you need to go west, over to the city where filming on *The Shawshank Redemption* began in 1993, Upper Sandusky.

Sure, around the film's tenth anniversary, curiosity seekers and fans of the movie occasionally would show up in Mansfield or Upper Sandusky, looking for sites used in the movie. But there was nothing organized

Andy's escape tunnel rendered in chocolate for one of the tasty tableaus on display at the Squirrel's Den shop in Mansfield

PHOTO BY BECKY DAWIDZIAK

and nothing suggesting something should be organized as an attraction for tourists, film fans, and *Shawshank* devotees. There was no sense of, to paraphrase another movie, if you build it, they will come. It all kind of started in a building that was rapidly becoming a town eyesore—the former Stephan Lumber Company in Upper Sandusky. It had been used for the prison woodshop scenes filmed in August 1993. Five years later, the Stephan Lumber Company ceased operations. The building was sold to a construction company that only lasted about two years. Then the place was vacant. The historic middle part of the structure, the brick mill building, was in bad shape. Local kids found it an easy target for rocks scattered along the nearby railroad tracks, so almost every window was broken.

Andy and Red's reunion in Zihuatanejo depicted in chocolate at the Squirrel's Den
PHOTO BY BECKY DAWIDZIAK

It may well have faded into oblivion had it not been for Bill and April Mullen, who, ironically enough, were two Upper Sandusky residents not involved with the film on any level in 1993. They were living there at the time, all right, and they were aware of the movie, but they had slightly bigger cares on their minds.

"We were too busy trying to save our business when they came to film here," Bill Mullen said. "We'd had a fire in our building and it almost destroyed it. We did have a 1949 Olds convertible at the time, and we saw a request in the newspaper for old automobiles. We submitted a picture and didn't hear anything for months. So we decided to just sell it and help with a down payment on a home. And it wasn't two weeks after we sold it that they wrote back and said they wanted it in the movie. That's the closest I got to being in the film. My car almost got in."

Bill Mullen grew up in the big city, Cincinnati. He moved to Upper Sandusky at the age of sixteen when his father, an engineer, got a job at a plastics plant. After a few years of Upper Sandusky living, he fell in love with the place and had no desire to return to Cincy.

"I graduated from tech school in heating and air-conditioning and refrigeration," he said. "I went to work as a service tech for a local company and got to know everyone in the community and the county. Then, when April and I went into business for ourselves, everybody was so supportive of us. It's a wonderful place to raise kids—great neighbors, low crime, good schools. I always wanted to give back to the community in some way, but I hadn't really thought about *Shawshank*. It sort of found me."

It began with his reluctance to see a building with town history leveled. "I knew a movie had been made there, and I just hated to think about it being torn down," Bill Mullen said. So, the Mullens took out a mortgage and took over the former Stephan Lumber Company. They rented out parts of the structure to other businesses, using what funds they could scrape together to fix up the old mill building. Gradually, it was being restored to how it looked when Darabont and his film crew set up shop in there. Also in dire need of repair was the other Upper Sandusky location used in the film, the Wyandot County Courthouse.

"Our courthouse is sort of the jewel of the county, but it wasn't nearly as beautiful as it had been in 1993," Mullen said. "Ten years later, it was in terrible shape."

By 2006, the Mullens were working on an idea for a fundraiser to restore the ten-foot statue of Lady Justice that stands atop the courthouse. How about a *Shawshank* reunion? The first order of business was for Bill Mullen to acquaint himself with the film.

"I hadn't even seen the movie at this point," he said. "So I rented every version I could get my hands on—every way it was released, the British release, everything I could find. It was a real crash course, and, of course, I fell in love with it."

The Mullens worked on the reunion throughout 2007, reaching out to actors and waiting on responses. Finally, Bob Gunton got in touch. And Darabont sent a video expressing his great affection for the people of Upper Sandusky, Mansfield, and Ashland. The first reunion event became a reality in 2008, raising about $10,000 of the $22,050 needed to restore Lady Justice. When work was completed and she was hauled back in place with a time capsule, a copy of *The Shawshank Redemption* went with her. It was an appropriate touch. Just as the movie had saved the

April and Bill Mullen started the Shawshank Woodshop museum in Upper Sandusky and organized the first reunion event in 2008, fifteen years after *The Shawshank Redemption* filmed in Ohio.

PHOTO BY BECKY DAWIDZIAK

Ohio State Reformatory from the wrecking ball, it now had played a part in restoring a symbol of local pride in Upper Sandusky. The courthouse subsequently underwent a $2 million restoration, thanks to a tax levy that passed by an overwhelming margin.

But in order to make the 2008 event more interesting for fans, the Mullens arranged for two buses to take people over to the filming sites, including Malabar Farm, the E&B Market in Mansfield, the bank in Ashland, and, of course, the Ohio State Reformatory. "The intention was just to get a bunch of the local people together and reminisce," said Upper Sandusky resident Bob Wachtman, an extra hired for the courtroom scenes. "Bill got that rolling, and it turned into something much bigger."

It wasn't long before the tourism-minded folks at Destination Mansfield, Lee Tasseff and Jodie Snavely, were getting in touch.

"We had no money," Bill Mullen said with a laugh. "We had donated it all. But we developed a relationship with the folks at the tourism bureau in Mansfield, which is one of the best in the state, so now things really got rolling. And it was a complete win-win for all the communities associated with the movie."

The Mullens have created a woodshop museum devoted to *The Shawshank Redemption*, and, like the Wyandot County Courthouse and the Ohio State Reformatory, it now boasts an Ohio state historical marker as well as a sign designating it as part of The Shawshank Trail. The old mill building part of the former lumber company is packed with displays about and memorabilia from the film. It also has become a popular spot for wedding receptions, reunions, and fundraisers. And, on any given day, Bill Mullen, April Mullen, or Wachtman can be found guiding *Shawshank* fans, on pilgrimage, through the woodshop where Red listened to the music that, for a few moments, made every man in Shawshank State Prison feel like a free man.

But, back in 2008, back in Mansfield, the response to the event planned by the Mullens got the attention of two people who had been deeply involved with the film company's 1993 stay in Ohio, Tasseff and Snavely.

"When people would show up and ask about the movie, it was just a kick at first," Tasseff said. "There wasn't enough to put the dots together. It wasn't until the fifteenth anniversary reunion that we really started thinking there was something more here."

Gradually, they realized that the "something" that was there had an international draw. They started noticing an increase in visitors dropping by their offices, wanting to know where certain sites used in the movie could be found. These visitors were from all over the United States, but they also were from Australia, Canada, England, France, Germany, Italy, Ireland, Japan, New Zealand, and South Korea.

"Then we realized it was time to put something together," Snavely said. "That's when we developed The Shawshank Trail, and, gradually,

Jodie Snavely and Lee Tasseff of Destination Mansfield talk *Shawshank* under the watchful eyes of Red, Andy, and Brooks.

PHOTO BY BECKY DAWIDZIAK

the town started to realize what we had. This is a major tourism product. People are coming in from all over the world to see these sites."

The casual evidence was overwhelming.

"We had a Korean businessman who showed up randomly, wanting to see Shawshank locations," Tasseff said. "We had a guy from England who, after he got to the United States, hitchhiked his way here in January, just to get to the prison."

Meanwhile, with Mansfield now on board, the reunions got bigger and more ambitious. There was a twentieth anniversary for the filming in 2013, followed by a twentieth anniversary for the movie's release in 2014. As of the writing of this book, plans were underway for the biggest event yet—a twenty-fifth anniversary reunion/fan gathering in August 2019. Mansfield also holds an annual Shawshank Hustle 7K race each June, starting with a mass "escape" from the Ohio State Reformatory and running past five of the filming sites. With each event, more and more of the Ohio residents who worked on the film get involved.

"It's like our Woodstock," Tasseff said. "Were you there? Because they did hire a lot of locals to do all kinds of stuff."

"And there's usually a connection if you're talking to someone here," Snavely said. "If they weren't in the movie, they're related to or know someone who was. Almost everybody has a connection."

Tasseff credits Snavely, the group tour and media director at Destination Mansfield, with being "the architect of The Shawshank Trail." "She planned it out," he said. "She drove the distances, timed them. Jodie was the one who did all of that and pulled it all together."

What emerged were a widely circulated brochure and a much-visited website (ShawshankTrail.com) that charted fifteen filming sites (a sixteenth, the E&B Market, was added in 2018). The current tour, starting at OSR, is as follows:

MANSFIELD (SIX STOPS):

1. **Ohio State Reformatory:** Shawshank State Prison. Drive up the prison entrance, following the path of the bus taking Andy to Shawshank. Then drop by Warden Norton's office. Descend the steps Andy uses when asking Norton if he can request funds from the legislature for the prison library. You can walk through the hotel room where Brooks checked in (and checked out) and look into the sewer pipe where Andy crawled to freedom. Take a seat in the room where Red faced the parole board three times. Stand in the very spot where Gunton stood and gave his famous "welcome to Shawshank" speech.

2. **Bissman Building:** Gaze on the impressive structure used as the Brewer Hotel, imagining Brooks dodging traffic in a world that went and got itself in one big hurry. You can also step inside to the first-floor room used as the editor's office at the *Portland Daily Bugle*.

3. **Carousel Antiques:** Stop at the pawn shop window where Red sees the guns and then spots the compass he'll use to guide him to the rock wall where Andy buried something for his friend.

4. **Central Park:** Pose for a picture on Brooksie's bench.

5. **Renaissance Theatre:** Visit the movie palace where *The Shawshank Redemption* had a special premiere on September 13, 1994.

6. **The KV Market:** Remember to double bag in this store, which, in 1993 was the E&B Market, doubling for the Food-Way, where Brooks and Red worked after getting out of prison.

BUTLER (TWO STOPS):

1. **Corner of Snyder Road and Hagerman Road:** Walk the spot where Red got out of the red pickup truck looking for the rock wall in Buxton.

2. **Hagerman Road and Route 95:** Drive down the stretch of road that the Trailways bus takes on its way, with Red, to Fort Hancock, Texas.

LUCAS (THREE STOPS):

1. **The Oak Tree:** Stand near the fence on Pleasant Valley Road and gaze at the site where the tree once stood.

2. **Malabar Farm State Park:** Visit novelist Louis Bromfield's home, where James Whitmore and Clancy Brown were given a tour in 1993.

3. **Pugh Cabin:** Drop by the cabin at Malabar Farm used as the rendezvous spot for Andy's wife, Linda Dufresne, and her lover, golf pro Glenn Quentin, but always be on the lookout for a lurking Elmo Blatch.

ASHLAND (TWO STOPS):

1. **Crosby Advisory Group, LLC:** Walk into the bank where Andy withdraws Warden Norton's ill-gotten money.

2. **Revivals 2 Thrift Store:** Stand in the store that doubled for the Trailways Bus Station where Red stood in line to buy his ticket to Fort Hancock, Texas.

UPPER SANDUSKY (TWO STOPS):

1. **Wyandot County Courthouse:** Enter the courtroom and face the judge's chair, standing where Andy stood while receiving two life sentences.

2. **Shawshank Woodshop:** Visit the former Stephan Lumber Company, used as the Shawshank prison woodshop and imagine the sound of opera music emerging from the speakers. Take a gander at such vehicles as the bus that took Andy to Shawshank and the ambulance that took Bogs away.

ST. CROIX, US VIRGIN ISLANDS (ONE STOP):

1. **Sandy Point, National Wildlife Refuge:** Saunter along the beach used for Zihuatanejo and the reunion of Andy and Red.

The sixteenth stop, of course, is the more elusive and most exotic one on the list, but, hey, it is the Zihuatanejo of the movie, and the movie makes it clear that you have to work at getting there.

Complete with maps and detailed directions, the brochure encourages fans to make the fifteen Ohio stops a self-guided driving tour, allowing plenty of time to make the entire circuit. How much time? Well, you can spend an entire day exploring the Ohio State Reformatory. And the drive from Mansfield to Upper Sandusky takes about forty-five minutes. Two or three days would be a good start for full immersion in the Shawshank Experience.

For the *Shawshank* fan, these locations aren't merely parts of towns in Ohio. Put The Shawshank Trail together, and you're looking at one giant movie set. Most films are shot on Hollywood soundstages, and, when production is over, there's nothing left of the constructed sets. Even when films are shot on location, there's seldom much left behind that's

Bill Mullen, left, and Michael A. Evans, federal wildlife officer with the US Fish & Wildlife Service, make the beach at Sandy Point National Wildlife Refuge an official stop on The Shawshank Trail.

PHOTO COURTESY OF DESTINATION MANSFIELD—RICHLAND COUNTY

recognizable and accessible while also inspiring an emotional connection. And if you need some guidance or quick directions, you always can stop by the Destination Mansfield office and ask Lee or Jodie for Trail tips. In *Shawshank* terms, their office is located across the street and up the hill from the Brewer Hotel and just a few doors down from the pawn shop.

"We had a fellow from New Zealand stop in, and it was his goal to go to all of the filming sites," Snavely said. "With most movies, you don't have that physical contact with the film. Here, you're going to stand in those actual locations. You're going to be in those actual places where those actors filmed those scenes. You can put yourself in their place. You can go into the warden's office and put your hand in his safe. You can stand where the editor of the *Portland Daily Bugle* gets the package about corruption at the prison. You can throw a jacket over your shoulder and walk the road to Buxton that Red walks on at the end of the film."

"You can immerse yourself," Tasseff said.

When the oak tree was still standing, Tasseff and Snavely would get regular requests from couples wanting to be engaged underneath its branches. It was on private property, so some settled for getting engaged while looking at the tree from the road. "Or you'd see people gazing at it with tears running down their face," Snavely said. "What other movie can do that?"

The other sites, too, including Brooksie's bench and OSR, have prompted extreme emotional responses from visiting fans. "The places evoke feelings," Amber Bissman said. "They're not just buildings and places. They tap into how people feel about the movie."

Following The Shawshank Trail "makes you feel like you're part of the movie," April Mullen said. "You make an actual connection."

⌐ ⌐

Ashland University professors Maura Grady and Richard Roberson also had a passion for the film and decided to do research on the *Shawshank* following. They asked Tasseff and Snavely about doing a survey of fans visiting the *Shawshank* sites. "Yes," the Destination Mansfield team happily responded. "In fact, you can help us figure out what fans want when they get here." So the professors started collecting data, surveying more than 250 people. Then they did a second survey in 2014. Then Grady teamed up with Tony Magistrale on the book *The Shawshank Experience*.

"Maura wanted to study the fan attraction to this film, and she kept coming back to the word *pilgrimage*," Tasseff said. "If you're a fan, you're drawn here and it has a sense of pilgrimage. They have to be here."

The Shawshank Trail, in a very real sense, is a pilgrimage trail. Grady also was able to pinpoint several specifics that fans wanted to get out of The Shawshank Trail and reunion events.

"Fans want to interact with each other," she said. "They want to interact with specific places. They want to be able to touch the places and take pictures. They want to be able to buy stuff—merchandise is important. They want to be able to meet the people who were involved with making the movie, or at least hear them on a panel. They want to have a good time and create their own experience."

The research and advice have been taken to heart, and the effort has been made to provide everything that Grady recommended to fans on pilgrimage as individuals, with families, or in large groups. And nowhere is the pull stronger than at OSR.

"The influence of nostalgia is great in this film," Grady said. "And the Ohio State Reformatory allows you to go back simultaneously to two different time periods: to when it was used as an actual prison and to when it was used for filming. People love that building. People are devoted to that building. There's something about that building that just draws people in. It's creepy and alienating the first time you go in, and then you start to feel that real affection for it."

The affection is from the fans, the people who work at the building, and the people of Mansfield. "There's a tremendous sense of civic pride about this film and this building that you feel in Mansfield," Magistrale said.

An estimated 120,000 people visit the prison each year.

"Even if there wasn't this wonderful movie associated with it, it would be an incredibly impressive building," said Dan Smith, the creative marketing director at the Ohio State Reformatory historic site. "But the movie is the main reason people come here. Some are into history. Some are into the paranormal. But the movie is the main draw. They drive in here and recognize the building, and it takes them to why they love this movie."

OSR has been featured on many of the cable shows dealing with haunting. For that matter, so has the Bissman Building. And ghost tours are regular offerings at both Mansfield locations. The greater draw, though, is not the spirits of OSR but the spirit of *Shawshank*.

"You meet people from all walks of life, and the emotion on their faces is amazing, sometimes overwhelming," Smith said. "It's a movie that is so relevant to people's lives. To many people, we are the Shawshank

State Prison. When you tell people, I work where *Shawshank* was shot, their eyes light up."

One stop not on the Trail is the cellblock set built in the old Westinghouse warehouse. The cellblock, of course, was torn down by the film company before they left town. About twenty years later, the warehouse also was torn down.

"They just flattened it," Tasseff said. "There's nothing to see."

"You really have to use your imagination if you make that part of the tour," Snavely added.

Other parts of the Trail keep growing, though, in Mansfield and at "*Shawshank* West," as the Upper Sandusky folks sometimes call themselves.

"Lee and Jodie have just done an electrifying job of keeping this kindled in this town," Ben Bissman said. "I think it would have faded away if they hadn't embraced it and promoted it. It went from nothing to solid to, 'Wow, this got big!'"

The sign outside of Mansfield on Route 30, guiding travelers to The Shawshank Trail and the Ohio State Reformatory

PHOTO BY BECKY DAWIDZIAK

For Tasseff, the twenty-five-year association with *Shawshank* is something that never gets old and never loses its magic: "If we're anywhere and we say we're from Mansfield, we can make a connection by saying, 'Have you ever seen *The Shawshank Redemption*? That's our prison. That's our town.' It's an immediate conversation starter. It's an immediate connection."

And if you want to keep making those *Shawshank* connections, there's a trail. You'll find it in "The Heart of Ohio," and it will take you directly through the heart of the movie. The lead characters in the film are trying to get far away from Shawshank and the surrounding area. The fans of the film, some with a near-religious fervor, are drawn to the places where these characters do penance and find redemption.

THE *SHAWSHANK* FANS

It is a brutally hot day in Mansfield as we trudge up the Main Street incline that takes you from the Bissman Building, at the bottom of the hill, to Central Park, at the top. It's a punishing walk as we pass the Destination Mansfield office, the storefront that became the pawn shop in *The Shawshank Redemption*, the carousel, and the Squirrel's Den shop filled with chocolate and fudge treats, candied popcorns, gourmet nuts and snacks, and *Shawshank* candy bars that would quickly be reduced to a liquid state on a day like this. It is a climb to grab one more picture for the day. We're toting along a couple of sweating Prison Break soda bottles to place on the bench where Brooks (James Whitmore) fed the birds. It's not the actual bench, mind you. It's a replica. And it's not in the precise spot where Brooksie's bench was located in the movie. And it doesn't matter. It's one of the spots on The Shawshank Trail that attracts fans seeking a physical and emotional connection with their favorite film.

The top of the hill finally attained, we make our way into Central Park and toward the bench. Coming toward us is a deeply tanned woman with long brown hair and a blonde daughter at her side. The mother looks to be in her thirties. The daughter looks about twelve. My daughter, Becky, about ten years older, is toting her camera and some equipment for this last shot of the long day. It's clear that mother and daughter are making their way toward Brooksie's bench, also wanting to take a picture (or pictures). It's also clear we'll get there first. We do, and we wait for them to arrive.

"Want to take some pictures sitting on the bench?" I ask them.

"You were here first," the mother says with an accent that strongly suggests the Lone Star State.

"That's all right," I tell her. "It's going to take some time to set up our shot. You go ahead."

She smiles, thanks us, and then turns to look at the bench. She's still smiling, but it's a different kind of smile. It's almost beatific. She and her daughter take turns posing on the bench, using a phone to grab the memory pictures. My daughter and I wait silently by, not wanting to intrude on what's clearly a moment that means so much to both of them. After a few minutes of *Shawshank* connecting, they thank us again and start to leave.

"Fans of the movie?" I ask, treading in the obvious (blame the heat of the day).

"It's our favorite movie," she says. "We drove all the way from Texas to spend our vacation here. We just spent the day at the prison, and tomorrow we're going out to other sites."

"This is your vacation?"

"Yes, and it's been just wonderful. We want to come back."

This encounter could have been duplicated anywhere along The Shawshank Trail. The type of person might well change. You never know. You might find yourself talking to an ex-convict in front of the Ohio State Reformatory, wanting to tell you what the film means to him, "because you're the people writing that *Shawshank* book." *Shawshank* fans come in all shapes and sizes, backgrounds and occupations, ages and experiences . . . and they come from everywhere.

"When they first announced the film, we couldn't even figure out what 'Rita Hayworth and Shawshank Redemption' meant," said Lou Whitmire, the *Mansfield News Journal* reporter who plays a reporter in the film. "So no one ever guessed people would end up loving it the way they do. People travel here for their vacation, and they come from all over. It has a cult following, and, on any day, you can walk around town and see people posing and taking pictures in front of the Bissman Building or on Brooksie's bench."

Although she played a major part in getting the movie to Ohio in 1993, former Film Commission manager Eve Lapolla hadn't been to OSR for several years. "I had a niece come up to visit this past summer, and I told her I'd take her to see the prison." she said. "It was a Sunday,

Two cold *Shawshank*-themed Prison Break sodas await visitors to Brooksie's bench on a blisteringly hot day in Mansfield, Ohio.

PHOTO BY BECKY DAWIDZIAK

so I said, 'Probably no one will be there, but I haven't been back there in years and years.' We got here, and there was a line of people out the door. One fellow said, 'Me and buddies, about twenty of us, rode six hours on motorcycles because we wanted to see Shawshank.'"

Everyone connected with a site on The Shawshank Trail has a thick file of stories like that. "And the stories that people tell us are amazing," said April Mullen, who talks to fans visiting the Shawshank Woodshop in Upper Sandusky. "They want to share why this movie means so much to them."

It took a while for the penny to drop at the visitor and tourism bureau in Mansfield. People asking about *The Shawshank Redemption* were common enough, but it took a very special visitor in August 2011 to make Jodie Snavely realize how special the film was—and how passionate its fans are.

"I didn't get it at first," Snavely said. "I didn't get why people loved this movie so much. It wasn't until I met this fellow from Canada out at the reformatory. I happened to be going out there for something, and I saw him taking one of our brochures."

Delighted, she good-naturedly shouted to the visitor, "Hey, that's our brochure!"

"I'm only taking one," he told her.

"Take as many as you want," she replied. "We have like 90,000 of them. We crave that."

Then he told her, "I'm the world's biggest fan of this movie."

His name was Rick Ayres. He was visiting Mansfield with his wife of six years, Roxanne. They had traveled from Dutton, Ontario, which Ayres joked was "a place a lot like Green Acres." When Roxanne suggested a vacation to, oh, maybe Cuba or Las Vegas, Rick said, "Let's go to Mansfield, Ohio." He wanted to do as many stops on The Shawshank Trail as possible. At fifty-four, Ayres had been diagnosed with cancer and he was suffering from severe arthritis that made sitting for prolonged stretches extremely difficult. He also had survived a heart attack. The four-and-a-half-hour trip to Mansfield had been tough. There was a pillow and an air mattress in the back of their blue Ford pickup for emergency stops, but Rick managed to make the entire drive sitting upright.

Why did he need to make the pilgrimage to Mansfield? Why was the film so special to him? A DVD copy of the movie had been Roxanne's gift for their first Christmas together. It proved to be the gift that kept on giving. If he had a rough day at work, he'd text his wife to say, "Have my movie ready, I need it when I get home." No matter how low he was, *The Shawshank Redemption* would bring him up, making him feel like "a million bucks." He told Snavely that he watched it at least two times a week . . . sometimes four times a week.

"He does," Roxanne told Snavely. "We go to bed with it on. We wake up with it on."

The movie pulled him through, Rick told Snavely. It gave him hope. And he tried to pass along that hope to others. When not working as a custodian at the McCormick spice company, he was a volunteer hospice worker and crisis counselor.

Rick and Roxanne were armed with the Shawshank Trail map and were planning to visit as many of what was then thirteen sites as possible in two days.

The couple from Canada and Snavely were about to have an incredibly moving and memorable day.

Moved by Rick's devotion to his favorite movie, Snavely told the couple, "Let me call my boss. Let me show you around and take you to the places where it was filmed."

"You've got to be kidding me," Rick said. She wasn't.

They toured OSR. They went out to the Shawshank Woodshop in Upper Sandusky and met the Mullens.

"He told us that he watched the film all the time because, if Andy and Red could make it through all of that, maybe he could, too," April Mullen said.

Rick enjoyed a Shawshankwich (roast beef with Red's onion and Andy's Aioli, all confined in a warden's wrap) at Ed Pickens' Cafe on Main. They went to site after site, guided by Snavely.

"Every time we stopped, we'd get out and he'd recite what happened in the movie," Snavely recalled. "He was thrilled beyond belief. At the end of two days, we went out to the tree."

Some of the many items on display at the Shawshank Woodshop museum in Upper Sandusky
PHOTO BY BECKY DAWIDZIAK

The tree had been damaged a few weeks earlier by heavy winds, and only half the tree was left standing. "If it was just a stump, I'd still go," Rick said. He gazed at what was left of the tree from Pleasant Valley Road.

"He's looking at the tree, and he starts crying," Snavely said. "And then he said, 'If I die tomorrow, this is the best thing that has ever happened to me. If I die tomorrow, I die a happy man.' It was such an emotional thing to watch him and his wife."

The next day, Roxanne came into the office and presented Snavely with a little wooden angel. "I can't thank you enough for spending time with us," Roxanne said.

And like so many other fans who have made the pilgrimage to Mansfield, they stayed in touch. As of this writing, they're still in touch, exchanging Christmas wishes seven years and four months after that sunny day on Pleasant Valley Road.

"So we'd send them Shawshank shirts and stuff over the years, because they were such good people and really loved this movie," Snavely said. "But that was the moment I realized how special this movie is, how special these fans are, and how special everything that we have is."

Other fans also have made profound impressions on Snavely. There was the fan with the tattoo of the tree. There was the fan who made his own video travelogue, soundtrack and all.

"There was Mike Demetriades, this fellow who traveled all the way from Florida," Snavely said. "Mike kept calling my cell phone, and I thought, 'I don't know this guy. I'm not calling him back.' But he was coming up to see the *Shawshank* sites, and he was a great guy. He comes in with his father-in-law. And he has a binder with more than one hundred printed pictures from the film and notes and everything on *Shawshank*."

He also had a GPS programmed with the precise locations of various sites and a copy of the movie's soundtrack to listen to while visiting stops on the trail. "I don't want to sound like too much of an extremist," Demetriades told NPR reporter Cory Turner for a 2011 feature on Mansfield's *Shawshank* attraction. "But I was definitely prepared."

And there was Abe Klein, who has made several trips to Mansfield from his home in Massachusetts. He has a room dedicated to *The Shawshank Redemption*.

"I was in high school and actually kind of oblivious to it when it first came out," Klein said. "I think I was in my senior year when I first saw it at my parent's house. It had just come out on VHS, and I was standing by the door when it started. And I never sat down. I just kept watching it. I just loved it from the first. I was a fan. I liked the music. I liked the plot. I like the use of color. I loved the acting. And my father loved it, so it was something we shared."

During a visit, Klein's dad passed one of the many *Shawshank* posters in his son's house. "I'm going to go home and watch that movie," he told Abe.

"That was my last conversation with him," Klein said. "It was right before he passed. We always talked about how much we loved this movie. It was something we shared."

It has remained special to Klein. He has the posters of Rita Hayworth, Marilyn Monroe, and Raquel Welch. He has a replica of the postcard Andy sends to Red. He has three of the tins that Andy buried at the rock wall for Red to find. He has a couple bottles of the Stroh's Bohemian Beer. He has a replica of that red pickup truck that took Red to Buxton. And he has a rock hammer. Not just any rock hammer, by the way.

He has one of the rock hammers crafted by another *Shawshank* uber-fan, Brian McNeal, of Delaware, Ohio. What makes Brian's rock hammers so special is that they're fashioned from the wood of the fallen oak tree. McNeal, a woodcarver, is in partnership with the tree's owner. He produces everything from commemorative plaques, signs, and tables to keychains and, yes, rock hammers for fans who want to literally own a piece of the film (each item coming with a certificate of authenticity identifying it as part of The Shawshank Oak Tree Ltd. collection).

"I am blessed beyond my understanding to have such a unique role in designing and crafting items sent to almost 4,000 *Shawshank* fans around the world," McNeal said. "It's a humbling experience to be able to allow people to not only have a memorabilia item but also a symbol to hold on to."

Those items symbolize the great love fans have for all things *Shawshank*.

"Seeing the prison for the first time, and Brooksie's bench, I was like a kid, but every trip is special," Klein said. "A couple of years after my father passed, I proposed to my fiancée in Butler, Ohio, at the spot where Morgan Freeman gets out of the red pickup truck," Klein said. "We got engaged on the road to Buxton. My original plan was to propose at the tree. But I learned at the prison that the tree had completely fallen and was on private property. So the other spot felt right."

We've seen *Shawshank* superfans reach the pilgrimage trail from the north, south, and east. Emily Pugh traveled from the southwest: Texas, to be precise. She was eighteen when she first saw the film. That was in 2009, when she was determined to see all the movies on the American Film Institute's top-100 list.

"I actually didn't want to watch it, as it is a prison film and my dad always loved it," Pugh said. "I grew up with him quoting it. Immediately upon watching it I was raving. It became my favorite movie right away. Around this time I started collecting 'Hope' memorabilia. I'd say I have about fifty knick-knacks, clothes, plaques, notebooks, etc."

Two years later, she was visiting her sister in Kentucky. She looked up how close the Ohio State Reformatory was. Her search led her to the Facebook page for The Shawshank Trail. She hit the "like" button and started engaging with people of like minds. At this point, *The Shawshank Redemption* felt "like more than a movie" to Pugh.

"Then in 2013 I saw that they were holding the twentieth anniversary of the filming of the movie and I booked a flight," Pugh said. "At this point I was watching the film at least three times a year, not including TV showings! I went to Ohio for the next two years to celebrate the film. I can't tell you how amazing it was to be able to walk around and take pictures at all of the filming locations."

Tom Clark is a *Shawshank* fan who has become part of The Shawshank Trail. Originally from Mineola, New York, he was a former English and social studies teacher who segued into a career in pharmaceutical advertising (with occasional thoughts about stand-up comedy). Work brought him to Ohio in late 2015 and a house near Mansfield. Eventually, he was told over a meal that he was living where *The Shawshank Redemption* was filmed.

"I literally dropped my fork," Clark said. He showed up at an open audition for tour guides at the Ohio State Reformatory and started taking visitors through the structure in April 2018. Clark quickly established himself as one of the liveliest, most knowledgeable, most enthusiastic, and most engaging guides at OSR. He's the one who dresses as a convict and engages visitors with the gift of gab befitting, well, a stand-up comic.

"I came for *Shawshank*, but I stayed for the building," Clark said. "It feeds my soul being a guide here. I always ask people what they think this amazing building looks like. The number-one answer is a castle, but others are a church, a university building, Hogwarts. Nobody says it looks like a prison."

Even actors in other Stephen King movies are superfans of *The Shawshank Redemption*. When the movie was mentioned during an interview, Jerry O'Connell immediately exclaimed, "Best film ever made, *The Shawshank Redemption* . . . best . . . movie . . . ever!" I remind him that he played Vern in director Rob Reiner's *Stand by Me*, which many believe is in the discussion for finest adaptation of a King work. It's a great film,

Two old cons, Ohio State Reformatory guide Tom Clark and the author, visit Warden Norton's Shawshank State Prison, wondering if they have time to case the safe.
PHOTO BY BECKY DAWIDZIAK

O'Connell agrees, but he doesn't back off his praise for *The Shawshank Redemption.*

The actors in the movie who encounter the fans typically are impressed with the deep need to share their feelings for *The Shawshank Redemption.*

"It's not just, 'Hey, loved you in that' kind of thing," Tim Robbins said. "There's the need to impress on you why the film means so much to them, and what they tell you often is quite profound. It goes very deep."

The top-billed players don't get fans quoting famous lines at them, at least not all that much. But the actors with smaller roles do. It's a fan's way of showing how well they know the film and how true the devotion is.

"I've met fans, and when I tell them I'm the bank teller, they quote my lines, word for word, to me," Claire Slemmer said. "Now, I only have a few lines. That always amazes me."

Charlie Kearns, who also had a small role in the film, tells the story of being bedraggled in Mendoza, Argentina, having spent a frustrating day trying to fly to the Iguazu Falls Park. He finally got on a plane and had a mid-plane window seat, and a woman breast-feeding a baby sat down next to him. Her young husband had the aisle seat, holding the diaper bag. Kearns, who played the 1966 district attorney in *The Shawshank Redemption*, learned that the couple was taking the baby to see a grand-father for the first time in Buenos Aires. He learned that she was a singer before the baby. She pulled out a photo of her singing in a recording studio. He mentioned that he used to be in show business, particularly commercials. Then he added, oh, he also had been in one movie. He didn't know the Spanish name for it, but told her the English title.

"The husband loves that movie and before we are told to turn off our phones, he whips his out and Googles YouTube and proudly flashes my scenes," Kearns said. "Yes, the lord works in strange ways."

Scott Mann, who plays Linda Dufresne's lover, credits the fans with turning around his perspective on the film. When Jodie Snavely asked him about attending the 2013 reunion, he wasn't interested, at first.

"It didn't really matter much to me anymore," he said. "I wasn't going to go. I just didn't think my part in the film was that important. But both of my parents had passed away in 2012, and my wife said, 'You should go.' And it was actually the fans of the movie that made me look at it from a whole different angle. They taught me to appreciate it and my role in it. Now if they ask me to go to Mansfield for something, I'm there to answer questions and tell stories."

For Dan Smith, his vantage point as event and social media coordi-nator at the Ohio State Reformatory is an ideal one for interacting with fans and gleaning insight on its popularity and appeal.

"I get to ask them why this place and this film is so important to them," Smith said. "And so many say, 'I went through this terrible time, I was in this horrible place, and this movie spoke to me about hope and showed me the idea of redemption.' So, no matter what you're going through, you can find comfort and guidance and inspiration in that. You can relate to that. It's why people are still talking about this movie twenty-five years after it was made. And it's why people will still be talking about this movie fifty or sixty years from now. It is timeless."

THE ROAD TO ZIHUATANEJO

"TERRIBLE THING TO LIVE IN FEAR," RED TELLS US NEAR THE END OF *The Shawshank Redemption.* Terrible thing to be ruled by it, to be overwhelmed by it, to be engulfed by it. At a time when there seems to be so much fear loose in the world, Red's observation, spoken in such a quiet and solemn way, seems to reverberate more loudly and alarmingly than it did when first heard in theaters twenty-five years ago. For every generation, fear is a constant. It's always there, even at the best of times, lurking just out of view. It's an opportunistic little monster, this thing, eager to pounce and tear happiness to tear-soaked tatters. And yet, the recognition of this is not despair. It is the beginning of hope.

If *The Shawshank Redemption* does owe something to Mark Twain's *Adventures of Huckleberry Finn,* and it probably does, then perhaps it's appropriate to listen to Twain on this subject. "Courage is resistance to fear, mastery of fear—not absence of fear," he advised us. This is what makes Andy and Red heroic in *The Shawshank Redemption.* They recognize fear, and if at times threatened to be mastered by it, they persist and master it instead. This is a big part of the reason we cheer for them and are so happy that they find Zihuatanejo. A vision of Heaven? I don't think so, but maybe an escape from Hell. It's really just that place they've worked so hard to earn. They've persisted. They've endured. They've pushed back fear with the greater force of hope. And they've reached a bright, sunny place by dispelling the darkness. "Get busy living or get busy dying." The ultimate power of *The Shawshank Redemption* isn't so much that we want this for them but that we might dare to want it for ourselves. And then there is hope. Listening to the many people interviewed for this book, you hear again and again how they relate to Andy and Red because of something in their own lives. If they can vanquish fear and, no matter how much hard work and suffering is involved, keep hope alive, maybe redemption is a possibility, after all.

It's often categorized as an outlier among Stephen King's stories, but this is a monstrous lie told by people who think the absence of actual monsters makes it atypical. Keep in mind that this is the writer who famously declared, "Monsters are real, and ghosts are real too. They live inside us, and sometimes, they win." And sometimes, they don't. *The Shawshank Redemption* is all about not letting those monsters win.

King also once said, "You can, you should, and if you're brave enough to start, you will." He was talking about writing, but that advice might apply to any road that leads to a Zihuatanejo. We find much to admire

The stretch of Route 95 in Ohio that was used for the shot of the Trailways Bus taking Red to Fort Hancock, Texas

PHOTO COURTESY OF DESTINATION MANSFIELD—RICHLAND COUNTY

in Andy's persistence and patience in using that little rock hammer to carve out an escape tunnel. All it takes is pressure and time. Oh, how King must have enjoyed putting those words into the story. Yet the most admirable thing about Andy is his finding the courage to start. Then he can. Then he will. And then maybe we will.

There is immense satisfaction in watching Andy outwit the forces arrayed against him and then seeing Red profit from Andy's insistence that hope is a good thing, maybe the best of things. But this is a challenge to individuals, nations, and the planet.

For much of the movie, an argument can be made that Andy would be foolish to believe so. Red seems the more practical of the two when he says that hope is a dangerous thing that has no place in prison. Andy not only proves Red wrong, Red proves Red wrong by opting for hope.

Red finally knows he's free when he's brave enough to start and to say yes to hope. Red is feeling the excitement "only a free man can feel, a free man at the start of a long journey whose conclusion is uncertain." Precisely. There's no certainty. But if he's brave enough to start his long journey, then he should and he will.

"I hope I can make it across the border. I hope to see my friend and shake his hand. I hope the Pacific is as blue as it has been in my dreams. I *hope*."

This is where Stephen King ended his novella. They are the last lines we hear in Frank Darabont's screen version. I hope this ending is our start. Then this story truly becomes *Our Shawshank Redemption*. I hope we—all of us—are brave enough to want that. I hope.

APPENDIX 1

The following close encounter of the King kind occurred in January 1994. It is a snapshot of the writer as he stood about four months after shooting had wrapped on The Shawshank Redemption *and about eight months before the release of director Frank Darabont's film version of his story. It is a profile of Stephen King at forty-six, when no one yet knew what kind of film had been made from his novella* Rita Hayworth and Shawshank Redemption, *but we were soon to find out. Not an inconsiderable amount of discussion centered on adaptations of his works up to that point . . . the good, the bad, and the extremely ugly.*

Stephen King takes his stand in what is now the quietest corner of a noisy hotel ballroom packed with journalists, network executives, and the stars of ABC's eight-hour miniseries version of his novel *The Stand.* But the reigning King of Horror is not dwelling on such mundane matters as an apocalyptic plague or the survival of the human race. No, standing in a buffet line, King is using these few relatively calm moments to consider the impressive selection of pasta dishes spread before him. Surrounded by opulence and clamorousness, the horror master makes his choices and turns to the fellow with a tape recorder ready for action.

"Sorry about the rush, man," King says as a white-aproned hotel employee spoons out portions onto his plate. "It's just been that kind of day. Let's walk and talk, okay?"

We don't get very far, however, before Ossie Davis drops by to say hello. King greets the venerable actor warmly and chats with him for a few minutes. "Sorry," he explains, returning his attention to the tape recorder, "but this is the first chance many of us have had to see each other since the filming. You understand. It's sort of like a class reunion. Now, you wanted to talk about?"

Plenty. But let's start with horror writing. Does he mind analyzing the process? Or is he uncomfortable with press conferences and interviews and buffet lines stocked with tape recorders?

"Well, to tell you the truth, I don't really know how to do this," the master of the macabre says. "I mean, sure, I talk about it all the time, but nobody can adequately talk about what goes on in his head when he's making up stories. It's like cotton candy. It all melts away in your mouth. You think you've got the words to describe it, and they melt away in your mouth. All I can do in interviews is run my mouth and hope it comes out somewhat coherent. Being interviewed is tiring and sort of stressful, but not because of the interviewers. The people involved are always pretty nice. You can't control what they write. You can't control if they'll like something you've done. You can't make them like something. If they like it, they like it. If they don't, they don't. That's fine, either way. And either way, like I said, they're usually pretty nice. What's stressful to me is trying to put into words what can't be adequately described with words."

If there is another point, he doesn't get the chance to make it. Director Mick Garris (*Critters 2, Psycho IV*) wants a few words with him. King excuses himself for another minute or two. "I'll schmooze a little bit," the six-foot-four writer confides with a wide conspiratorial smile. "It's a wonderful chance to see Mick and Gary Sinise and Kareem [Abdul-Jabbar] again." This will be the pattern of the interview—five minutes of talk, a couple of minutes of schmooze. It works well because of King's down-to-earth demeanor and straightforward manner. No pretentious author poses or obscure academic palaver for this literary landlord with the skeleton key to such grisly properties as the Overlook Hotel, the Dark Tower, 'Salem's Lot, a Pet Sematary, and the entire town of Castle Rock. Indeed, dressed in black jeans and striped dress shirt over a black T-shirt, King seems out of place in the posh Ritz-Carlton Huntington Hotel, a hilltop slice of Pasadena elegance recalling long-gone decades ("Didn't I write a book about this hotel?" King jokes). You get the idea that the author prefers a small-town diner to these plush and proper surroundings.

Stephen King in 1994, the year *The Stand* aired on ABC and *The Shawshank Redemption* was released in theaters

The striped shirt is not tucked in or buttoned. It's open and the sleeves are rolled up, comfortably and casually. He is dressed for comfort, right down to the white socks and black sneakers that carry him from Garris to Sinise and back to the waiting tape recorder. King also is wearing his winter beard, which is showing hints of gray now that its owner is forty-six. A decade ago, when the beard was all black, King told a *Playboy* interviewer that creating horror stories was an ongoing psychoanalyzing that allowed him to, in the words of poet Anne Sexton, "write himself sane." Like Robert Bloch, the author of *Psycho* and other landmark terror tales, he believes that the horror writer continually exorcises the demons by putting them on paper. "That certainly is still my viewpoint," he says. "It's the way it works for me. It keeps me centered. You get rid of all the infection and insanity. Some people say horror writers are nice because of some kind of defense mechanism. You've heard that, right?"

Sure, as a matter of fact, from Robert Bloch.

"Well, I think, to a degree, it is a defense mechanism," King explains. "I'd agree with that. This defense mechanism kicks in because we know what we're doing is not normal. I mean, just writing is not normal, and writing the stuff we are writing, you get even more defense mechanisms kicking in. Besides, you have to have the defense mechanisms, man, because you can't really talk about it. You try, when people ask you questions, but, whatever I do, I can't really describe it. How can I? I mean, the guy standing in front of you right now is not the guy who writes those stories. He steps out for coffee when I step out from behind the typewriter. That guy is now on vacation. I'm not even sure he's checked into the hotel with me. I don't know. I don't know where it comes from. Everything seems normal and then I sit down at the typewriter or the word processor and Charlie Starkweather comes out. I don't know. I can't explain it at all. I just think up stories that I like to tell and I try to think up ways to get readers to be really upset and lock their doors and worry and not be able to go to sleep. I like that. That gives me a feeling of power, because I'm twisted and strange."

But is it possible to write yourself completely normal? Will there come a time when the stories just stop?

"I don't know if that will ever happen," King had told a group of television critics at a press conference earlier that day. "For all I know, I've told the best stories that I have to tell. I hope that's not true. So I guess you could say, in a way, that it's hope that keeps me going. I never wrote for money. People who write for money are not successes anyway. I wrote from love and to get rid of whatever it was that kept me awake at night and give it to somebody else. I've been successful at that. But that has almost been a side effect, if you will. I can't foresee a time when I would stop. But, sooner or later, God just tells you, 'You're out of the game, hang up your jock, that's it, you're through.'"

If the guy behind the word processor mystifies King, he seldom scares him.

"Sometimes I scare myself when I'm writing," King admitted to critics assembled to discuss *The Stand*. "Sometimes I've seen things on TV that have been made from my work that scares me. There's a sequence in the miniseries [version of the 1986 novel] *It*, where a light comes through this pipe that's got a lot of holes in it. That really gave me the creeps. There's a scene that scared me to write that's set in the tunnel in *The Stand* when these people get out of New York, and when I saw it on film, it scared me. And there's a sequence, too, in *The Stand* where Stu Redman [Sinise] is trying to escape from this facility that's really full of dead people. It's become a graveyard. And, for me, that's scary. And some of the dream sequences are scary. When I read the stuff over, I don't think I scare myself. What I'm trying to judge then is whether or not it will scare anybody else. And if I think it will, I get this kind of little maniacal grin that's trying to surface on my face now because, underneath, of course, I'm quite insane."

At the ABC press conference for *The Stand*, a reporter asked King if he could describe the most frightening moment of his life. He responded without hesitation.

"The most frightening moment of my life? I could, but I'm not gonna."

There must be some secrets in this very public life.

Born Stephen Edwin King on September 21, 1947, in Portland, Maine, the future horror king arrived on the scene as the second son of Donald and Nellie Ruth King. Donald King deserted the family in 1949, and was not heard from again. The raising and supporting of two sons fell exclusively to Nellie, whom King remembered as "a wonderful" and "very brave lady." Moving her boys from Fort Wayne, Indiana, to Stratford, Connecticut, back to Maine, she worked at one low-paying job after another—housekeeper, laundry presser, doughnut maker, anything to keep the family going.

Robert Bloch says that a Universal horror picture, Lon Chaney's *The Phantom of the Opera* (1925), was a turning point in his young life. The first film King can recall seeing is a Universal horror film, *The Creature from the Black Lagoon* (1954). By the early '60s, King was submitting short stories to magazines. The first to be accepted, "I Was a Teenage Grave Robber," was published by a comic book fan magazine in 1965. He was still attending high school in Lisbon Falls, Maine. But he also was collecting enough rejection slips to wallpaper a dungeon. One of his stories was rejected by Forrest J Ackerman, editor of *Famous Monsters of Filmland* magazine. "He showed me the piece a few years ago," King recalls. "I was plenty used to rejection at that stage of my life. When I saw it again, it was like a distant voice from the past."

Ackerman laughs about letting the young King slip through his clutches: "Can you believe it? I rejected Stephen King. So what do I know? He sent me a story when he was fourteen years old. I should have got him when he was cheap. He gets a $10 million advance now before he writes word number one."

Still, Ackerman wasn't the only editor rejecting King stories. Although King had completed three novels by 1971, the year he married Tabitha Jane Spruce, his future as a writer looked far from promising. In 1973, King was teaching English at Hampden Academy in Maine. They were living in a trailer and driving a wheezy 1965 Buick. At the end of the work day, King would squeeze himself into the trailer's furnace room, a portable Olivetti typewriter balanced on his knees.

The story has taken on the proportions of a literary legend. Tabitha King rescued the manuscript of *Carrie* from a wastepaper basket. Submitted to Doubleday in 1973, the novel was published the following year. The money from the sale of the paperback rights to the New American

Library allowed King to quit teaching and devote himself entirely to writing. In 1975, King's second novel, *'Salem's Lot*, appeared. In 1976, director Brian De Palma's film version of *Carrie*, with Sissy Spacek in the title role, hit the screens. In 1977, his third novel, *The Shining*, became his first hardback bestseller. It was followed by *The Stand* and *Night Shift*, his first collection of short stories, in 1978. He closed the remarkable rags-to-riches decade with another novel, *The Dead Zone* (1979), which again demonstrated King's ability to charge up the bestseller list.

Stephen King, raised on a diet of EC Comics' *Tales from the Crypt* and '50s science-fiction thrillers, had become a household name in less than seven years. Stephen King, with his thorough understanding of such horror royalty as Richard Matheson and Shirley Jackson, was hitting a pop-culture nerve with astounding accuracy. Stephen King, with that driving need to write himself sane, had established himself as a franchise author with a regular home on the bestseller lists—common enough for mystery and spy novelists, yet an almost-impossible feat for a horror writer until King and Anne Rice emerged in the 1970s.

It would be unfair and wildly inaccurate to say that King singlehandedly started the horror boom of the late '70s. After all, Bloch, Matheson, and Ray Bradbury—that triumvirate of terror from the 1950s—hardly had been dormant in the '60s and '70s. And the stage had been set on the bestseller lists by the success of such horror novels as Ira Levin's *Rosemary's Baby*, William Peter Blatty's *The Exorcist*, and Tom Tryon's *Harvest Home*. King, however, proved that horror could reach the mass audience, not as an occasional sensation, but again and again and again. If the stage had been set for King by the likes of Bloch, Matheson, Jackson, Charles Beaumont, Harlan Ellison, and Blatty, then King set the stage for Anne Rice, Clive Barker, and Robert McCammon.

The Stand went into production as a miniseries twenty years after the publication of *Carrie*. During those two decades, the incredibly prolific King had seen thirty-three books in print and seven original screenplays made into films.* It was a dizzying output that has, in many ways, defied and befuddled critics trying to determine his place in the literary or pop-culture landscapes. The books included *The Talisman* (his 1984

---

* King's 2019 book tally stands at more than eighty-five.

collaboration with fellow horror master Peter Straub), *Danse Macabre* (his 1981 nonfiction study of the horror genre), three entries in the *Dark Tower* series, two volumes of novellas (*Different Seasons* and *Four Past Midnight*), five novels written under his Richard Bachman pseudonym (*Thinner, Rage, The Long Walk, Roadwork,* and *The Running Man*), collections of short stories (*Night Shift* and *Skeleton Crew*), and such novels as *Firestarter* (1980), *Cujo* (1981), *Christine* (1983), *Pet Sematary* (1983), *It* (1986), *Misery* (1987), *The Tommyknockers* (1987), *The Dark Half* (1989), *Needful Things* (1991), *Gerald's Game* (1992), and *Dolores Claiborne* (1993). Those who argue that King has been too prolific (writing too fast, publishing too often) should reverse the timeframe. Consider that, by the age of thirty, King had written two of the horror genre's finest novels, *'Salem's Lot* and *The Shining*. No matter what else he has written (or will write), these two books, at the very least, will forever be mentioned by horror fans in the same league with Bram Stoker's *Dracula*, Jackson's *The Haunting of Hill House*, Matheson's *I Am Legend*, and Bradbury's *Something Wicked This Way Comes*.

Hollywood, of course, was quick to latch on to King's creepy stories. By the time *The Stand* appears, there will have been twenty-three films made from King concepts.* Just two of these movies, both directed by Rob Reiner, truly stand out from the mediocre mess: *Stand by Me* (1986, based on the *Different Seasons* novella, *The Body*) and *Misery* (1990), which won Kathy Bates an Oscar. The rest range from superior supernatural fare (*The Dead Zone, Carrie, Creepshow*) to fairly horrible (*Children of the Corn, Maximum Overdrive, Needful Things*). King has developed a philosophical attitude toward the Tinseltown mangling of his books.

"In the course of selling things that I've written to various people, I mean, some of the things have turned out to be real coleslaw," he said. "You know? *Graveyard Shift* is not going to stand in film history. Neither is *Children of the Corn*. But on the other hand, when Rob Reiner wanted to do *Stand by Me*, he had no money and I was advised against doing the deal, because it was a real question about whether he could ever finish production. I'm not trying to pat myself on the back. My view is just,

---

* By 2019, there were more than one hundred film and TV adaptations of King's work, with many more in development.

here it is, here's this story. Somebody wants to make it into a movie. I love movies."

Even when King is involved in a film as a writer or producer, he believes in letting the director and actors have enormous leeway.

"If you try to control it completely, you go nuts," he says. "You go mad. You have to start with the idea that things are going to change if you let it out of your own backyard, same way your kids are going to change when you send them off to school. They meet other kids, and the kid you sent off to school isn't the same when it comes back. If I wasn't willing to subscribe to that philosophy that James Cain subscribed to—that is, that the book is always the book—I'd go nuts. My view is that books are long-distance runners, and they're there long after the films are forgotten. I did not care for the Arnold Schwarzenegger film that was made out of *The Running Man*—not very much at all. It's not very much like the book and I like that book a lot. I relate it to a period of my life that I enjoyed and I remember the writing of it with great affection. So I didn't like the movie, but I kept my mouth shut and now the movie is gone. It shows up once in a while on cable TV. But, otherwise, the book rules. It's in the bookstores. It's in print. And a lot more people are ultimately going to be familiar with the book than they are with the movie, because movies don't have the staying power that books have."

There also have been King episodes of such anthology series as the CBS revival of *The Twilight Zone* and the syndicated *Tales from the Darkside*, a TV movie (*Sometimes They Come Back*), a 1991 CBS series (*Stephen King's Golden Years*) and four miniseries: *'Salem's Lot* (1979), *It* (1990), *The Tommyknockers* (1993), and *The Stand*, scheduled for May. *Golden Years*, which is available on home video, was canceled before King had the chance to complete the story of an elderly custodian contaminated when an experiment goes wrong at a top-secret government laboratory.

Despite the number of King Kong–size King disappointments on the big screen and TV, there always seem to be more adaptations on the Hollywood horizon. Count on it. There are, in various stages of development, at least three TV movies (*The Langoliers*, *The Night Flier*, and an animated *Creepshow 3*) and three features (*Dolores Claiborne* with Kathy Bates, *Thinner*, and, later in 1994, director Frank Darabont's *The Shaw-*

shank Redemption, a film version of another *Different Seasons* novella, "Rita Hayworth and Shawshank Redemption," starring Tim Robbins and Morgan Freeman).

"What I do is split everything that I sell to film into two groups," King says. "In one group are the things where I say to the book, the way that you would to a kid you were sending off to summer camp, 'Enjoy yourself, have a good time. I hope you don't get banged up too bad, that you don't get homesick, that you don't come home with poison ivy. See you later. Bye-bye.' The other is the group where you get involved."

The writer has a cameo in the miniseries, just as he did in three other projects produced by one or both members of his *Stand* partners, Richard Rubinstein and Mitchell Galin—as a minister in *Pet Sematary*, a cemetery caretaker in *Sleepwalkers*, and a bus driver in *Golden Years*. He also starred in one of the five *Creepshow* sequences as bovine bumpkin Jordy Verrill

"But I wanted to trade up, you know?" King says of his role as Teddy Weizak in *The Stand*. "I've gotten typecast in my parts. I get to play sort of the country idiot, somebody whose IQ and pants size are pretty much interchangeable. And I told Mick I would play the part if I could step up to an IQ of possibly as high as 65, and he said, 'Sure, if you can really emote that high.'"

King and his wife still live in the twenty-three-room Victorian house they bought in 1980. Bangor, Maine, is home.* They are the parents of three children. The two oldest, Naomi Rachel and Joseph Hillstrom, are in their early twenties. The youngest, Owen Philip, is a teenager.

And King still writes on the word processor he has used since the '70s.

"I'm not very computer-savvy," he admits. "It's a very old word processor. It's a Wang word processor. And sometimes people will call up and my wife will say, 'Steve can't talk to you now, he's pounding his Wang.' She gets a kick out of that because she's as twisted as I am, essentially. And I'm proud that I played a part in that. Anyway, I have this mastodon

---

* Twenty-five years after this interview, the Kings divide their time between their Maine house and a Florida winter home; and both of their sons have become successful writers, Joseph using Joe Hill as his pen name.

of a word processor. On a trip like this, I use a pen. I have a ledger book and I write long hand. A lot of *The Stand* is actually in a ledger book that I have with mc on this trip."

For relaxation and kicks, King plays guitar in what might be described as the ultimate garage band.

"It is the ultimate garage band, that's right," he says. "It's a band called the Rock Bottom Remainders, and it's Amy Tan and Dave Barry, and you can tell that associating with Dave Barry a lot, some of his smart-ass has rubbed off on me. It's a whole bunch of writers and we're sort of maintenance level instrumentally and vocally."

Yet his principal method of remaining sane continues to be writing.

"I didn't decide to be a writer," he says. "I didn't have any choice. It's the only thing I can do. I can barely change my own guitar strings . . . It's therapy, but you know what else it is? It's a gas. It's a real stone gas. It's a blast. It's great. Don't you feel that way? You write. Don't you feel that way? Don't you have fun when you're doing it? It's the best reason to write. It's a complete blast."

APPENDIX II

Frank Darabont: Adapting King and Remembering *Shawshank*

A few directors—very few—have the magical movie touch when it comes to translating Stephen King stories to the screen. Why has Frank Darabont succeeded in such spectacular fashion where so many other filmmakers have flopped? Maybe it's because the director of *The Shawshank Redemption* was a writer first.

"I think that's very fair to say," Darabont agreed. "It always surprises me how many directors don't really view a script the way a writer does. So I think being a writer first certainly makes a big difference, especially when you're adapting another writer's story."

Still, there's something about King's approach to storytelling that resonates deeply with Darabont, whose other film adaptations of the author's works include *The Green Mile* and *The Mist*.

"To me, it's always character first," he said. "With Steve, it's always been character first, and all the groovy stuff trails in the wake of that, and that's certainly true with 'Rita Hayworth and Shawshank Redemption.' We also had many of the same influences, Richard Matheson being a profound one. So I connected on a very deep gut, heart, and brain level with Steve's work. Directors can go wrong when they focus too much on plot. Now, plot is an important mechanical function of what we do. But if it's just plot, you've got a transmission for a car, but it won't go anywhere because you've forgotten the rest of the car."

Darabont remembers the 1993 filming of *The Shawshank Redemption* as "a dream gig," but he also recalls the pressure of making his first feature film and the intensity of a three-month shoot on location.

"It was a tiger by the tail, no doubt," he said. "There was so much pressure to get this wonderful story right, and, well, self-doubt is the rational response of any rational mind. So there was many a night when I thought, 'Am I screwing this up?' On top of that, we were doing six-day weeks. My weekend was Sunday. I'd wake up late in the day, just in time to do my week's worth of laundry, maybe watch my tape of *Goodfellas*, then go back to sleep, then go back to the set. There was no time or energy to do anything else. It was a forced march."

Was it fun?

"No. Oh, no. No, no," Darabont said. "I didn't really start to enjoy directing until I did an episode of *The Shield* for [writer–executive producer] Shawn Ryan. And they shot fast. That was very liberating. That's about when I started enjoying directing. I really started loving directing with the first episode of *The Walking Dead*. That's when I felt like I had all of the tools in my toolbox. But in terms of the people I was working with, *Shawshank* was a wonderful experience."

That started with Rob Reiner and the people at Castle Rock.

"I knew I was in a fortunate position as a filmmaker, especially one just starting out, to be supported so completely by everybody at Castle Rock," Darabont said. "I wish I'd known how fortunate I was. I learned that they were the wonderful exception in a town filled with greedy, malevolent people. When you encounter that typical lack of integrity and humanity and decency, all you can do is think back to when you encountered the most decent and most human people, and thank God that they were there and supported my vision and let me make the movie I wanted to make."

Darabont, therefore, is happy that the record is being set straight on a Hollywood myth about Reiner's involvement as a Castle Rock founder and executive: "Sometimes a story gets recounted and hardens into legend. The story gets told that I got all of this pressure from Rob Reiner to let him direct it. You hear they pushed this check in front of me and I tore it up and threw it in his face. None of that happened. Yes, Rob wanted to direct it. But when I thought about it and said I wanted to direct and not sell off my dream, Rob took no as graciously for an answer as anyone I've ever seen. From that moment on, Rob was such an incredibly generous supporter and booster. He is a paragon of integrity, kindness, and decency, which is not easy to find in Hollywood."

Twenty-five years after the release of *The Shawshank Redemption*, that memory is just one of many things that bring a smile to Darabont's face.

"Some others?" he said. "That there is this Shawshank Trail that brings people to Mansfield to connect with what we did. That the movie saved the Ohio State Reformatory. That we did right by Stephen King's story, and not just because we say so but because he says so. That the movie we made matters so profoundly to so many people. It's pretty amazing. Words do fail at some point, but the smiles never stop."

APPENDIX III

Cast and Credits for *The Shawshank Redemption*

Running time: 142 minutes
Production company: Castle Rock Entertainment
Distributed by Columbia Pictures
Release date: September 23, 1994 (United States); September 10, 1994 (Toronto)

Cast

Andy Dufresne	Tim Robbins
Ellis Boyd "Red" Redding	Morgan Freeman
Warden Samuel Norton	Bob Gunton
Heywood	William Sadler
Captain Byron Hadley	Clancy Brown
Tommy Williams	Gil Bellows
Bogs Diamond	Mark Rolston
Brooks Hatlen	James Whitmore
1946 District Attorney	Jeffrey DeMunn
Skeet	Larry Brandenburg
Jigger	Neil Giuntoli
Floyd	Brian Libby
Snooze	David Proval
Ernie	Joseph Ragno
Guard Mert	Jude Ciccolella
Guard Trout	Paul McCrane
Linda Dufresne, Andy's wife	Renee Blaine
Glenn Quentin	Scott Mann
1946 Judge	John Horton
1947 Parole Board Hearing Man	Gordon C. Greene

Fresh Fish Con ....Alfonso Freeman

Hungry Fish Con...V. J. Foster

New Fish Guard ....John E. Summers

Fat Ass .... Frank Medrano

Tyrell...Mack Miles

Laundry Bob... Alan R. Kessler

Laundry Truck Driver... Morgan Lund

Laundry Leonard ....Cornell Wallace

Rooster..Gary Lee Davis

Pete .... Neil Summers

Guard Youngblood.. Ned Bellamy

Projectionist ....Joseph Pecoraro

Hole Guard.. Harold E. Cope Jr.

Guard Dekins ....Brian Delate

Guard Wiley ....Don R. McManus

Moresby Batter .... Donald E. Zinn

1954 Landlady ....Dorothy Silver

1954 Food-Way Manager ....Robert Haley

1954 Food-Way Woman.. Dana Snyder

1957 Parole Board Hearing Man..............................John D. Craig

Ned Grimes ....Ken Magee

Mail Caller...Eugene C. De Pasquale

Elmo Blatch ....Bill Bolender

Elderly Hole Guard .... Ron Newell

Bullhorn Tower Guard...John R. Woodard

Man Missing Guard ....Chuck Brauchler

Head Bull Haig.. Dion Anderson

Bank Teller...Claire Slemmer

Bank Manager..James Kisicki

Bugle Editor ....Rohn Thomas

1966 District Attorney..Charlie Kearns

Duty Guard ....Rob Reider

1967 Parole Board Hearing Man...............................Brian Brophy

1967 Food-Way Manager ....Paul Kennedy

PRODUCTION CREDITS

Directed by..Frank Darabont

Produced by.. Niki Marvin

Screenplay by ....Frank Darabont

Based on the short novel "Rita Hayworth and Shawshank
    Redemption" by .... Stephen King

Executive Producers .... Liz Glotzer
                                  David Lester

Director of Photography.............................. Roger Deakins B.S.C.

Edited by.. Richard Francis-Bruce

Production Designer .... Terence Marsh

Costume Design by...Elizabeth McBride

Music by... Thomas Newman

Casting by ....Deborah Aquila C.S.A.

Unit Production Manager.. David Lester

First Assistant Director..................................... John R. Woodward

Key Second Assistant Director .... Thomas Schellenberg

Art Director ....Peter Smith

Set Decorator.. Michael Sierton

Production Supervisors ....Kokayi Ampah
                              Sue Bea Montgomery

Script Supervisors .... Sioux Richards
                                    James Ellis

First Camera Assistants ....Eric Swanek
                                 Robin Brown

Second Camera Assistants... Andy Harris
                               Bill Nielsen Jr.
                             Bobby Mancuso

Steadicam Operator ....Gerrit Dangremond

Production Sound Mixer..Willie Burton

Boom Operator...MarvinLewis

Cable Person .... Kevin Boyd

Location Manager..Kokayi Ampah

2nd 2nd Assistant Director............................ Michael Greenwood

First Assistant Editor...Patty Galvin

Second Assistant Editor.. Robert Lusted
Apprentice Editor ....Jeff Canavan
Editorial Assistant... David Johnson
Casting Associate...Jane Shannon
Production Office Coordinator .... Beth Hickman
Assistant Office Coordinator ....Margaret Orlando
Office Assistant...Anne Hilbert
Office Intern .... Amie Tschappat
Property Master ....Tom Shaw
Gaffer.. Bill O'Leary
Key Grip ....Don Cerrone
Key Makeup Artist .... Kevin Haney
Makeup Artists ....Monty Westmore
                                                                            Jeni Lee Dinkel
Key Hairstylist .... Phillip Levy
Hairstylists .... Roy Bryson
                                                                            Pamela Priest
Senior Set Designer .... Antoinette Gordon
Set Designer...Joe Hodges
Storyboard Consultant.. Peter Von Sholly
Special Effects...Bob Williams
Animal Trainer.. Scott Hart
Additional Animal Wrangler .... Therese Amadio
Assistant to Frank Darabont................................. Robert Barnett
Assistant to Niki Marvin ....Sophia Xixis
Wardrobe Supervisor...Taneia Lednicky
Key Costumers.. Mira Zavidowsky
                                                                            Kris Kearney
Costumers .... Eva Prappas
                                                                            Donnie McFinely
Seamstress ....Carol Buckler
Wardrobe Assistant.. Cookie Beard
Construction Coordinator.......................................Sebastian Milito
Transportation Coordinator .... David Marder
Transportation Captain.. Fred Culbertson

Stunt Coordinator...Jerry Gatlin
Construction Foreman .... Dixwell Stillman
Production Accountant .... Ramon Waggoner
Assistant Production Accountant................................Jane Estocin
Accounting Assistants..Kelley Baker
                  Michael Vasquez
                  Karin Mercurio
Set Estimator .... Susan Fraley
Assistant Art Director..Jack Evans
Decorating Consultant...Bobby Baker
Art Department Assistant...Rhonda Yeater
Still Photographer..Michael Weinstein
Unit Publicist..Erine Malik
Publicity .... Nancy Seltzter & Associates, Inc.
Video Assist Operator ....Van Scarboro
Video Assistant..Judy Scarboro
Ohio Casting .... D. Lynn Meyer
Background Casting..Ivy Weiss
Casting Assistant ....Julie Weiss
Background Casting Assistant .... Brent Scarpo
Background Casting Intern..Adam Moyer
Lead Person .... Alba Leone
On Set Dresser... Lee Baird
Set Dressers...Christopher Neely
                John M. Heuberger
                  Jack Hering
Propman... Carey Harris
Best Boy Electric..Jeremy Knaster
Rigging Gaffer .... Richie Ford
Rigging Best Boy ....Tony Corapi
Lamp Operators...Bill Moore
               William Kingsley
                Ruben Turner
                Quincy Koenig

Electric Riggers	Joseph Short
	James Gribbins
Best Boy Grip	Keith Bunting
Rigging Grip	Charley Quinlivin
Second Rigging Grip	John Archibald
Dolly Grip	Bruce Hamme
Grips	Eugene DePasquale III
	Kenneth McCahan
	Russell Milner
	Brian Buzzelli
	Thomas Guidugli
	James Harrington
Rigging Grips	Rex Buckingham
	Jorgen Christensen
Film Loader	Hope Nielsen
First Aid	Frank McKeon
Stunt Players	Tom Morga
	Ben Scott
	Dan Barringer
	Mickey Guinn
	Dick Hancock
	Allen Michael Lerner
	Fred Culbertson
Lighting Stand-Ins	James Burke
	Dexter Hammett
	Max Gerber
	David Gilby
	Tim Amstutz
	Bill Martin
	Jon Stinehour
Drivers	Chick Elwell
	Ray Greene
	Mickey Guinn
	Chuck Ramsey
	David Turner

Chip Vincent
William Culbertson
Douglas Miller
Ken Nevin Jr.
Scott Ruetenik
Harold Garnsey
Dick Furr
David Smith
Ronald Hogle
Judith Reed
Glen Murphy
James Graham
Tom Park
J. D. Thomas
Robert Conrad
William Davis
Sally Givens
Neil Knoff
Roland Maurer
Gary Mishey
Donald Snyder

Propmaker Foreman..Earl Betts
Propshop Foremen ....Isadora Raponi
Jim Henry
Propmaker Gang Bosses ....Scott Mizgaites
Chad Goodrich
Key Carpenter..Paul Wells
Plasterer ....Glen Blanton
Labor Foreman ....Barrett Fleetwood
Labor Gang Boss ....John Barbera
Paint Foreman..Peter J. Allen
Paint Gang Bosses ....Robert Hawthorne
James Hawthorne
Standby Painter...Todd Hatfield

Painters	Blair Gibeau
	Kelley Collopy
Helicopter Pilot	Robert "Bobby Z" Zajonc
Gyroscope Operator	Mike Kelem
Gyroscope Assistants	Ed Gutentag
	Richard Burton
Location Assistants	Scott Stahler
	Chris Cozzi
Set Producton Assistants	David McQuade
	Jesse Johnson
Assistant to Tim Robbins	Tom Cotter
Assistant to Morgan Freeman	Alfonso Freeman
Craft Services	Mark Moelter
	Don Speakman
	Brian Boggs
Caterer	Joe Schultz
	Carlos Garcia
	Jose Lopez
Post Production Sound	Bald Eagle Sound, Inc.
Supervising Sound Editor	John M. Stacy
Re-Recording Mixers	Robert J. Litt
	Elliott Tyson
	Michael Herbick
Mixing Recordists	Jack Keller
	David Behle
Sound Editors	Bill Manger
	Jeff Clark
	Zack Davis
	Dale Johnston
	Larry Lester
	Bruce Bell
	Richard Oswald
ADR Supervisor	Petra Bach
ADR Editors	Robert Ulrich
	Shelley Rae Hinton

Assistant Sound Editors ....Lori Martino
Bill Weinman
Janelle Showalter
Foley Artists.. Kevin Bartnof
Ellen Heuer
Foley Mixer ....Marilyn Graf
ADR Voice Casting .... Barbara Harris
ADR Mixer...Tom O'Connell
Additonal ADR Mixers ....Paul Zydel
Doc Kane
Foley Recordist .... Ron Grafton
ADR Recordist .... Rick Canelli
Additional ADR Recordists................................. Michael Cerone
Mike Boudry
Music Editor... Bill Bernstein
Assistant Music Editor ....James C. Makiej
Music Orchestrator... Thomas Pasatieri
Music Scoring Mixer .... Dennis Sands
Music Contractor...Leslie Morris
Music Preparation..Julian Bratolyubov
Music Consultant...............................Arlene Fishbach Enterprises
Titles and Opticals...Pacific Title
Color Timer.. David Orr
Negative Cutter..D. Bassett & Associates
Digital Special Effects .... Motion Pixel Corporation

ACKNOWLEDGMENTS

THIS BOOK HAD FRIENDS. LOTS AND LOTS OF FRIENDS. ONE OF THE early champions of this *Shawshank* celebration was Gere Goble, the editor at the *Mansfield News Journal*. We met at a book fair in Cincinnati, Ohio, in October 2017, when the idea of doing something on *The Shawshank Redemption* was restricted to a lengthy chapter in a bigger book about Stephen King. She was incredibly enthusiastic and encouraging. The next time we met was at a book fair in Columbus, Ohio, in April of 2018, and, by then, the idea had shifted to a book-length study for the twenty-fifth anniversary of the film largely shot in Mansfield. Gere was even more enthusiastic and encouraging than she had been six months earlier. She put me in touch with *Mansfield News Journal* reporter Lou Whitmire, who covered the making of the film for the paper and ended up being in it as an extra. Lou, in turn, put us in touch with many of the key people we needed to meet to flesh out the *Shawshank* story. We appreciate their guidance and generosity.

And by "we" I mean me and my daughter, Becky, a gifted writer and photographer who accompanied me on research trips to Mansfield, Upper Sandusky, and other locations, taking many of the pictures for this book. I am grateful not only for the wide selection of wonderful photographs, but for her company, her ideas, and the smiles we shared along the way.

When Becky and I made our first trip to Mansfield, our first stop was the *Mansfield News Journal* building, where Gere and Lou continued to bowl us over with their graciousness and kindness. They offered us a desk to use when we were in Mansfield. They shared their memories and insights on all things *Shawshank*. And they handed us the newspaper's files on both the Ohio State Reformatory and *The Shawshank Redemption*, an invaluable record.

The A-Team in Mansfield and Upper Sandusky also included: Lee Tasseff, president of Destination Mansfield, who was instrumental in getting the film to set up headquarters in the city; Jodie Snavely, the group tour and media director at Destination Mansfield (and the creator of the Shawshank Trail tour); Dan Smith, event and social media coordinator at the Ohio State Reformatory, who arranged unlimited access to the historic prison and its grounds; Bill and April Mullen, who own and operate the *Shawshank* museum in the Upper Sandusky woodshop used as a location in the film (and who shared pictures from their collection with us); Bob Wachtman, a regular presence at the woodshop and an extra in the film; Ron Metzger, the Wyandot County commissioner who permitted us to roam through the Wyandot County Courthouse, where the trial scenes were shot; and Ben and Amber Bissman, who were our genial hosts in their family building used as the Brewer Hotel in the film. Lee and Jodie, the dynamic Destination Mansfield duo, also offered splendid suggestions for interviews and offered use of their meeting room (and sent some pictures to be used in the book). Before long, Becky and I were walking around Mansfield and people would be approaching us to say, "You're the folks writing the book about *Shawshank*." It didn't take long to feel at home.

Something quite beyond thanks is owed Eve Lapolla, who, in 1993, was the manager of the Ohio Film Commission. In that capacity, she kept me informed at all phases of the filming (I was a film critic at the time) and set up several interviews for me, including an on-set chat with Morgan Freeman. This book was a terrific excuse to catch up with Eve, who shared not only memories but several pictures relating to *Shawshank*.

Also providing lively recollections and delightful pictures were Renee Blaine, who played Linda Dufresne in the film, and four area residents chosen as extras in *Shawshank*: reporter Jane Imbody, who like Lou Whitmire, appears as a reporter in the film; Steve Oster, who plays a guard; Jodiviah "Joe" Stepp, who is one of the "fresh fish" new convicts; and Brian Connell, who was one of the Core Cons around for most of the filming.

Many thanks to the many actors interviewed about their *Shawshank* experiences, starting with Freeman in 1993 and including those reached twenty-five years later: Tim Robbins, Clancy Brown, Jeffrey DeMunn, Scott Mann, Frank Medrano, Morgan Lund, Dorothy Silver, Rohn Thomas, Claire Slemmer, Charlie Kearns, and Paul Kennedy. Bob Gunton warmly responded to e-mails, kindly sharing and pointing to recorded interviews that best reflect his thoughts on the film and his memorable role in it.

Other extras eagerly responding to requests for interviews included Bob Cassity, Max Gerber, Chris Hershberger, Dick Jourdan, Brenda Kelly, David Lessig, Tracy Love, Bob Nachbar, Steve Oster, Mike Thatcher, and Doug Wertz. Thanks also to Marilyn Irey Burchett for heartfelt recollections of her mother, Janet Kelly Irey, and her experiences as an extra in *The Shawshank Redemption*. Time did not permit me to get back to all of the dozens of extras who responded to Lou Whitmire's *Mansfield News Journal* story about the research phase for this book, and to them both my thanks and regrets.

For providing insight into that incredible structure known as the Ohio State Reformatory, I am indebted to Dennis Baker, a corrections officer at OSR and later (when *Shawshank* was being filmed) the warden of the Mansfield Correctional Institution, and Harold Cope, who spent five years as an officer at OSR. Both ended up as extras in the film. For providing expert analysis of the film and its international fandom, I am deeply thankful to Maura Grady and Tony Magistrale, authors of *The Shawshank Experience: Tracking the History of the World's Favorite Movie*.

I also need to acknowledge the marvelous time spent talking to those who worked behind the cameras on *Shawshank*, including first assistant director John R. Woodward, location manager and a production supervisor Kokayi Ampah, construction coordinator Sebastian Milito, and animal trainer/wrangler Therese Backowski. Others interviewed for this book were: LaDonna Secrist, owner of the Squirrel's Den chocolate and fudge (and candy and popcorn) store in Mansfield, who also granted us permission to take pictures in the Den for this book; Mike Koser, a student interviewer when *Shawshank* came to town; Brian McNeal, the wood carver who fashions collectible items from the fallen Shawshank

Oak Tree; and "superfans" Tom Clark (a guide at OSR), Emily Pugh, Abe Klein, and actor Jerry O'Connell.

Among those generously assisting with the research were librarian and King fan Patrick Manning, who dipped into his own library and lent me a box of pertinent volumes, and Rebecca Showman, who quickly tracked down materials in the early going. Much appreciated, as were the enthusiastic responses for permissions from Richard (Rick) and Roxanne Ayres, Mike Demetriades, and Willie Hunn, the director of the Richland Carrousel Park in Mansfield.

Thanks for the advice and feedback from photographer and longtime pal Mandy Altimus Pond, ace agent Charlotte Gusay, and Lyons Press editor Stephanie Scott.

And there would be no *Shawshank* study without the author of "Rita Hayworth and Shawshank Redemption," Stephen King. So, thanks for that story (and so many others) and for the interviews (especially those touching on *Shawshank*).

There also would be no *Shawshank* film without the vision and passion of its director, so thank you, Frank Darabont, for sharing the insights and memories . . . and for the warm and generous support of this book.

And there also would be no book without the support and understanding and patience of the two angels going by the names of Sara and Becky. Everyone seeks his or her own Zihuatanejo. For me, it's where they are.

BIBLIOGRAPHY

Although interviews were the primary sources for this examination and celebration of *The Shawshank Redemption*, several books and magazine articles proved incredibly valuable.

BOOKS

Beahm, George. *The Stephen King Companion* (Kansas City: Andrews and McMeel, 1995 revised edition).

———. *The Stephen King Companion: Four Decades of Fear from the Master of Horror* (New York: Thomas Dunne Books/St. Martin's Press, 2015).

———. *Stephen King from A–Z: An Encyclopedia of His Life and Work* (Kansas City: Andrews and McMeel Publishing, 1998).

Bishop, Jim, ed. *Hearts in Suspension* (Orono: The University of Maine Press, 2016).

Browning, Mark. *Stephen King on the Big Screen* (Bristol, UK: Intellect, 2009).

———. *Stephen King on the Small Screen* (Bristol, UK: Intellect, 2011).

Darabont, Frank. *The Shawshank Redemption: The Shooting Script* (New York: Newmarket Press, 1996). (Anyone interested in comparing the screenplay to what ended up on the screen should seek out this volume. It features a foreword by Stephen King and illuminating, amusing, and highly detailed notes by Darabont.)

Darbey, Nancy K. *Images of America: The Ohio State Reformatory* (Charleston, SC: Arcadia Publishing, 2016).

Freeman, Brian James, Hans-Ake Lilja, and Kevin Quigley. *The Illustrated Stephen King Movie Trivia Book* (Baltimore: Cemetery Dance Publications, 2013).

Grady, Maura, and Tony Magistrale. *The Shawshank Experience: Tracking the History of the World's Favorite Movie* (New York: Palgrave Macmillan, 2018).

Herron, Don, ed. *Reign of Fear: The Fiction and the Films of Stephen King* (Novato,CA: Underwood-Miller, 1988).

Horsting, Jessie. *Stephen King at the Movies* (New York: Starlog Press/Signet, 1986).

Kermode, Matt. *The Shawshank Redemption* (London: British Film Institute/Palgrave, 2003).

James, Joe. *The Ohio State Reformatory: An Overview* (Bloomington, IN: AuthorHouse, 2011).

Jones, Stephen. *Creepshow: The Illustrated Stephen King Movie Guide* (New York: Billboard Books, 2002).

King, Stephen. *Different Seasons* (New York: The Viking Press, 1982).

———. *On Writing* (New York: Scribner, 2000).

Lloyd, Ann. *The Films of Stephen King* (New York: St. Martin's Press, 1993).

Magistrale, Tony. *Hollywood's Stephen King* (New York: Palgrave Macmillan, 2003).

Mavis, Brad. *Rita the Shawshank Dog: The True Story of Making a Movie and a Best Friend* (CreateSpace Independent Publishing Platform, 2014).

Raush, Andrew J., and R. D. Riley. *The Stephen King Quiz Book* (Albany, GA: Bear Manor Media, 2011).

Underwood, Tim, and Chuck Miller, eds. *Fear Itself: The Horror Fiction of Stephen King* (New York: Plume, New American Library, 1984).

Underwood, Tim, and Chuck Miller (produced by), written by Jeff Conner. *Stephen King Goes to Hollywood* (New York: Plume, New American Library, 1987).

Von Doviak, Scott. *Stephen King Films FAQ* (New York: Applause, 2014).

Winter, Douglas E. *Stephen King: The Art of Darkness* (New York: New American Library, 1986 expanded and updated edition).

MAGAZINES AND WEBSITES

Heidenry, Margaret. "The Little-Known Story of How *The Shawshank Redemption* Became One of the Most Beloved Films of All Time." *Vanity Fair*, September 22, 2014.

Probst, Christopher. "Flashback: *The Shawshank Redemption*." *American Cinematographer*, August 23, 2017.

Schulz, Bill. "20 Things You Didn't Know About *The Shawshank Redemption*." *The Daily Beast*, August 27, 2014.

INDEX

ABOUT THE AUTHOR

PHOTO BY BECKY DAWIDZIAK

MARK DAWIDZIAK HAS BEEN THE TELEVISION CRITIC AT THE *CLEVELAND Plain Dealer* since July 1999. During his sixteen years at the *Akron Beacon Journal*, he held such posts as TV columnist, movie critic, and critic-at-large.

Before moving to Ohio in 1983, he worked as a theater, film, and TV critic at newspapers in Tennessee and Virginia. He began his journalism career in the late '70s at the Associated Press and Knight-Ridder bureaus in Washington, DC.

Also an author and playwright, his many books include two histories of landmark TV series: *The Columbo Phile: A Casebook* (1989) and *The Night Stalker Companion* (1997). *Everything I Need to Know I Learned in The Twilight Zone*, his lighthearted tribute to Rod Serling's celebrated anthology series, was published in 2017.

A recognized Mark Twain scholar, his acclaimed books on the author include *Mark My Words: Mark Twain on Writing* (1996), *Horton Foote's The Shape of the River: The Lost Teleplay About Mark Twain* (2003), *Mark Twain in Ohio* (2015), *Mark Twain's Guide to Diet, Exercise, Beauty, Fashion, Investment, Romance, Health and Happiness* (2015), and *Mark Twain for Cat Lovers* (2016). He frequently is invited to lecture on Twain or television history at universities, libraries, and museums. A contributing scholar to several prestigious anthologies about Twain, he has been the guest lecturer three times at Elmira College's Center for Mark Twain Studies. He also has presented papers on Mark Twain at five consecutive State of Mark Twain Studies conferences at Elmira College. No less an authority than Ken Burns has said, "Nobody gets Mark Twain the way Mark Dawidziak does."

In addition to *The Night Stalker Companion*, a history of the Carl Kolchak character, his work on the horror side of the street includes the 1994 novel *Grave Secrets*, a play (*The Tell-Tale Play*), such nonfiction books as *The Bedside, Bathtub, & Armchair Companion to Dracula* (2008), short stories, and comic book scripts. Several of his essays and introductions appear in *Richard Matheson's Kolchak Scripts* (2003) and *Bloodlines: Richard Matheson's Dracula, I Am Legend, and Other Vampire Stories* (2006), two books he edited for Gauntlet Press. He contributed the career appreciation and overview to *Produced and Directed by Dan Curtis* (2004), and he is the creative consultant to Moonstone's comic book series *Kolchak: The Night Stalker*.

Written with Paul J. Bauer, the literary biography *Jim Tully: American Writer, Irish Rover, Hollywood Brawler* was published by the Kent State University Press in 2011. It's the first full-length biography of "hobo writer" Jim Tully, a forgotten author hailed as "America's Gorky" and as a literary superstar in the '20s and '30s. In preparation for the biography, he and Bauer have edited and written introductions for four Kent State University Press reprints of books by Tully: *Beggars of Life, Circus Parade, Shanty Irish* (with a foreword by John Sayles), and *The Bruiser*.

Dawidziak and his wife, actress Sara Showman, founded the Largely Literary Theater Company in 2002. Dedicated to promoting literacy and literature, the company has staged his three-person version of Charles

Dickens' *A Christmas Carol* and his two-act play based on sketches by Mark Twain, *The Reports of My Death Are Greatly Exaggerated*. In addition to directing the Largely Literary plays, he portrays Twain and Dickens. He met his wife when both were cast in a production of Neil Simon's *The Good Doctor* (he played the Anton Chekhov role, later appearing with her as the H. L. Mencken character in *Inherit the Wind*). He and Showman have developed play versions of several of his books, including *Everything I Need to Know I Learned in The Twilight Zone* and *Mark Twain's Guide to Diet, Exercise, Beauty, Fashion, Investment, Romance, Health and Happiness*, which they've performed in several states.

As a performer, he has been a member of two comedy teams (using the stage name Mark Daniels). In 1993, he reunited with one of his former partners to win the routine contest at the first-ever Abbott & Costello Convention.

His Critics' Classics video essay on director Frank Capra's *Meet John Doe* was shown regularly on the American Movie Classics cable channel, and he has appeared in such documentaries as the A&E *Biography* profile of Peter Falk and *AMC's Visionaries: James Cameron's Story of Science Fiction*. He has written the liner notes for the Columbia House Video Library's Collector's Editions of several TV series, including *Columbo, Kolchak: The Night Stalker, Quincy, The Odd Couple, 3rd Rock from the Sun, The Carol Burnett Show, F Troop, Hart to Hart, Magnum, P.I.*, and *Murder, She Wrote*.

Dawidziak also has been a regular contributor to such magazines as *TV Guide, Commonwealth, Cinefantastique, Scarlet Street, Mystery Scene, Sci-Fi Universe, Not of This Earth, Knoxville Lifestyle, Self-Reliant, Ohio Magazine*, and *Parent's Choice*. A member of the Television Critics Association's board of directors for five years, he has won five Cleveland Press Club awards for entertainment writing, as well as a Society of Professional Journalists award for coverage of minority issues. In 2015, he was inducted into the Press Club of Cleveland Journalism Hall of Fame.

A journalism graduate of George Washington University, he was born in Huntington, New York. He lives in Cuyahoga Falls, Ohio, with his wife and their daughter, Rebecca "Becky" Claire.